*World Food*

# THAILAND

## Joe Cummings

**WORLD FOOD Thailand**
1st edition

**Published by**
Lonely Planet Publications Pty Ltd A.C.N. 005 607 983
192 Burwood Rd, Hawthorn, Victoria 3122, Australia

**Lonely Planet Offices**
**Australia** PO Box 617, Hawthorn, Victoria 3122
**USA** 150 Linden Street, Oakland CA 94607
**UK** 10a Spring Place, London NW5 3BH
**France** 1 rue du Dahomey, 75011 Paris

**Photography**
All of the images in this guide are available
for licensing from Lonely Planet Images.
email: lpi@lonelyplanet.com.au

**Published**
March 2000

ISBN 1 86450 026 3

text & maps © Lonely Planet Publications Pty Ltd, 2000
photos © photographers as indicated 2000

**Printed by**
The Bookmaker Pty. Ltd.
Printed in China.

## About the Author

Joe Cummings ate his first Thai meal at San Francisco's Racha Café on March 15, 1977 while on his way to Thailand for the first time. Upon arrival in Bangkok, one of the first Thai culinary lessons he learned was that there is often little connection between Thai food served outside Thailand and the cuisine found in its native land. Joe has since chased bowls of noodles and plates of curry through all 76 Thai provinces, and counts Thai cuisine among the foremost pleasures of life. All recipes that appear in this book started from original Thai sources and were modified according to 22 years of experimentation and peeking over great Thai cooks' shoulders.

## About the Photographer

Jerry Alexander provided most of the photographs in this book, with other Lonely Planet photographers providing the balance. The photography credits are on page 280. Jerry is a highly experienced food & travel photographer with extensive experience working in South-East Asia, particularly Thailand. When he's not travelling around the world – leaving behind a trail of crumbs from eating his props – Jerry lives in California and tends to his vineyard in the Napa Valley.

## From the Publisher

This first edition of *World Food Thailand* was edited by Patrick Witton at Lonely Planet's Melbourne office. Joanne Adams and Brendan Dempsey designed the book, Paul Piaia mapped with finishing touches provided by Natasha Vellelley. Tim Uden and Andrew Tudor provided technical know-how.

Olivier Breton, Vicki Webb, Patrick Marris, Quentin Frayne, Kerrie Hicken, Gushi Soda, Paul Clifton and Guillaume Roux provided essential bits and pieces. Valerie Tellini, Lonely Planet Images (LPI) co-ordinated the supply of photographs. Author, Joe Cummings, co-ordinated the language section and Peter D'Onghia oversaw its production.

Sally Steward, publisher, developed the series and Martin Hughes, series editor, nurtured each book from the seeds of ideas through to fruition, with inimitable flair.

## Acknowledgements

Thanks to Allison Jones, London, for helpful suggestions, and Guy Mirabella for design concepts. Thanks to Jeerapa Rugtuam for supplying the Thai script, and to Joe Cummings for going the extra yards.

For their insights into Thai cuisine, the author wishes to thank Theerada 'Jan' Suphaphong, Jeerapa Rugtuam-Schuett, Sopavadee Bejrajati, Andrew Forbes, Steven Martin, Simon Robson, Boonpian Sirirat and Pensri Saenyot. In Chiang Mai, Pia Wunna was of major assistance with everything from language to photography. Thank you Sara-Jane's and the Fabb Fashion Café in Bangkok, along with Heuan Phen and the Riverside Pub in Chiang Mai, for allowing us to shoot photos on the premises. Further thanks to Bangkok jâo meuang Jerry Hopkins and Christopher Moore. A nod to Larry Nahlik and Peter Ford for chronographic info. Finally, thanks to Jerry Alexander for putting so much energy into this project.

**Warning & Request**
Things change; markets give way to supermarkets, prices go up, good places go bad and not much stays the same. Please tell us if you've discovered changes and help make the next edition even more useful. We value all your feedback, and strive to improve our books accordingly. We have a well-travelled, well-fed team that reads and acknowledges every letter, postcard and email and ensures that every morsel of information finds its way to the appropriate people.

Each correspondent will receive the latest issue of Planet Talk, our quarterly printed newsletter, or Comet, our monthly email newsletter. Subscriptions to both are free. The newsletters might even feature your letter so let us know if you don't want it published.

If you have an interesting anecdote or story to do with your culinary travels, we'd love to hear it. If we publish it in the next edition, we'll send you a free Lonely Planet book of your choice.

Send your correspondence to the nearest Lonely Planet office:
Australia: PO Box 617, Hawthorn, Victoria 3122
UK: 10a Spring Place, London NW5 3BH
USA: 150 Linden St, Oakland CA 94607
France: 1 rue du Dahomey, Paris 75011

Or email us at: talk2us@lonelyplanet.com

# contents

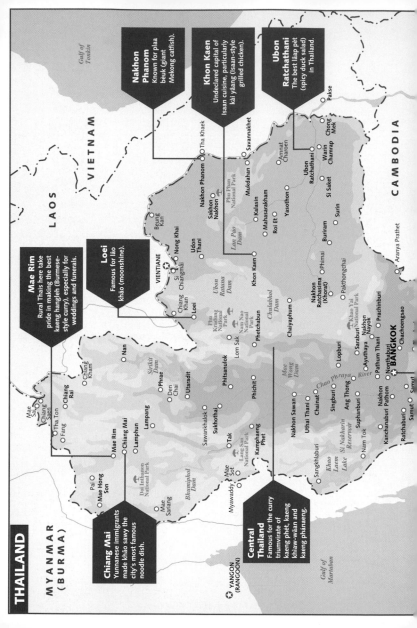

# THAILAND

**MYANMAR (BURMA)**

*Gulf of Tonkin*

**VIETNAM**

**LAOS**

**CAMBODIA**

**Nakhon Phanom**
Known for plaa beuk (giant Mekong catfish).

**Khon Kaen**
Undeclared capital of Isaan cuisine, particularly kài yâang (Isaan-style grilled chicken).

**Ubon Ratchathani**
The best lâap pèt (spicy duck salad) in Thailand.

**Mae Rim**
Rural Thais here take pride in making the best kaeng hangleh (Burmese-style curry), especially for weddings and funerals.

**Loei**
Famous for lâo khǎo (moonshine).

**Chiang Mai**
Yunnanese immigrants made khâo sawy the city's most famous noodle dish.

**Central Thailand**
Famous for the curry triumvirate of kaeng phèt, kaeng khǐaw-wǎan and kaeng phánaeng.

Pakse
Tha Khaek
Savannakhet
Mukdahan
Amnat Charoen
Warin Chamrap
Chong Mek
Ubon Ratchathani
Si Saket
Surin

Beung Kan
Nong Khai
Si Chiangmai
*Phu Phan National Park*
Sakhon Nakhon
*Lam Pao Dam*
Kalasin
Mahasarakham
Roi Et
Yasothon
Buriram
Aranya Prathet

**VIENTIANE**
Udon Thani
Khon Kaen
Phimai
Nakhon Ratchasima (Khorat)
Pakthongchai

Nakhon Phanom

*Ubon Ratana Dam*
Chiang Khan
Loei
*Phu Kradung National Park*
*Nam Nao National Park*
Lom Sak
Phetchabun
*Chulabhol Dam*
Chaiyaphum

Nan
Chiang Khong
Chiang Rai
Chiang Saen
Mae Sai
Tha Ton
Fang
Phrae
Den Chai
Uttaradit
Phitsanulok

*Khao Yai National Park*
Saraburi
Nakhon Nayok
Prachinburi
Lopburi
Ayutthaya
Pathum Thani
**BANGKOK**
Nonthaburi
Chachoengsao

Pai
Mae Hong Son
Mae Rim
Chiang Mai
Lamphun
Lampang
*Doi Inthanon National Park*
*Bhumiphol Dam*

Sawankhalok
Sukhothai
Tak
Kamphaeng Phet
*Lan Sang National Park*
Mae Sot
Mae Sarang
Myawaddy

Nakhon Sawan
Uthai Thani
Chainat
Singburi
Ang Thong
Suphanburi
*Mae Wong Dam*
*Chao Phraya River*

*Sirikit Dam*
Phichit

Sangkhlaburi
*Khao Laem Lake*
*Si Nakharin Reservoir*
Nam Tok
Kanchanaburi
Nakhon Pathom
Ratchaburi
Samut
Samut

**YANGON (RANGOON)**

*Gulf of Martaban*

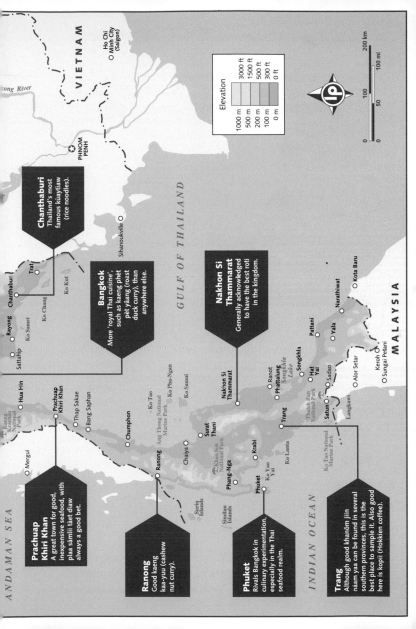

**VIETNAM**

Ho Chi Minh City (Saigon) ○

Mekong River

**PHNOM PENH** ◉

Sihanoukville ○

Elevation

| | |
|---|---|
| 1000 m | 3000 ft |
| 500 m | 1500 ft |
| 200 m | 500 ft |
| 100 m | 300 ft |
| 0 m | 0 ft |

**GULF OF THAILAND**

**Chanthaburi**
Thailand's most famous kuaytiaw (rice noodles).

Trat ○
Chanthaburi ○
Ko Kut
Rayong ○
Ko Samet
Ko Chang
Sattahip ○

**Bangkok**
More 'royal Thai cuisine', such as kaeng phèt pèt yâang (roast duck curry), than anywhere else.

**Nakhon Si Thammarat**
Generally acknowledged to have the best roti in the kingdom.

Mergui ○
Hua Hin ●
Kaeng Krachan National Park
Prachuap Khiri Khan ○
Thap Sakae ○
Bang Saphan ○

**Prachuap Khiri Khan**
A great town for good, inexpensive seafood, with plaa sâmlii tàet diaw always a good bet.

**ANDAMAN SEA**

Chumphon ○
Ko Tao
Ang Thong National Marine Park
Ko Pha-Ngan

**Ranong**
Good kaeng kaa-yuu (cashew nut curry).

Ranong ○
Chaiya ○
Surat Thani ○
Ko Samui

Surin Islands

Khao Sok National Park

Phang-Nga ●
Krabi ●
Ko Lanta

**Phuket**
Rivals Bangkok in culinary experimentation, especially in the Thai seafood realm.

(Similan Islands)

Ko Yao Yai
Phuket ●

**INDIAN OCEAN**

Ranot ○
Phatthalung ○
Songkhla Lake
Songkhla ○
Hat Yai ●

Thalè Ban National Park

Trang ●

Ko Tao National Marine Park

Satun ○
Sadao ○
Langkawi

Kroh ○
Sungai Petani ○
Alor Setar ○

Pattani ○
Yala ○
Narathiwat ○
Kota Baru ○

**MALAYSIA**

**Trang**
Although good khanǒm jiin náam yaa can be found in several southern provinces, this is the best place to sample it. Also good here is kopi (Hokkien coffee).

| | | |
|---|---|---|
| 0 | 100 | 200 km |
| 0 | 50 | 100 mi |

 Thailand lures more visitors than any other country in South-East Asia with its irresistible combination of natural beauty, historic temples, renowned hospitality and robust cuisine. From pulse-pounding Bangkok to tranquil villages moored along the Mekong River, Thai cooks concoct a seemingly endless variety of dishes, whether from 300-year-old court recipes, the latest in Euro-Thai fusion or simple dishes guided by seasonal and regional necessity.

Standing at the crossroads of traditions dominated by India, China and Asian Oceania, Thailand has adapted cooking techniques and ingredients from each of these major influences as well as the culinary kits carried by passing traders and empire-builders from the Middle East and southern Europe. Over the centuries, indigenous rudiments have fused with imported elements to produce a distinctive native cuisine.

Thai food's light and healthy nature, vast internal range, adaptability to other cooking styles and straightforward stovetop dynamics, raises it well beyond the ken of just another 'ethnic cuisine' to be struck off a list of palatal destinations. Today Thai cuisine has become so globally appreciated that in a survey polling travel agencies in over 25 countries, it ranked fourth after France, Italy and Hong Kong in the perceived excellence of cuisine. Nowadays most major cities have at least one Thai restaurant.

Although Thai chefs have become darlings of the international food set, there is still no place like the cuisine's home to experience the full depth and breadth of the Thai culinary palette. The alternately cooling and incendiary flavours exist not only abstractly, in recipes easily transported past any customs gate, but are linked to a complex set of private and public occasions that make up a less portable Thai culture.

Whether offering scoops of steamed rice and tiny plastic pouches of curry to a shaven-headed, barefooted Buddhist monk at dawn, or spreading out around a beach campfire for a weekend feast of barbecued fish, Thais connect food with all the important interstices of their lives. This is one reason why the cuisine has become so highly developed. Another is the important medicinal nature which Thais attribute to many foods.

Food lies very close to the heart of **khwaam pen thai** (Thai-ness), so much so that to truly appreciate Thai culture you must understand and appreciate the food. If you become comfortable with both, perhaps you will then become **kin jai** (eat heart), that is, truly impressed and absorbed in Thai food culture. Finally you may come to understand what Thais mean when they say they are ìm jai (full heart), an expression that fuses culinary satisfaction with general contentment.

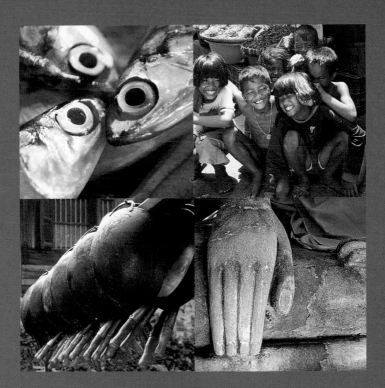

# the
# culture
## of thai cuisine

Food has always played a key role in the history and culture of Thailand. Kingdoms, ceremonies, customs and language have all been influenced by what Thais grow, eat, and how they eat it. Dig into a spicy curry and you'll soon find out what really fuels Thailand's vibrant culture.

Thais love to talk about their cuisine, but ask them to describe the essence of Thai food, and they're not likely to have a quick answer. They can be at a similar loss for words when attempting to describe their culture in general. In fact Thais don't really have a word that corresponds to the English term 'culture'. The nearest equivalent, **wátánátham**, emphasises fine arts and religious ceremonies over other aspects usually covered by the western conception of culture.

But ask what it means to be Thai, and the response is invariably two-fold: to speak Thai, and to eat Thai food. Appreciation for Thai food is so central to Thai cultural identity that many Thais naively assume that non-Thais are physically or mentally unable to partake of the cuisine. Long-time foreign visitors or residents won't be asked simply whether they *like* to eat Thai food. Rather they will be asked '**kin aahāan thai pen māi?**' (do you know *how* to eat Thai food?). It is almost assumed that to enjoy Thai cooking you must either be born Thai or trained in the difficult art of feeling exhilarated over a plate of well prepared **phàt thai** (stirfried noodles).

---

## DON'T BE LIKE LIME WITHOUT JUICE

Food plays an important role in Thai idioms and proverbs whose intended meanings have nothing to do with eating.

**kin hâew**
'eat water chestnuts', to fail at something

**kwàa thùa jà sùk ngaa kâw mâi**
'before the peanuts are done, the sesame will burn', an admonition to do things in the proper order. This saying offers added poetry in the way all words in the first clause – 'before the peanuts are done' – are spoken in parallel low tones, while two of three words in the second clause – 'the sesame will burn' – are falling tones.

**mâi kin sên**
'not eating noodles', when two people refuse to speak to one another due to a falling out

**mánao mâi mii náam**
'like lime without juice', dull

**phàk chii rohy nâa**
'coriander leaf sprinkled on top', performing a deed for appearances only

**sên yài**
'big noodle', important person

**wǎan yen**
'sweet cool' (a type of iced Thai dessert), an easy-going person

Of course the one aspect of the cuisine that does require getting used to for many people, even other Asians, is Thai food's relatively high chilli content (see Phrik in the Staples & Specialities chapter). This is why the second most common question asked of a foreigner about to slip a tablespoon into a bowl of **kaeng khǐaw-wǎan** (green curry) is '**kin phèt dâi mǎi?**' (can you eat spicy food?).

Thailand stakes its national reputation on producing a cuisine that Thai chefs and local food critics sum up with the phrase '**rót châat phèt ráwn**' (literally, 'tastes original spicy hot') often shortened to **rót châat** (from the Pali-Sanskrit *rasa jati*, 'birth flavour'), a highly complimentary term generally applied only to Thai cooking. Other kinds of cooking, by implication, are considered **jèut** (bland) and Thais who go to visit or live in western countries often return home remarking how plain they found **faràng** (western) cuisine.

Thai cuisine employs a stock variety of cooking techniques and ingredients to achieve this vaunted originality, and many of these are covered elsewhere in this book. One major cultural aspect contributing to the wonderful life found in Thai food is the Thai insistence on freshness. Quick culinary techniques such as blanching, flash frying, parboiling and poaching produce dishes in which the vegetables, for example, maintain most of their just-picked freshness and flavours are effectively sealed in. Unlike their Indian counterparts, Thai cooks assemble curry pastes and other relatively elaborate seasoning concoctions quickly from fresh rather than powdered, dried or preserved ingredients. Exceptions include the fermentation and pickling processes favoured for certain condiments and seasonings (see Herbs, Spices & Other Seasonings in the Staples & Specialities chapter).

In classic Thai dishes, the use of butter or lard is extremely rare and probably limited to east-west fusion experiments. From the Thai perspective, the freshness and rót châat of their cuisine means diners can easily discern and appreciate all the component flavours, a fact that has contributed to Thai cuisine's rapid expansion in the increasingly health-conscious and gourmet-shop-around-the-corner west.

Quick techniques and relatively simple recipes (save for the curry pastes, and even these are easy compared to their Indian progenitors) also mean less time spent in the kitchen and thus more time available for enjoying the company of fellow diners, whether guests or family. Internationally renowned Thai chef, Vatcharin Bhumichitr, probably surprised many readers when he confessed, in *The Taste of Thailand*, that few Thai dishes take longer than eight to 12 minutes to cook.

*Peasant farm girl, Chiang Mai, Chiang Mai Province*

It was only natural that the Thais would have developed a cuisine that emphasised ease of preparation since, if any one element typifies Thai culture more than any other, it is the imperative for life to be **sanùk** (fun). In Thailand anything worth doing – even work – should have an element of sanùk, otherwise it automatically becomes drudgery. This doesn't mean Thais don't want to work or strive, just that they tend to approach tasks with a sense of playfulness. Nothing condemns an activity more than the description **mâi sanùk** (not fun).

When you're in Thailand, sit down beside a rice field and watch workers planting, transplanting or harvesting rice. That it's back-breaking labour is obvious, but participants inject the activity with lots of sanùk – flirtation between the sexes, singing, trading insults and cracking jokes. The same goes in an office or a bank, and certainly for a kitchen, where Thais reach for a higher level of playfulness and humour than just about anywhere else.

Sanùk also comes into play when Thai cooks experiment with **tamráp kàp khâo** (formula with rice), the name given to basic recipes handed down from previous generations, traded among friends or clipped from popular magazines like *khrua* (Kitchen), *sut sapda* (Weekend) or *khwan reuan* (House Spirit). One riverbank restaurant in the tiny Mekong town of Khong Jiam has served us a different version of **yam mét má-muang hìmáphaan** (spicy cashew nut salad) each time we've visited, yet it has been excellent every time. One imagines the kitchen staff merrily improvising, tossing in ingredients according to what's available since the last grocery trip to Ubon Ratchathani, or what's flourishing in the garden behind the proprietor's house that month.

Such experimentation is itself a tradition in a country that has long functioned as an Asian crossroads, where Indian, Arab and European traders arrived from the west, intersecting trade routes emanating from southwestern China. Unlike China and Japan, whose cultures remained largely insulated for thousands of years, Thailand has always thrived on foreign influence. Its kitchen doors have stood wide open to admit new ideas, new ingredients and new cooking techniques. Undoubtedly one of the reasons Thai cuisine has gained international popularity comes from the fact that it successfully blends so many different taste sensations. Typically, the blend is seamless and it's almost impossible to separate the strands of influence.

This can be explained by the fact that Thais adopted and adapted outside culinary influences not so much out of necessity – Thailand has always been a fertile land of plenty – but because they love to eat and they love to cook, and, like great cooks and diners everywhere, they love to improvise with food. Furthermore, Thais harbour a very strong notion of what food should taste like and what it should look like, and all outside influences have had to submit to this central gustatory vision.

As a result, even the most discriminating diner would be hard-pressed to identify the direct links between the curries of India and those of Thailand (other than the presence of chilli, native to neither). In fact, it can be argued that Thailand had its own native **kaeng** (curry) long before Indian influences began to arrive early in the first Christian millennium (see Kaeng in the Staples & Specialities chapter).

Moving from the kitchen to the dining room – even when the latter is merely a space on the floor where plates and bowls may be spread out upon a **sèua** (rice mat) – you will quickly discover that eating is one of the great pleasures in life here. Thais have one of the most varied cuisines in the world and enjoy eating so much that they appear to want to sample this variety as often as possible. The average urban Thai takes time out to eat, not three times per day, but four or five. Sitting down at a roadside **rót khĕn** (vendor cart) after an evening of cinema or nightclubbing, a Thai may barely have finished one steaming bowl of noodles before ordering a second round, just to revel in the experience a little longer. The array of condiments, even at a noodle stand, allows Thais to improvise and to indulge their individualism by arranging the taste to suit their respective palates.

The general lightness of Thai cuisine, along with the way food may be shared among a group at main meals (see Etiquette later in this chapter), allows the diner considerable latitude in deciding how little or how much to consume without paying much regard to weight gain. The rate of obesity in Thailand is, in fact, very low on a world scale.

Food plays an important role not only in the purely personal and social dimensions of Thai life, but in the ritual and ceremony of their spiritual life as well. Over 90% of all Thais are Buddhists, and one of the most important Buddhist acts is the daily feeding of the monks (see the boxed text 'Making Nutritional Merit'). Food is offered at numerous other types of religious shrines throughout the country, from Brahman temples and Chinese ancestor shrines to the all-important **làk meuang** (city pillar) where a city's guardian earth deity resides.

*Young monks collecting alms, Chiang Mai*

CULTURE

## MAKING NUTRITIONAL MERIT

Every dawn throughout the kingdom nearly a half million Thai monks – shaven-headed, barefoot and wrapped neck to ankle in saffron robes – leave the compounds of around 32,000 **wát** (monasteries). Each monk carries with him a black lacquered alms bowl, either cradled in his hands or supported by a woven shoulder sling. Slowly, and in single file, the monks walk along the streets and footpaths of virtually every village, town and city in the country.

Stopping in front of homes and shops along the way, they receive their daily sustenance in a practice known as **bintàbàat**, the 'alms round' of Theravada Buddhism.

Lay people who come out to meet the monks usually prepare for the encounter by bringing along individually wrapped food portions. As each monk stops, the devotee will squat or kneel as a sign of respect, and place one of the food packets in the monk's alms bowl. Keeping his eyes cast toward the ground, the monk may offer a few words of blessing in return, then slowly and mindfully move on.

Any type of food may be offered, whether **kaeng** (curry), **yam** (hot & tangy salad), **khanŏm** (Thai sweets) or other dishes. The amount of food in each portion typically amounts to no more than a bite or two. This allows many lay people to share in the **bun** (religious merit) earned by feeding the monks, and avoids overloading the alms bowl. In poorer areas of North and North-Eastern Thailand, lay people may offer plain rice rather than **kàp khâo** (any dish eaten with rice). In such cases, the wát provides an accompaniment for the monks when they return from bintàbàat.

Once a monk has either filled his bowl or come to the end of his route (most urban monks follow the same route daily), he returns to his monastery with the food. At this point the monks will pool the day's offerings and then share them among all the members of the **sangha** (Buddhist community) present.

During certain annual religious festivals, lay people prepare special dishes for the Sangha. One of these, **kràyaasàat** (a rice, sesame, coconut and peanut sweet), must be stirred for hours in a giant pot using large wood paddles before it's ready to offer, first to the Buddha and then to the monks. It is served between 1 and 5am on the morning of Loy Krathong, an important harvest festival. Such festival specialities are taken directly to the monasteries for offering to the monks, or may even be prepared on the wát grounds themselves. It's also common for Thais to host an elaborate meal for a group of monks, either at the monastery or at the home of the host, usually in return for performing a house blessing, marriage ceremony or other private religious function.

## Geography

Thailand's culinary evolution owes much to its charmed geographical position. Roughly equivalent in size to France, this 517,000 sq km kingdom straddles the Indochinese and Sundaic biogeographic realms for over 1800km north to south, and hosts a vast range of flora from both zones. The entire country falls between the tropics of Cancer and Capricorn, so tropical temperature and rainfall patterns predominate. Its northward position above the equator means that highland winters are sufficiently cool for the cultivation of a wide variety of vegetables, including temperate varieties introduced from Europe and the Americas after the 15th century.

In Northern Thailand the southeastern escarpment of the Himalayan mountain range and Tibetan Plateau crests at between 3000 and 3500m, providing an important watershed for much of the country. Rivers springing from these heights drain southward into the fertile river basins of Central Thailand – where the nation's famous **khâo hǎwm málí** (jasmine rice) is cultivated in abundance – before emptying into the Gulf of Thailand. Farms in Central Thailand also fill a large portion of the bounteous Thai fruit basket (see Phon-la-mai in the Staples & Specialities chapter).

The shelf-like Khorat Plateau in North-Eastern Thailand borders Laos and Cambodia. Rivers and streams in this region feed into the Mekong River, the world's 12th longest inland waterway. Freshwater fish from these rivers, especially the national favourite, **plaa châwn** (serpent-headed fish), have long formed an important daily source of nutrition and eating pleasure for a vast number of Thais.

South of Bangkok, the slender Thai-Malay Peninsula is characterised by tropical rainforests, stunning limestone outcrops and smaller mountain ranges that leave very little arable land for rice cultivation. Instead the seafaring Southern Thais depend on the oceans to stock their pantries and provide an income.

The Andaman Sea, part of the Indian Ocean, faces the peninsula's west coast. The Gulf of Thailand, itself an extension of the South China Sea, sweeps along the east coast from Malaysia all the way to Cambodia. The country's marine harvest graces tabletops all over Thailand with enough left over to export sea products – particularly tuna, mackerel and shrimp – around the world.

Thus from the very start of human habitation in what is now Thailand, food abundance was ensured. Still, the Thais have come a very long way since their social origins as a loose collection of city states concentrated in extremely fertile river valleys.

## History

What most distinguishes the history of Thailand from that of any other South or South-East Asian country is the simple fact that it was never ruled by a European power. Whether this was a simple historical accident or whether the structure of Thai society itself is responsible for resisting European colonisation remains a burning debate among today's scholars. What is certain, however, is that Thailand's Mekong River valley and Khorat Plateau display ample archaeological evidence of agricultural settlement beginning 10,000 years ago.

Rice found deep underground at archaeological sites in Ban Chiang in North-Eastern Thailand, and the remains of cucumber, gourd and water chestnut found in Central Thailand's Kanchanaburi, date from 8000 to 4000 BC. These discoveries demonstrate that Thailand was probably the first rice-growing country in Asia and possibly the first in the world to practise riziculture. At Ban Prasat in the northeast, rice was cultivated as early as 4000 BC. China, by contrast, was growing and consuming millet at that time.

*Rice harvest, Northern Thailand*

During India's Ashoka period, in the 3rd century BC, Indian Buddhist missionaries were said to have been sent to a land called Suvannabhumi (Land of Gold). Suvannabhumi most likely corresponds to a remarkably bounteous area stretching from southern Myanmar, across the centre of Thailand, to eastern Cambodia. Two different cities in Thailand's central river basin, in fact, have long been called Suphanburi (City of Gold) and U Thong (Cradle of Gold). By the 6th century, an important network of agricultural communities was thriving as far south as modern-day Pattani and Yala, and as far north and northeast as Lamphun and Muang Fa Daet.

Indian and Chinese records reported the existence of simple Thai **meuang** (loosely affiliated settlements or principalities under the control of local meuang princes) along the Mekong, Nan, Ping, Kok, Yom and Wang rivers in the 8th to 10th centuries. It was probably at this time, as the Thais were gaining power over larger tracts of land and establishing a greater agricultural reach, that a native Thai cuisine began developing. Seasoned with native herbs and roots such as **tà-khrái** (lemongrass) and **khàa** (galangal), and possibly cooked with pastes or sauces made from cured fish or shrimp, this early menu may have borne recognisable similarities to Thai food today, minus a millennium of culinary experimentation and adoption of imported elements.

*Pak Khlong Market, Bangkok*

CULTURE

Agricultural communities in Surat Thani and further south also became active during this period, with ties to the Malay-Indonesian Sriwijaya dynasty. Cambodia's Angkor empire exerted substantial influence on central and eastern Thailand from the 8th to 13th centuries. It is likely that influences from Malay-Indonesian and Cambodian cuisines may have begun to seep into Thai food culture at this time.

As the Cambodian sphere of influence waned due to the collapse of the Angkor empire, the northern meuang expanded southeastward and, in 1238, a number of Thai princes in the north consolidated their power and declared an independent kingdom called Sukhothai (Arising of Happiness) under King Ram Khamhaeng.

Thais consider Sukhothai to have been the first true Thai nation, a golden age when everyone had plenty to eat and the kingdom was without enemies. A famous royal inscription from the era begins its lengthy narrative with a comment on the two most important Thai food staples:

> This land of Sukhothai is thriving. There is fish in the water and rice in the fields.

Further south, in what is today Central Thailand, a second Thai kingdom emerged during the 14th and 15th centuries. Encircled by rivers with access to the Gulf of Thailand, Ayuthaya became one of the wealthiest and most powerful cities in Asia, a flourishing seaport beside which London and Paris paled in comparison. All of Siam (as Thailand was called until 1939) eventually came under Ayuthaya dominion, and the kingdom's borders extended far beyond those of today's Thailand.

*Temple of the Big Buddha, Ko Samui*

CULTURE

"Among the Asian nations", wrote London visitor Engelbert Campfer, "the Kingdom of Siam is the greatest. The magnificence of the Ayuthaya Court is incomparable". Throughout 400 years of Ayuthaya reign, the Portuguese, Dutch, English, Danish and French courted the kingdom, trying without success to establish colonial relationships. Thai cuisine flourished in the court of Ayuthaya, and many recipes were carefully recorded for posterity.

During the Ayuthaya period, Europeans managed to wield considerable influence over Siam, particularly in the food realm. The Portuguese, who were the first westerners to make contact with Thailand in the 16th century, introduced what has perhaps become the most well known hallmark of Thai cuisine. **Phrík** (chilli), a robust native of Latin America added a large dollop of fire to the Thai culinary toolkit (see Phrik in the Staples & Specialities chapter).

Many contemporary Thai **khanōm** (sweets) owe a debt to travelling Portuguese chefs, who taught the Thais how to make rich and flavourful pastries using flour, sugar and egg. **Mákhēua-thêht** (tomatoes), **man faràng** (potatoes), **khâo phôht** (corn), **mákhēua** (eggplant) and other New World vegetables also journeyed to Thailand some time between the 16th and 18th centuries.

A brutal Burmese invasion in 1765 razed the royal capital and ended the Ayuthaya era. Many royal archives, including crucial medical and culinary records, were unfortunately destroyed. Phaya Taksin, a half-Chinese, half-Thai general, expelled the Burmese and moved the capital to Thonburi on the banks of the Chao Phraya River in 1769. The capital was moved again in 1782, across the river to its present site. During the early Bangkok era, European influence declined as Thailand shunned all outside powers following the fall of Ayuthaya.

Rama IV (more commonly known in the west as King Mongkut) re-cultivated relations with western powers while keeping colonialism at bay during the mid-19th century. His Majesty also loosened trade restrictions, established Siam's first printing press and introduced the European fork and spoon to the Thai court so that they wouldn't have to sully their hands eating like commoners. His son, King Chulalongkorn (1868-1910), furthered Mongkut's reforms, but diplomatic compromise forced him to concede Siamese territory to French Indochina in 1893 and 1907, and to British Burma in 1909. Frequent Burmese, Shan and Yunnanese contact with Northern Thailand during this period brought such now-famous delicacies as **kaeng hangleh** (a rich Burmese-style curry), **khâo sawy** (adapted from a popular Shan noodle recipe) and **khanōm jiin náam ngíaw** (a sweet and spicy Yunnanese noodle dish).

*Floating market at Damnoen Saduak*

Before WWII, very few restaurants could be found in Thailand, and those that did exist – mostly in Bangkok – focused on Chinese or European food. On the rare occasion when Thais had enough cash to eat out, they hungered for something different from their usual home fare. Indigenous cuisine thus remained confined to Thai homes and market vendors.

Only with the post-WWII influx of foreigners and Thailand's rapid economic development did Thai cooking begin to be appreciated as worthy of a night out. A similar process can be seen in neighbouring Myanmar and Laos, where stagnant economies minimised demand for local cuisine in restaurant settings. It has only been with recent economic growth – and a keen outside interest – that Burmese and Lao restaurants have begun appearing in large numbers. Back in Thailand, Thai restaurants are now the norm and foreign ones the exception, at least in most towns and cities – beach resorts remain an exception.

The current craze for 'authentic' Thai cuisine, though admirable, belies the internationalisation of Thai food culture which began centuries ago when the first trading ships entered the wide mouth of the Chao Phraya River bearing foods from Europe, the Americas and India. Step back another few centuries and you would find mule caravans driven down from China and Central Asia stocked with herbs, spices and tea. As a result of these early trade connections, many ingredients from outside the Thai diaspora in South-East Asia have found a permanent place in Thai kitchens. The process has worked in the opposite direction as well, and Thai seasonings and cooking techniques are finding their way into all sorts of world fusion experiments, from kitchens in Los Angeles to London, Paris and Perth. In every country bordering Thailand you will find a version of **tôm yam** (chilli & lemongrass soup) on local menus.

Beyond the kingdom, Thai cuisine took a long time to reach the west and it is yet to find its way to Africa or Latin America. Britons brought Indian food back to Europe, the French brought Vietnamese and the Dutch brought Indonesian, but there were no empire-builders to export Thai cuisine. Instead it was the travel explosion of the 1960s and 70s, particularly the growing popularity of the Asia trail among backpackers, that was responsible for spreading the word about Thai cooking and ultimately bringing it to Europe, America and Australia. In these corners of the globe Thai cuisine is once again meeting with new influences, and importing (or re-importing) them back to Thailand via techniques and ingredients found in other ethnic cooking styles. Its flexibility in either direction has made it all the more popular, and Thai cuisine clearly influences other cuisines more than it is influenced itself these days.

CULTURE

## How Thais Eat

Aside from the occasional indulgence in deep-fried savouries, most Thais sustain themselves on a varied and healthy diet filled with many fruits, carbohydrates and vegetables mixed with smaller amounts of animal protein and fat. The Thais' main culinary satisfaction seems to come not from eating large amounts of food at any one meal – 'all-you-can-eat' deals and even set multicourse meals are a rarity reserved for foreigners here – but rather from nibbling at a variety of dishes with as many different flavours as possible throughout the day.

In Thai, the word for 'meal', **méu**, is a close homonym with the word for 'hand', and Thais appear to extend a hand towards a bowl of noodles, a plate of rice or a banana leaf-wrapped snack with amazing frequency. There are no 'typical' times for meals, though the Anglo-American influenced noon to 1pm lunch break in urban Thailand tends to cluster diners in local restaurants at that hour. Even so, it's not at all unusual for a bank clerk or shopowner to order in a bowl of **kŭaytĭaw** (rice noodles) some time mid morning, and perhaps again around 3 or 4pm.

Nor are certain genres of food restricted to certain times of day. Practically anything can be eaten first thing in the morning, whether it's

*Digging into an Isaan meal in Bangkok*

sweet, salty or chilli-ridden. **Khâo kaeng** (curry over rice) is a very popular morning meal all over Thailand, as are **khâo mŭu daeng** (red pork over rice) and **khâo man kài** (sliced steamed chicken cooked in chicken broth and garlic and served over rice).

Lighter morning choices, especially for Thais of Chinese descent, include deep-fried chunks of **paa-thâwng-kōh** (fried wheat pastry) dipped in warm **náam tâo-hûu** (soya milk). Another early morning favourite is **kúay jáp**, a thick broth of sliced Chinese mushrooms and bits of chicken or pork. Thais also eat noodles, whether fried or in soup, with great gusto in the morning, or as a substantial snack food any time of day or night.

But **khâo** (rice) is taken at least once a day, preferably twice, in order for Thais to feel 'normal'. As the staple with which almost all Thai dishes are eaten – noodles, after all, are still seen as a Chinese import – it is considered an absolutely indispensable part of the daily diet (see Khao in the Staples & Specialities chapter). Most Thai families will put on a pot of rice, or start the rice cooker, just after rising in the morning to prepare a base for the day's menu. All other dishes, aside from noodles, are considered **kàp khâo** (side dishes) which supplement this central **aahāan làk** (staple).

**Plaa** (fish), finds its way into almost every meal, even if it's only in the form of **náam plaa** (a thin, clear, amber sauce made from fermented anchovies) which is used to salt Thai dishes, much as soy sauce is used in eastern Asia. The next favourite source of protein is **kài** (chicken), which is prepared in a variety of ways from curries to stirfries to barbecues. A very close third is **mŭu** (pork), particularly enjoyed by Chinese Thais while shunned by most Muslim Thais. Although **néua** (beef) isn't as popular as fish or chicken, there are some regional favourites such as Central Thailand's **néua phàt náam-man hăwy** (beef stirfried in oyster sauce) and North-East Thailand's **néua náam tòk** (literally, 'waterfall beef'). Most beef in Thailand comes from locally raised cattle, including water buffalo.

Thais are prodigious consumers of fruit. You'll find vendors pushing glass-and-wood carts filled with a rainbow of fresh sliced papaya, pineapple, watermelon, coconut and a more muted palette of salt-pickled or candied seasonal fruits. These are usually served in a small plastic bag with a thin bamboo stick to use as an eating utensil.

Because many restaurants in Thailand are able to serve dishes at an only slightly higher price than it would cost to make at home, Thais dine out frequently. One reason eating out is so cheap is that the most common type of Thai eatery – the true **ráan aahāan** (food shop) – has very low

*Doi Hoi Lord Restaurant, Bangkok*

overheads since the proprietor spends little on decor or presentation. Thai diners don't expect much more than great food, though a pleasant **banyaakàat** (ambience), perhaps simply an afternoon breeze, is always a bonus.

More commonly in the cities than in the countryside, Thais indulge in **aahāan wâang**, literally 'empty food' but perhaps better translated by the English 'junk food'. Teenagers, like teens all over the world, appear to be the main consumers of the myriad of plastic-bagged, mass-produced fried chips made from rice flour, wheat flour or less commonly corn flour.

*The classic yam plaa mèuk (hot & tangy salad with squid)*

CULTURE

## THE RIGHT TOOL FOR THE JOB

If you're not offered chopsticks, don't ask for them. When faràng ask for chopsticks to eat Thai food, it only puzzles the restaurant proprietors. An even more embarrassing act is trying to eat sticky rice (popular in the North and North-East) with chopsticks. You should use your right hand instead.

Chopsticks are reserved for eating Chinese-style food from bowls, or for eating in all-Chinese restaurants. In either case you will be supplied with chopsticks without having to ask. Unlike their counterparts in many western countries, restaurateurs in Thailand won't assume you don't know how to use them.

Flavourings for such crispy snacks run the gamut from a little salt to more heady components such as squid or shrimp. Shrimp crisps, in fact, are probably the most popular and widely available snack in any grocery store or corner convenience shop, including the ever-spreading, Japanese-owned 7-eleven chain.

More traditional aahāan wâang can be picked up in markets and from street vendors who fry up their fare in large oil-filled woks, to be served hot to passers-by. These include **klûay thâwt** (batter-fried bananas), **phêuak thâwt** (batter-fried taro) and a wide variety of deep-fried or barbecued meatballs.

Any evening of the week you'll see small groups of Thais – usually males – clustered around roadside tables, in outdoor restaurants or at the back of their homes, drinking Thai-brewed Singha beer or Mekong rice liquor while picking from an array of common dishes, one morsel at a time. These are **kàp klâem**, dishes specifically meant to be eaten while drinking alcohol, often before an evening meal or while waiting for the larger courses to arrive. Kàp klâem can be as simple as a plate of **mét má-mûang thâwt** (fried cashews) or as elaborate as one of the many types of **yam**, (hot & tangy salad) containing a blast of lime, chilli, fresh herbs and a choice of seafood, roast vegetables, noodles or meats (see the boxed text Kap Klaem in the Drinks chapter).

## BEACH MEMORIES

When I was a kid, we used to spend school holidays in Cha-am. In those days the only places to stay were simple, large wooden beach houses on stilts, designed so that the sea breezes circulated all around the house, keeping them amazingly comfortable even in the hot season. One of my aunts owned one of these old wooden places, and because it was closed up most of the year, we all had to pitch in and clean it up the first day we arrived, sweeping out the dust and spiders.

It took about four hours to drive to Cha-am from Bangkok then – nowadays it takes longer because of Bangkok traffic – and along the way we'd stop for lunch in Mae Klong (Samut Songkhram). Our favourite stop was an old Chinese eatery, Meng Khao Muu Daeng, for plates of really good **pèt yâang** (roast duck) and **mǔu daeng**, (barbecued pork), served with a half dozen **náam jîm** (dipping sauces). Because there were usually six or eight of us, depending on which relatives came along, my father always picked out their largest table. He made sure the restaurant staff set up a floor fan near our table, and ordered everyone around like we were in the army.

Back on the road we'd start getting excited about our stay at the beach. After we'd arrive, in the late afternoon when the fishermen's boats were pulled up at the centre of Cha-am's long sand beach, father would go out to chat with the fishermen. We'd usually stay two and sometimes three nights, and he wanted to make sure there would be plenty of fresh seafood for our visit.

The boats always had **puu thaleh** (sea crab) and **plaa mèuk klûay** (squid) on hand, so we ate lots of these. Some ladies with foodstalls along the beach would cook for us for very little money. Steamed crab claws, crab stir-fried in curry powder, roast squid and spicy squid yam were some of the dishes I can remember eating on every single visit, and they were always delicious. Often we could also buy our family's favourite fish, **plaa sǎmlii** (cottonfish). For this we'd build a little fire on the beach, wrap the fish in banana leaves, roast it over the coals and eat it with our hands, dunked in **náam jîm aahǎan thaleh** (seafood dipping sauce). My aunt's bungalow had a gas burner and steel counter on the back terrace upstairs, and she or my mother would prepare a few things, mainly sauces for the seafood, or stuffed omelettes using leftover crab. Sometimes mother would make a **hàw mòk thaleh** (mixed seafood souffle) using a curry paste she had made herself and brought down from Bangkok; she didn't like the local ones.

I've been back to Cha-am as an adult, with my friends. Now there are multi-storey hotels all along the northern end of the beach, and it probably won't be long before all the wooden beach houses to the south are also gone. My aunt sold hers long ago, making enough money to retire on her small guava farm on the banks of the Chao Phraya River in Thonburi. Cha-am still has great seafood. All of the dishes we used to eat 20 years ago can still be found there. I don't think you can build a fire on the beach anymore, but you can order **plaa sǎmlii phǎao** (fire-roasted cottonfish) at local restaurants.

*– Suksawat Sabaijai*
*Suksawat is a poet and musician living in Saraphi.*

*Dried Star and Puffer fish for sale – Ban Phe, Rayong*

## Etiquette

Eating in Thailand is nearly always a social event and people avoid eating alone whenever possible. When forced to fly solo by circumstance – such as during lunch breaks at work – a single diner usually sticks to one-plate dishes such as fried rice or curry over rice. Dining with others is always preferred from the Thai perspective because it means everyone has a chance to sample several dishes.

While Thai table manners would hardly ever be described as 'formal' in the western sense, there are plenty of subtleties to be mastered. Using the correct utensils and eating gestures will garner much respect from the Thais, who generally think western table manners are coarse.

Originally Thai food was eaten with the fingers, and it still is in certain regions of the kingdom and for certain foods such as **khâo nǐaw** (sticky rice). In the early 1900s, Thai restaurateurs began setting their tables with fork and spoon to affect a 'royal' setting (see History earlier in this chapter), and it wasn't long before fork-and-spoon dining became the norm in Bangkok and later spread throughout the kingdom.

The **sâwm** (standard fork) and **cháwn tó** (tablespoon) are placed to the left of the plate, and usually wrapped in a paper or cloth napkin. In simpler restaurants, these utensils are laid bare on the table or may not arrive until the food is served. Some restaurants place a steel or glass container on each tabletop in which a supply of clean forks and spoons are kept.

At informal eateries, you'll wipe your hands using a roll of **kràdàat cham-rá** (tissue) placed in the centre of the table, often in a plastic dispenser with one end of the rolled tissue protruding from a round opening. Visitors are often surprised to discover that this is the same sort of tissue used exclusively in western toilets.

To most Thais, pushing a fork into one's mouth is almost as uncouth as putting a knife in the mouth in western countries. Thais do use forks, however, to steer food onto the spoon, to eat chunks of roasted meat served as **kàp klâem** and to spear sliced fruit served at the end of the meal. Even so, the fork is never placed all the way into the mouth.

**Tà-kìap** (chopsticks) are reserved for dining in Chinese restaurants or for eating Chinese noodle dishes. Noodle soups are eaten with a spoon in the left hand (for spooning up the broth) and chopsticks in the right.

Another exception to the fork-and-spoon routine is sticky rice (common in the north and northeast), which is rolled into balls and eaten with the right hand, along with the accompanying food.

Whether at home or in a restaurant, Thai meals are always served 'family style', that is, from common serving platters. Traditionally, the party orders one of each kind of dish, perhaps a curry, a fish, a stirfry, a yam, a vegetable dish and a soup, taking care to balance cool and hot, sour and sweet, salty and plain. One dish is generally large enough for two people. One or two extras may be ordered for a large party.

Dishes are typically served more or less all at once rather than in courses. If the host or restaurant staff can't bring them all to the table at the same time, then the diners typically wait until everything has arrived before digging in. One exception to this rule is if a yam or other kàp klâem is ordered, as these are sometimes served as an appetiser with drinks before the main meal. When these dishes come out with everything else they will be eaten first.

Thais aren't fussy about dishes being served piping hot, so no one minds if the dishes sit untouched for a while. In fact it's considered impolite to take a spoonful of steaming hot food, as it implies that you're so ravenous or uncivilised that you can't wait to gorge yourself. The one exception to the cooling rule is noodle dishes, which are typically served right from the pan.

Whenever dining with Thais it's good to remember not to touch any of the food before the host (or oldest or wealthiest person present) announces 'kin khâo' (eat rice) often spoken rather quietly and informally rather than with any sort of grand gesture.

Empty plates are placed in front of every person at the beginning of the meal, and the diners take a little from each serving platter onto these plates. When serving yourself from a common platter, put no more than one or two spoonfuls onto your plate at a time. It's customary at the start of a shared meal to eat a spoonful of plain rice first – a gesture that recognises rice as the most important part of the meal. If you're being hosted by Thais, they'll undoubtedly encourage you to eat less rice and more curries, seafood etc as a gesture of their generosity (since rice costs comparatively little). The humble guest, however, takes rice with every spoonful.

For the most part, tôm yam and other soups aren't served in individual bowls except in tourist restaurants or in more elegant restaurants. You serve yourself from the common bowl, spooning broth and ingredients over your rice or into your own spoon. Sometimes serving spoons are provided. If not, you simply dig in with your own spoon.

Don't pick up a serving plate to serve yourself. Proper Thai food etiquette means leaving the plate on the tabletop and reaching over to it with your spoon, even if it means stretching your arm across the table. If you can't reach the platter at all, it's best to hand your plate to someone near the serving platter, who can then place some food on your plate. Most Thais will do this automatically if they notice you're out of platter range. Whatever you do, don't incline a serving plate over your individual plate – this is considered a very rude and greedy gesture.

Never ask for someone to pass food your way, but rather wait for someone to offer you more. Thais are constantly looking out for each other at mealtimes – making sure no one's plate is empty – and will usually give you more food than you can eat. Don't be surprised if another diner in your party, usually a woman sitting nearby, spoons food directly onto your plate, just like your mother did when you were a child. This is a completely normal gesture in Thai dining custom and carries no particular import other than showing compassion for a foreign guest.

Thais want you to enjoy the food, and at some point in the meal your host or one of your dining companions will pause for a second, smile and ask 'àràwy mãi?' (is it delicious?) The expected answer, of course, is 'àràwy' (delicious) or 'àràwy mâak' (very delicious). If you don't like the food, and don't mind a loss of face for everyone at the table, then you can boorishly reply 'mâi àràwy' (not delicious).

Always leave some food on the serving platters as well as on your plate. To clean your plate and leave nothing on the serving platters says to your hosts 'you didn't feed me enough'. This is why Thais tend to over-order at social occasions – the more food is left on the table, the more generous the host appears.

Cigarettes often appear both before and after a meal, but it is considered impolite to smoke during a meal. Thais will often step away from the table to smoke, mainly because ashtrays aren't usually placed on dining tables. It's not customary in Thailand to ask permission to smoke before lighting up, though this is beginning to change in Bangkok society. To be on the safe side, always ask 'sùup bùrì dâi mãi?' (Is it OK to smoke?).

# staples
## & specialities

Thailand is famous for its quality of rice, the grain which finds its way onto Thai tables everyday. Along with noodles, rice creates the cushioning for the kingdom's curries, salads, stirfries and sauces. The balance of hot, salty, sour and sweet in these dishes is maintained through the use of a wide range of fresh and preserved ingredients, with the infamous chilli providing the punch.

# Khao (Rice)

A tugboat pulls a ponderous train of aircraft hangar-sized barges along the Chao Phraya River into the middle of downtown Bangkok. Inside the creaking cargo-holds sit mountains of milky-coloured grains brought to feed this city of seven million, or perhaps to continue down river into the Gulf of Thailand, bound for world markets.

Thais, thought to be the world's first rice cultivators (see History in The Culture of Thai Cuisine chapter), carried rice with them wherever they went during their early migrations throughout South-East Asia, South Asia and China. In fact their sole concern, when choosing land on which to settle, appears to have been whether or not there was enough water to **plùuk khâo** (plant rice). The vast river valleys and deltas, known today as Thailand, suited this purpose so well that the Thais finally organised themselves into a single nation here nearly a thousand years ago.

Established by a people who seem to have a spiritual connection with the grain, **muang thai** (Land of the Thais) seemed destined to become the rice bowl of Asia. Thailand has led the world in rice exports since the 1960s, and the quality of Thai rice, according to the perception of many discerning Asians, is considered the best in the world. Thailand's **khâo hăwm málí** (jasmine rice) is so coveted that there is a steady underground business in smuggling bags of the fragrant grain to neighbouring Malaysia, Laos, Cambodia, Myanmar and even as far away as India and Nepal. The government of Thailand recently sued a US company for allegedly attempting to steal a Thai patent on jasmine rice, and no doubt there will be more litigation as Thai rice increases in popularity around the world.

More than just a culinary staple on the Thai table, the growing of rice is the primary farming activity nationwide, part and parcel of a way of life often romanticised in Thai novels and films. The all-purpose Thai word **chao naa** (farmer; literally, 'rice field person'), conjures up a figure dressed in a collarless **sêua mâw hâwm** (blue cotton tunic), holding a crescent-shaped rice cutter in one hand and a sheaf of rice ears in the other. A brightly chequered, folded **phâakhamáa** (short sarong) fastened sash-like around the waist, along with a wide-brimmed straw hat, complete the picture. Of course, the reality of rice farming doesn't quite measure up to this romantic vision. Conflicts between growers, landlords, rice millers, rice wholesalers and retailers are constant, and rice farmers earn incomes only slightly above that of the average unskilled labourer. Still, as long as Thailand remains competitive in the global market, there will always be work for the chao naa.

STAPLES

*Fanning rice to remove chaff*

Rice cultivation begins in a specially prepared corner of the field where rice seeds – unhusked rice grains – are germinated in the early monsoon season (typically July) to produce a thick crop of **klâa** (rice sprouts). When they reach a height of about 20cm, these are pulled out of the ground, tied into bunches, and transplanted in thinner rows throughout the remainder of the field. In typical lowland rice cultivation, the fields are kept flooded with water until the end of the monsoon season, and when the rice has grown tall and begins turning brown, the harvesting begins.

Not all rice, even of the same variety, matures at the same time. Rice that ripens early is called **khâo bao** (light rice) or **khâo tôn rá-duu** (early season rice), while rice that matures late is **khâo nàk** (heavy rice). In between is **khâo klaang** (middle rice). Discerning Thais claim to be able to taste the difference between rice harvested at different times, much like a gifted wine connoisseur can distinguish between wine vintages.

*Varieties of Thai rice.*

At least 75% of all rice produced in Thailand, up to 15 million tonnes in an average year, is **khâo naa pii** (one-field-per-year rice), planted during the traditional southwest monsoon season – roughly July to October. Depending on local water conditions, some rice farmers will be able to plant and irrigate a second crop after November to produce **khâo naa prang** (off-season rice). In sloped areas where field flooding would be impossible, **khâo râi** (plantation rice) is grown. After harvesting the **ruang khâo** (ears of rice) are threshed – often beneath the hooves of a water buffalo yoked to a post – and the loosened grains are winnowed in huge, flat woven baskets to remove the **ram khâo** (chaff).

Winnowed rice is traditionally stored in **yawng khâo** (round bins of woven bamboo plastered with mud or buffalo dung), which are usually constructed behind the villagers' houses on stilted and roofed platforms. Once the village's yawng khâo have been filled, the rest of the **khâo sāan** (unmilled rice) goes to market via direct or cooperative-supervised transactions with local **rohng sīi** (rice mills). After polishing the rice, the millers package it in strong burlap bags and sell it to wholesalers who may repackage it again.

Rice is so central to Thai food culture that the most common term for 'eat' is **kin khâo** (literally, 'consume rice') and one of the most common greetings is '**kin khâo láew rēu yang?**' (have you consumed rice yet?). All the dishes eaten with rice – such as curries, stirfries or soups – are simply classified as **kàp khâo** (with rice). Only two dishes using rice as a principal ingredient are common in Thailand, **khâo phàt** (fried rice) and **khâo mòk kài** (Southern Thai-style chicken biryani), neither of which is native to Thailand.

Most Thais eat **khâo jâo** (white rice), which is prepared by boiling it in a covered pot, a task known as **hūng khâo**. Before cooking, Thais rinse the raw rice grains in cold water to remove unwanted rice powder, which if left in produces sticky, starchy rice rather than the preferred slightly separated grains. Traditionally the cook rinses the rice three times in a row, the more devout Buddhists among them silently dedicating this task to the **triratana** (triple gems of the faith). Extra-finicky cooks may rinse a number of additional times until the water runs clear.

The amount of water added to the rice for boiling is crucial, although Thais don't use measuring cups as there's a much easier way: simply add enough water above the top of the rice to meet the first joint of your index finger. Every cook adjusts the 'rule of finger' more or less according to experience (all digits aren't of equal length, after all) and according to the age of the rice. Young rice needs to be cooked in less water, as it still contains natural moisture. Cooking time averages about 20 minutes, but this again will vary according to the type of rice.

## SPEAKING OF RICE

Khâo, so essential to the Thai identity, has taken on shades of meaning well beyond 'rice' or even 'food' in everyday speech. For example, if a Thai waiting for a phone line to be installed says it's like '**khâo khawy fõn**' (rice awaiting rain), it's a comment on the slowness of the phone company.

A Thai way of describing the honeymoon stage of a romantic relationship is to say '**khâo mài plaa man**' (new rice, juicy fish). The opposite? A long-term relationship gone bad is described as '**khâo bùut plaa ráa**' (spoiled rice, rotten fish). Another expression, '**khâo nâwk naa**' (rice outside the field), refers to the offspring of a racially mixed marriage.

In contemporary Thailand, rice is never scarce and betelnut is relatively inexpensive, so the expression '**khâo yâak màak phaeng**' (rice scarce, betelnut expensive) means times are tough. On the opposite side of that metaphorical fence, a contented, self-sustaining home or village may be described with the phrase '**khâo lẽua, kleua ìm**' (rice left over, salt full/satisfied).

Once the pot has been removed from the heat, the lid is kept in place to allow the rice to sit for 10-15 minutes before serving, and is then usually scooped onto serving plates without fluffing. Many Thais nowadays use automatic electric rice cookers (paying no attention whatsoever to the measuring instructions since they know their 'rule of finger' is more reliable), which will keep cooked rice warm for long periods of time. Cooked rice is usually referred to as **khâo súay** (literally, 'beautiful rice'), yet another clue as to how thoroughly Thais esteem this staple. When you order plain rice in a restaurant you may use this term or **khâo plào** (plain rice). Restaurants may serve rice by the **jaan** (plate) or you can order a **thõh** (large bowl), which is lidded to keep the rice warm and moist, and notched along the rim to accommodate the handle of a rice scoop. Thõh may be practical thick-sided plastic containers or more elaborate engraved, footed aluminium bowls with fancy serving spoons to match.

Most people living in Northern and North-Eastern Thailand prefer **khâo nĩaw** (sticky rice) over khâo jâo. In fact, many dishes from these regions are always served with khâo nĩaw, which you eat with your hands. You can easily tell uncooked sticky rice because it's much whiter – a rather opaque white – than white rice, and the grains are usually a bit shorter and more oval-shaped. Once it's cooked, however, sticky rice loses some of its whiteness and becomes almost translucent. Uncooked white rice is the opposite, appearing translucent before cooking and more opaque after.

Sticky rice is prepared using a cooking process known as **nêung khâo**. First, the uncooked rice is soaked in cold water overnight or for at least three hours. It is then drained, rinsed thoroughly and placed in a **hùat** (crescent-shaped bamboo steamer). The narrow end of the hùat is then fitted into the neck of a rounded **mâw khàek** (Indian pot) filled with boiling water, and the rice is left to steam for around 30 minutes. Cooks who don't have the traditional hùat and mâw khàek may use a western-style steamer, as long as the upper apparatus is first lined with muslin or cheesecloth so that rice grains don't fall into the water below.

Once the sticky rice is cooked, it's usually inserted into short, cylindrical, lidded baskets of woven reed or bamboo called **krà-tìp khâo**. Diners usually receive their own krà-tìp khâo to pluck individual servings of rice from.

Thais also grow **khâo nĭaw dam**, a deep purple sticky rice used in desserts and, in Northern Thailand, to produce a mild homemade rice wine called **khâo klam**. Thailand's famous Mekong whisky (see Rice Whisky in the Drinks chapter) comes from regular sticky rice. **Khâo klâwng** (brown rice) is traditionally thought of as something fed to prisoners and pigs. It has become only slightly more popular with health- and nutrition-oriented Thais over the last 15 years or so.

In the spiritual life of Thai food, rice once again takes centre place. The most common type of offering at spirit shrines is a small fistful of rice placed on a saucer. **Phǐi** (spirits) are thought to be particularly fond of sticky rice. During Buddhist festivals, many devotees will leave small lumps of rice called **khâo pràdàp din** (literally, 'earth-adorning rice') as offerings at the base of temple stupas or beneath banyan trees – *Ficus religiosa* – considered symbolic of the Buddha. Also nearly a half million Buddhist monks are offered rice each day, thus sustaining their monastic lives and earning religious merit for those who provide the rice.

Rice fields have their own wood and bamboo spirit shrines dedicated to Jao Mae Phosop (Mother Deity Phosop), where rice farmers leave offerings of unhusked rice, flowers, candles, incense and cups of Chinese tea to ensure Phosop's favour. At the beginning of the rice-growing season, the farmers hold a more elaborate ceremony in which rice grains from the last harvest are mixed with new rice seed and prayers for an abundant harvest are chanted. Later, as the first ears of rice appear – when the rice is 'pregnant' – the villagers make special offerings of fruits that pregnant women suppos-edly favour, such as tamarind, banana and sugarcane, along with betel and chewing tobacco. These are placed in a woven basket suspended from a cane pole in the middle of the rice field. A young woman from the village may also add such items as a hair comb, fragrant oils and powders and even a shawl and vanity mirror, to support Mae Phosop in her pregnancy.

STAPLES

## Kuaytiaw & Ba-mii (Noodles)

Exactly when the noodle reached Thailand is difficult to ascertain, but it almost certainly arrived along trade routes from China, since the preparation styles in contemporary Thailand are similar to those found in China's south.

Four basic kinds of noodle predominate in Thailand. Hardly surprising, given the Thai fixation on rice, is the overwhelming popularity of **kǔaytǐaw**, made by mixing pure rice flour with water to form a paste which is then steamed to form wide, flat sheets. These sheets are then folded and sliced into **sên yài** (flat 'wide line' noodles 2-3cm wide), **sên lék** ('small line' noodles about 5mm wide) and **sên mìi** ('noodle line' noodles only 1-2mm wide). **Sên mìi** dry out so quickly that they are usually sold only in their dried form.

The king of Thai noodledom, kǔaytǐaw comes as part of many dishes. The simplest, **kǔaytǐaw náam**, is kǔaytǐaw served in a bowl of plain chicken or beef stock along with bits of meat and pickled cabbage, with **phàk chii** (coriander leaf) as garnish. Season your noodle soup according to taste, dipping from a rack of small glass or metal containers on the table (see the boxed text Perk Up Your Noodle on the next page).

Another dish, **kǔaytǐaw phàt**, involves the quick stirfrying of the noodles in a wok with sliced meat (usually pork or chicken, occasionally beef), **phàk kha-náa** (Chinese kale), soy sauce and various seasonings. Aside from being found in any kǔaytǐaw stand, kǔaytǐaw phàt is a favourite crowd-pleaser at temple festivals all over the country.

Two other ways to order Thai rice noodles include **kǔaytǐaw hâeng** (dry kǔaytǐaw) and **kǔaytǐaw râat nâa** (kǔaytǐaw with gravy). For kǔaytǐaw hâeng, rice noodles are momentarily doused in very hot water to heat them up and soften them, then tossed in a soup bowl with garlic oil and topped with the usual ingredients that make up kǔaytǐaw náam, save the broth. Kǔaytǐaw râat nâa involves braising the noodles in a light gravy made with cornstarch-thickened stock, adding meats and seasonings and serving the finished product on an oval plate. **Kǔaytǐaw râat nâa tháleh** (a seafood version of kǔaytǐaw râat nâa) is popular throughout Thailand, particularly along the coast. **Râat nâa** (or lâat nâa in Bangkok and Central Thailand), the shortened name for any kǔaytǐaw râat nâa dish, is frequently used when ordering.

Chilli-heads must give **kǔaytǐaw phàt khîi mao** (drunkard's fried noodles) a try. A favourite lunch or late-night snack, this spicy stirfry consists of wide rice noodles, fresh basil leaves, chicken or pork, seasonings and a healthy dose of fresh sliced chillies. It's called drunkard's fried noodles because the blast of chilli is thought to be sobering.

*The rice harvest, Northern Thailand*

STAPLES

## PERK UP YOUR NOODLE

Much as chicken soup is viewed as something of a home cold remedy in the west, rice noodle soups in Thailand are often eaten to ward off colds, hangovers or general malaise. When you face a bowl of noodles and the array of condiments available to season them, you must be prepared to become your own pharmacist, mixing the ingredients to create the right flavour balance and, by implication, to set body and soul right.

If your table has a steel rack containing four lidded glass bowls or jars, the restaurant you're in serves **kŭaytīaw** (rice noodles). Typically these containers offer four choices:

**náam sôm phrík** – sliced green chillies, usually **phrík chíi fáa** (sky pointing chilli) or sometimes **phrík yùak** (banana-stalk chilli), in white vinegar

**phrík náam plaa** – **phrík khîi nŭu** (mouse-dropping chilli) in fish sauce

**phrík pon** – dried red chilli (usually phrík chíi fáa), flaked or ground to a near powder.

**náamtaan** – plain white sugar.

In typically Thai fashion, these condiments offer three ways to make the soup hotter – hot and sour, hot and salty and just plain hot – and one to make it sweet. Some kŭaytīaw vendors, particularly in Central Thailand, substitute **thùa pon** (ground peanuts) for the phrík náam plaa, which is provided in a separate bowl or saucer instead.

The typical noodle-eater will add a teaspoonful of each one of these condiments to the noodle soup, except for the sugar, which usually rates a full tablespoon. Until you're used to these strong seasonings, we recommend adding them a small bit at a time, tasting the soup along the way to make sure you don't go overboard. Adding sugar to soup may appear strange to some foreign palates, but it does considerably enhance the flavour of kŭaytīaw náam.

In addition to the condiments rack, a conscientious kŭaytīaw vendor will place a bottle of **náam plaa** (fish sauce), for those who want to make the soup saltier without adding the spice.

In North-Eastern Thailand, kŭaytīaw shops have a more elaborate set-up. Some follow the Lao and Vietnamese custom of serving a platter of fresh greens such as **phàk kàat hăwm** (lettuce), **phàk kàat náam** (watercress), **phàk phai** (Vietnamese mint), **bai hŏhráphaa** (sweet basil), **sàránàe** (mint) or **phàk chii** (coriander leaf) with an order of noodle soup. These are meant to be eaten raw along with the noodle soup, or they can be added directly to the bowl. Halved limes, a small bowl of **kà-pì** (shrimp paste) and a saucer of fresh whole phrík khîi nŭu completes the **Isaan** (North-Eastern) kŭaytīaw condiment array. In Isaan dialect, kŭaytīaw is often referred to as fŏe (from the Vietnamese, *pho*).

Probably the most well known kŭaytĭaw dish among foreigners is **kŭaytĭaw phàt thai**, usually called **phàt thai** for short, a plate of thin rice noodles stirfried with dried or fresh shrimp, beansprouts, fried tofu, egg and seasonings. Along the edge of the plate the cook usually places little piles of ground peanuts and ground dried chilli, along with lime halves and a few stalks of spring onion, for self-seasoning.

Some of Thailand's best noodle shops only operate late at night, to catch the crowds on their way home from an evening's entertainment. One well-known kŭaytĭaw vendor in Chiang Mai, Aung Phochana (situated south of the Chang Pheuak Gate), opens around 6pm and continues serving perhaps the best **kŭaytĭaw lûuk chín plaa** (rice noodles with fishballs) in Northern Thailand till just before dawn. Aung's noodle soups stand apart because the broth is incredibly tasty and the fishballs are fresh, delicate little orbs rather than the larger, chewy ones that are standard elsewhere.

As with most restaurants or vendor stands specialising in kŭaytĭaw, you can choose between sên yài or sên lék noodles when ordering your meal.

If you're buying kŭaytĭaw at a market or grocery store, you'll sometimes be able to choose between fresh noodles – best used within a few days before they harden – and dried noodles. Dried kŭaytĭaw are often called **kŭaytĭaw chanthabun**, in reference to Chanthaburi, a city along Thailand's eastern seaboard with a large Vietnamese population, which is the country's main production centre for dried rice noodles.

The second kind of noodle, particularly popular in Southern Thailand, is **khanŏm jiin**, produced by pushing rice flour paste through a sieve into boiling water. Although the name literally means 'Chinese pastry',

*Frying a large order of kŭaytĭaw phàt thai*

khanōm jiin developed its own culinary genre in Southern Thailand, where it is served doused with varying curries. The most standard curry topping is **náam yaa**, which roughly translates as 'herbal sauce'. The story behind this name lies in the presence of **krà-chai** (Chinese key), a root of the ginger family used as a traditional remedy for gastrointestinal ailments. The other spices are similar to those used in other Thai curries, one difference being that the main ingredient is ground or pounded fish, or **lûuk chín plaa** (fish balls) rather than whole pieces of fish or meat. In far Northern Thailand, khanōm jiin is often topped with **náam ngíaw**, a sweet and spicy sauce more akin to the original Yunnanese inspiration for this dish. Two other less common toppings, but also very tasty, include **sāo náam** (a scrumptious sauce of pineapple, dried shrimp, coconut, ginger and garlic) and **náam phrík** (spicy-sweet peanut sauce). In markets or grocery stores, khanōm jiin is always sold fresh, usually in small looped piles that look oddly like bird's nests.

The third genre of noodle, **bà-mìi**, is made from wheat flour and sometimes egg (depending on the noodle-maker or the brand). It's yellowish in colour and always the same size, about 1.5mm in diameter. Unlike kŭaytĭaw chanthabun, bà-mìi is sold only in fresh bundles, and unlike both kŭaytĭaw and khanōm jiin, it must be cooked immediately before serving. Cooking is simple; plunge a bamboo-handled wire basket full of bà-mìi into boiling water or broth and leave it for 2-3 minutes. Add broth plus meat, seafood or vegetables and you have **bà-mìi náam**. Serve in a bowl with a little garlic oil and no liquid, and you have **bà-mìi hâeng**.

Some restaurants serve both bà-mìi and kŭaytĭaw, but the best bà-mìi is found in shops or at vendor carts that specialise in bà-mìi and **kíaw** (won-ton). Kíaw is a triangle of bà-mìi dough wrapped around ground pork or ground fish (or a vegetable substitute at vegetarian restaurants). These dumplings may be boiled and added to soup, or fried to make **kíaw thâwt**. One of the most popular bà-mìi dishes in Thailand is **bà-mìi kíaw puu**, a soup containing kíaw and **puu** (crab).

Finally there's **wún sên**, an almost clear noodle made from mung bean starch and water. Sold in dried bunches, it's easily prepared by soaking it in hot water for 10-15 minutes. In Thailand, wún sên (literally, 'jelly thread') is used for only three dishes. The first and most native, **yam wún sên**, is a hot & tangy salad made with lime juice, fresh sliced **phrík khîi nŭu** (mouse dropping chillies), mushrooms, dried or fresh shrimp, ground pork and various seasonings. The second appearance is in **wún sên òp puu**, bean thread noodles baked in a lidded, clay pot with crab and seasonings. Wún sên is a common ingredient in **kaeng jèut**, (bland soup) a Chinese-influenced soup containing ground pork, soft tofu and a few vegetables.

*Fried bà-mìi to go*

## Kaeng (Curries)

The word 'curry' is said to come from the Tamil *kari*, meaning 'sauce', and the general assumption today is that all curry cooking descends from Indian models. If so, the spread of curry began early, as cooks in the Roman Empire mixed ground black pepper, ginger and cumin that came from Asia via the Silk Road in classic curry-like ways.

The importing of spices from east to west intensified following the 11th century Crusades, when Europeans ended their violent contact with the Middle Eastern Arab and Persian cultures. It's possible that curry recipes may have found their way to Europe during this period, though trade in spices between the European and Arab worlds had existed long before.

Of course no Indian curry contained chilli peppers until after this New World plant was introduced to South and South-East Asia by seafaring Portuguese traders in the mid-16th century. Until that culinary watershed, curries – spice concoctions of intense flavour intended to be eaten with rice, chapatis or other grain staples – depended upon **phrík thai** (black pepper), a South-East Asian native, for all of their gustatory heat.

What many westerners today know as 'curry' really originated in South India, when English colonisers modified local seasonings to create 'curry powder'. Although Thais are familiar with Indian-style **phŏng kàrìi** (curry powder), it's used only in a few Hokkien Chinese-influenced dishes such as **puu phàt phŏng kàrìi** (cracked crab stirfried with bottled curry powder and eggs). The only use of the term **kàrìi** in Thai cuisine is in **kaeng kàrìi kài**, the one Thai dish that most approximates a true Indian curry. The word **kàrìi** also happens to be Thai slang for 'prostitute', and is thus the source of endless puns intentionally confusing cooking with sex.

In Thai, kaeng (rhyme it with the English 'gang') refers to any dish with a lot of liquid and can thus refer to soups like **kaeng jèut** (bland soup) as well as the classic chilli-based curries such as **kaeng phèt** (hot curry) – for which Thai cuisine is famous. The preparation of all chilli-based kaeng begins with a **khrêuang kaeng**, created by mashing, pounding and grinding an array of ingredients to form an aromatic, extremely pungent-tasting and rather thick paste. Some khrêuang kaeng run to the consistency of fresh clay, while others are as soft as cornmeal dough. Although certain regional Indian curry preparations do consist of a paste, never are they as thick as a typical Thai khrêuang kaeng.

The moisture and viscosity of a khrêuang kaeng derives from the use of mostly fresh, rather than dried, herbs and roots, and from the inclusion of **náam plaa** (fish sauce) and/or **kà-pì** (shrimp paste). These ingredients appear to have been an essential part of Thai kaeng since before the arrival of the chilli pepper. Early Thai and Chinese historical records mention pungent food preparations containing native galangal, ginger, lemongrass, black pepper and shrimp paste. In 1687 French diplomat Simon de la Loubére noted that:

> the Siamese make a very good meal with a pound of rice a day, which amounts to not more than a farthing, and with a little dry or salt fish, which costs not much more. Their sauces are plain, a little water with some spices, garlic, or some sweet herb. They do very much esteem a liquid sauce, like mustard, which is only cray-fish corrupted because they are ill-salted [and] they call it Kepi.

Jesuit missionary Nicolas Gervaise recorded a kaeng recipe, in the 18th century, containing 'salt, pepper, ginger, cinnamon, cloves, garlic, white onions, nutmeg and several strongly flavoured herbs … mixed in considerable quantities with … shrimp paste'. Here we finally see the inclusion of ingredients (cinnamon, clove, nutmeg) that may have originated in India.

Today the use of these ingredients in Thai kaeng is limited to two curries with obvious Indian or Malay origins, the aforementioned kaeng kàrìi kài and **kaeng mátsàman** (literally, 'Muslim curry'). For all others the main ingredients are galangal, lemongrass, chilli and shrimp paste, with the addition of various other native rhizomes and herbs. It may be no coincidence that in most cases these herbs and spices are also considered **samũn phrai** (medicinal plants) with specific therapeutic attributes.

Thus it's entirely possible that kaeng developed on its own and that the same imported chillies that captivated Indian cooks – who, up to then, had depended on black pepper for culinary sting – found receptivity amid an indigenous kaeng tradition. Hence the only original link between Thai and Indian currydom may have been black pepper.

Whatever its origin, native or imported, each khrêuang kaeng derives character from the type and proportions of the spices chosen. Nowadays, the most basic will include:

**phrík hâeng** – dried chilli, usually phrík chíi fáa
  (see Phrik later in this chapter)
**khàa** – galangal
**tà-khrái** – lemongrass
**ma-krùt** – kaffir lime (peel, leaves or both)
**hãwm daeng** – shallots
**krà-thiam** – garlic
**kà-pì** – shrimp paste
**kleua** – salt

To this classic khrêuang kaeng, other ingredients will be added to make a specific kaeng. For example, **yíiràa** (cumin) and **mét phàk chii** (coriander seed) are important additions for making **kaeng khĭaw-wǎan** (see the boxed text Kaeng of Three beginning on the next page).

Once a khrêuang kaeng has been prepared, it will keep several days (longer if refrigerated or frozen) before it must be used, although for the full vibrancy of flavour it should be used immediately. Don't let any water come into contact with any khrêuang kaeng or it will spoil more quickly.

In Thai municipal markets, you will often see people selling various types of khrêuang kaeng, stored in large plastic or steel and porcelain bowls. Be aware, however, that freshness and quality of the pastes aren't always guaranteed. Check their smell, as older khrêuang kaeng will smell more strongly of shrimp paste, or stick with recommendations supplied by Thai acquaintances.

Nowadays vacuum-packed khrêuang kaeng can be purchased in most Thai supermarkets, but the flavour never comes close to the fresh-pestled, homemade versions. The better ready-made khrêuang kaeng are those crafted by specialist shops such as Nitaya and Mae Sri in Bangkok's Banglamphu district.

Most kaeng begin with the blending of the khrêuang kaeng into **hŭa kà-thí** (coconut cream) that has been brought to a quick boil in a saucepan or wok. From here on the rest of the ingredients (meat, poultry, seafood and/or vegetables) are added one at a time, along with **hǎang kà-thí** (coconut milk) to further thin and flavour the kaeng. A khrêuang kaeng should never be thinned with water, but rather with oil, coconut milk or the moisture found in other ingredients.

Some recipes will omit coconut milk entirely to produce a particularly fiery kaeng known as **kaeng pàa** (forest curry). Another kaeng that does not use coconut milk is **kaeng sôm** (sour curry), made with dried chillies, shallots, garlic and Chinese key pestled with salt, shrimp paste and fish sauce. Cooked with **náam mákhǎam** (tamarind juice) and green papaya to create an overall tanginess, the result is a soupy, salty, sweet-and-sour ragout that most westerners would never identify with the word 'curry'.

A few extra seasonings such as **phàk chii** (coriander leaf), **bai ma-krùt** (kaffir lime leaves), **bai hŏhráphaa** (sweet basil leaves) and **náam plaa** (fish sauce) may be added to taste just before serving. Unlike Indian curries, kaeng do not require long cooking times. With the khrêuang kaeng and all other ingredients at hand, most kaeng are thrown together in a matter of minutes.

*Dried chillies, shallots and garlic make up the foundation for many curry pastes*

*Four curries, clockwise from lower left: kaeng phèt; kaeng khĭaw-wăan; kaeng hangleh; kaeng phánaeng; surrounded by shallots, dried chillies, lemongrass, galangal, garlic, kaffir lime and kaffir lime leaves*

STAPLES

## Kaeng of Three

Of all the cooking techniques found in Thai **sìlàpaahãan** (food arts), the preparation of **khrêuang kaeng** (curry pastes) often appears the most difficult to the introductory student. Yet to the average Thai cook the procedure is very simple, like whipping up a Saturday morning omelette. While the proportions of ingredients are almost unwavering in traditional recipes, to put your own mark on the curry world you will have to experiment with different recipe ratios and the addition of other ingredients. Experienced cooks abandon recipes altogether and work by sight, smell and touch.

The main instruments needed to tackle a khrêuang kaeng are a **khrók** (mortar) and **sàak** (pestle), along with a sharp knife for those few ingredients that need slicing.

All the ingredients must be ground and mashed with mortar and pestle until they **khâo kan** (enter together), that is they are blended into a smooth paste. Start with a pounding, grinding motion focused on the bottom of the mortar until the coarser ingredients are equally pulverised, then switch to more of a whipping motion along the sides of the mortar, occasionally scraping the bottom to catch any 'escapees'. Mortars and pestles made of solid stone work best. Although some cooks try to speed up the process by using a blender or food processor, most Thai chefs and Thai food connoisseurs swear that the mortar and pestle better releases the aromatic oils that give each kaeng its characteristic flavour.

The three khrêuang kaeng featured here will produce classic Thai curries no matter what you choose for the main body – seafood, chicken, beef or vegetables. For vegetarian versions consider adding mushrooms (straw mushrooms work best) and cubes of tofu.

All curries are meant to be served with rice.

*Curry pastes on display in a municipal market*

# Kaeng Phet (Hot Curry)

Also known as **kaeng daeng** (red curry) and **kaeng phèt daeng** (red hot curry), this is the most traditional of Thai curries and is often used as a base to create other curries. This curry paste should be quite spicy, but the number of chillies can be reduced by half without seriously affecting the overall flavour.

Two of the most well loved versions of kaeng phèt are **kaeng phèt pèt yâang** (roast duck curry), a recipe confined to the royal court until the mid 20th century, and **kaeng phèt kài nàw mái** (chicken and bamboo shoot curry), a working-class mainstay of many rice & curry shops.

**khrêuang kaeng phèt** (hot curry paste)

| | |
|---|---|
| 15 | dried phrík chíi fáa (sky pointing chillies) |
| 15 | green peppercorns |
| 4 | tablespoons chopped garlic |
| 3 | tablespoons chopped shallots |
| 2 | tablespoons sliced fresh lemongrass |
| 2 | teaspoons chopped coriander root |
| 1½ | tablespoons chopped fresh galangal |
| 1½ | teaspoons roasted coriander seed |
| ½ | teaspoon roasted cumin seed |
| 1 | teaspoon shrimp paste |
| 1 | teaspoon salt |

Slice open the dried chillies, shake out and discard the seeds and soak the chillies in warm water until they are soft and flexible. Grind and mash all the ingredients together in a mortar until a thick, brick-red paste is formed.

**kaeng phèt pèt yâang** (roast duck curry)

| | |
|---|---|
| 1½ | tablespoons vegetable oil |
| 3 | tablespoons hot curry paste |
| 2½ | cups (625ml) coconut milk |
| 1 | roast duck, boned and sliced into 2-3cm pieces* |
| 8-10 | cherry tomatoes |
| 1 | cup (200g) whole Thai eggplants |
| ¾ | cup (150g) pineapple chunks |
| ½ | cup (125ml) clear chicken stock |
| 1 | teaspoon palm sugar |
| 2 | tablespoons fish sauce |
| ½ | teaspoon salt |
| 3 | kaffir lime leaves, sliced lengthways into 3cm strips |

* The duck skin may be removed, but much of the 'roast' flavour will be lost.

In a thick-bottomed saucepan, stirfry the curry paste in the vegetable oil on medium-high heat until fragrant. Add half the coconut milk, mix thoroughly, then add the duck and simmer for five minutes to allow the curry paste and coconut milk to permeate the meat.

Add the other half of the coconut milk and all the remaining ingredients except the kaffir lime leaves, and simmer another five minutes. Remove from the heat, garnish with sliced kaffir lime leaves and serve.

**kaeng phèt kài nàw mái** (chicken & bamboo shoot curry)
½    cup (125ml) coconut cream
1    tablespoon hot curry paste
300g chicken breast, sliced into rough 5cm pieces
1½   cups (375ml) coconut milk
300g fresh bamboo shoots, sliced*
1    fresh phrík chíi fáa (sky pointing chilli), seeded and thinly sliced
½    cup sweet basil leaves
1½   teaspoons sugar
2    tablespoons fish sauce
¼    teaspoon salt
     a few sweet basil leaves for garnish

*Canned bamboo shoots may be substituted, but rinse the shoots thoroughly in cold water first.

Heat the coconut cream in a saucepan or wok on medium heat till it begins to separate, then add the curry paste and stir-cook until the paste and cream are well blended and aromatic.

Add the chicken pieces to the pan, stir all ingredients and cook until the chicken is opaque and oil begins to appear.

Add the coconut milk and bamboo shoots, and stir on medium heat for 5 minutes.

Stir in the sliced chilli, basil, sugar, fish sauce and salt and cook another 1-2 minutes so the basil begins to wilt slightly. Remove from the heat, garnish with fresh whole basil leaves and serve with rice.

STAPLES

### Kaeng Khiaw-waan (Green Curry)

**khrêuang kaeng khĩaw-wãan** (green curry paste)

| | | | |
|---|---|---|---|
| 10-20 | fresh green phrík khĩi nũu (mouse-dropping chillies), depending on tolerance | | |
| 10 | chopped garlic cloves | 5 | chopped shallots |
| 1 | teaspoon chopped fresh galangal | 5 | green peppercorns |
| 1 | teaspoon roasted coriander seed | 1/2 | teaspoon salt |
| 1 | teaspoon shrimp paste | | |
| 1 | teaspoon chopped fresh coriander root | | |
| 1/2 | teaspoon ground roasted cumin seed | | |
| 1/2 | teaspoon chopped kaffir lime peel | | |
| 1 | tablespoon chopped fresh lemongrass | | |

Grind and mash all ingredients together in a mortar until a thick green paste is formed.

**kaeng khĩaw-wãan** (green curry)

| | | | |
|---|---|---|---|
| 3 | tablespoons green curry paste | 1/3 | cup (85ml) coconut cream |
| 2 | tablespoons fish sauce | | |
| 1/2 | cup sweet basil leaves | 1 1/2 | cups (375ml) coconut milk |
| 1/2 | cup whole coriander leaves | | |
| 1 1/2 | teaspoons sugar | | |
| 1/2 | cup (100g) pea eggplants | | |
| 300g | boneless chicken, pork or beef, sliced in rough 5cm strips | | |

Heat the coconut cream in a saucepan or wok on medium heat till it begins to separate, add the curry paste and stir until well blended and aromatic.

Add the meat to the pan and stir until the meat is opaque and oil begins to appear.

Add the coconut milk and pea eggplants, and continue to stir on medium heat for 5 minutes.

Stir in the basil, fish sauce and sugar and cook another 1-2 minutes so the basil begins to wilt slightly.

Garnish with coriander leaves and serve.

## Kaeng Phanaeng

The name for this relatively mild curry may be a Thai corruption of an English pronunciation of Penang, an island off the west coast of Malaysia not far from the Thai border. The seasonings, however, are more Thai than Malay.

**khrêuang kaeng phánaeng** (phánaeng curry paste)

| | |
|---|---|
| 5 | dried phrík chíi fáa (sky pointing chillies) |
| 5 | shallots |
| 10 | cloves of garlic, sliced |
| 1 | teaspoon minced fresh galangal |
| ½ | tablespoon minced kaffir lime peel |
| 1 | teaspoon chopped coriander root |
| 5 | green peppercorns |
| 1 | teaspoon shrimp paste |
| 1 | teaspoon salt |

Slice open the dried chillies, shake out and discard the seeds and soak the chillies in warm water until they are soft and flexible. Grind and mash all the ingredients together in a mortar until a thick red paste is formed.

**kaeng phánaeng kûng** (shrimp phánaeng curry)

| | |
|---|---|
| ½ | cup (125ml) coconut cream |
| 3 | tablespoons phánaeng curry paste |
| 1½ | cups (375ml) coconut milk |
| ½ | cup roasted, ground peanuts |
| 1 | fresh phrík chíi fáa (sky pointing chilli), seeded and thinly sliced |
| 3 | tablespoons palm sugar or coconut sugar |
| ½ | teaspoon salt |
| 500g | shrimp |
| ⅓ | cup sweet basil leaves |
| 5/6 | kaffir lime leaves, sliced length-wise into 2mm-wide strips |
| 2 | teaspoons fish sauce |

Heat the coconut cream in a saucepan or wok on medium heat until it begins to separate. Add the curry paste and stir until the paste and cream are well blended and aromatic.

Add the coconut milk, ground roasted peanuts, chilli, palm sugar and salt to the pan, lower the heat, stir all the ingredients and let simmer for about 10 minutes.

Stir in the shrimp and cook for about 5 minutes, or until the shrimp becomes opaque.

Add the basil, kaffir lime leaves and fish sauce, remove from the heat and serve with rice.

## Yam (Hot & Tangy Salad)

Equal to kaeng in terms of Thai-ness is the ubiquitous **yam**, a hot & tangy salad containing a blast of lime, chilli, fresh herbs and a choice of seafood, roast vegetables, noodles or meats. Thais prize yam dishes so much that they are often eaten on their own, without rice, before the meal has begun. Although food writers claim that the yam perfectly balances Thai cuisine's four basic flavours (tangy, salty, sweet and hot), the newcomer will counter that two sensations take centre place – tangy and hot.

Lime juice provides the tang, while the abundant use of chillies produce the heat. Other ingredients vary considerably, but plenty of leafy vegetables and herbs are usually present, including lettuce (often lining the dish) and mint leaves. Lemongrass, shallots, kaffir lime leaves and **khêun chàai** (Chinese celery) may also come into play. Most yam are served at room temperature or just slightly warmed by any cooked ingredients.

*Yam má-mûang - green mango salad to go*

Without a doubt, yam are the spiciest of all Thai dishes, and **yam phrík chíi fáa** (sky pointing chilli yam) is perhaps the hottest. A good yam to start off with if you're not so chilli-tolerant is **yam wún sên**, which consists of mung bean starch noodles tossed with shrimp, ground pork, coriander leaf, lime juice and fresh sliced chillies. Another tame yam that tends to be a favourite among Thais and foreigners alike is **yam plaa dùk fuu**, made from fried shredded catfish, chillies and peanuts with a shredded mango dressing on the side.

Many types of seafood yam – especially those made with squid and/or shrimp – are popular and very tasty. Yam may also be made with vegetables (**yam thùa phuu**, made with angle beans), fungi (**yam hèt hāwm**, made with shiitake mushrooms) or fruit (**yam sôm oh**, a delicious Chiang Mai speciality made with pomelo).

On many Thai menus, the yam section will be the longest. Yet often when these same menus are translated into English, most or all of the yam are omitted because Thai restaurateurs harbour the idea that the delicate **faràng** (western) palate cannot handle the heat or pungency. The usual English menu translation is either 'Thai-style salad' or 'hot and sour salad'.

### Yam Plaa Meuk (Squid Yam)

Yam plaa mèuk is probably the most common seafood yam, as squid is relatively inexpensive here and available all year round. It's also one of the simpler yam to prepare. The secret to a good squid yam is tender, rather than rubbery, squid, and the only way to cook tender squid is to parboil it quickly.

5      fresh phrík khîi nûu (mouse-dropping chillies)
5      garlic cloves, minced
¼     cup (60ml) fresh lime juice
4      tablespoons fish sauce
500g squid
½     cup mint leaves
2      shallots, thinly sliced
1      cup Chinese celery, cut into 3cm lengths
1      red phrík chii faa (sky pointing chilli), thinly sliced

Using a mortar & pestle, pound the garlic and phrík khîi nûu into a paste. Blend it with the lime juice and fish sauce to form a dressing. Set aside.

Carve a cross-hatch pattern into the squid and slice into 2 sq cm pieces. Drop the squid pieces into boiling water and parboil for no more than a minute. Remove with a wire strainer.

Toss the squid with the mint, shallots, Chinese celery and phrík chii faa, then add the dressing and toss again. Serve on a plate covered with lettuce leaves.

To give this yam a completely different flavour, leave out the Chinese celery and substitute one tablespoon of sliced kaffir lime leaves and two tablespoons of sliced lemongrass.

STAPLES

## Muat Phat (Stirfries)

Probably the simplest dishes in the Thai cooking repertoire are those prepared by stirfrying. This method of cooking was brought to Thailand by the Chinese, who are world famous for being able to stirfry a whole banquet in a single wok.

Despite its Chinese origins, **phàt** (stirfry) dishes are never served here with soy sauce as a condiment except in Chinese restaurants. Instead they come with **phrík náam plaa** (see Naam Jim & Naam Phrik later in this chapter) on the side – an instant way to give anything Chinese a predominantly Thai flavour.

The list of Thai dishes that you can stirfry is seemingly endless. Many of them are better classified as Chinese, such as **néua phàt náam-man hãwy** (beef in oyster sauce). Some are clearly Thai-Chinese hybrids, such as **kài phàt phrík khĩng**, in which chicken is stirfried with ginger, garlic and chillies – ingredients shared by both traditions – but seasoned with fish sauce. Also leaning toward the Thai side – if only because cashews are native to Thailand but not to China – is **kài phàt mét má-mûang hìmáphaan** (sliced chicken stirfried in dried chillies and cashews), a favourite with faràng tourists.

Perhaps the most Thai of the phàt genre is the popular lunch-time staple **phàt bai kà-phrao**, a stirfry of chicken or pork with garlic, fresh sliced chillies, soy and fish sauce and lots of holy basil. Order **khâo phàt bai kà-phrao** if you want this dish served over rice rather than separately. In a fancier version of this dish, the holy basil will be crisp-fried separately from the rest of the dish and served on the side.

Another classic Thai stirfry is **phàt phèt** (literally, 'hot stirfry'), in which the main ingredients are quickly stirfried with **khrêuang kaeng phèt daeng** (red khrêuang kaeng) and tossed with sweet basil leaves before serving. This recipe is most often applied to seafood or freshwater fish, such as shrimp, squid, catfish and freshwater eel.

*Ingredients for phàt thai*

Stirfry chicken, pork, beef or shrimp with **phrík thai** (black pepper) and **garlic** (krà-thiam) and you have **phàt phrík thai krà-thiam**, a relatively mild recipe often ordered more as a 'fill-in' dish during a larger meal.

For lovers of fresh vegetables, the dish **phàt phàk kha-náa** (Chinese kale stirfried in black bean sauce) is worth looking out for, as is **phàt phàk ruam** (literally, 'friendly mixed vegetables').

**Mùat thâwt** (deep-frying in oil) is a technique generally reserved for snacks like **klûay thâwt** (fried bananas) or **paw pía** (egg rolls). One exception is **plaa thâwt** (fried fish), which is the most common way you'll find any fish prepared. Many Thai recipes featuring whole fish require that it be fried first, usually in a wok filled with cooking oil to a depth of around 5cm. The fish is fried until the outside flesh is crispy to a depth of at least 1cm. Although this may appear to dry the fish out, in Thailand most fish fried in this way will then be topped with some sort of sauce – lime gravy or a cooked chilli-onion mixture – which will re-moisten the dish. Some fish, such as mackerel, will be steamed first, then lightly pan-fried in a smaller amount of oil to seal in the moisture.

A very few dishes require ingredients to be dipped in batter and then deep-fried. Two exceptions are **kài thâwt** (fried chicken) and **kûng chúp pâeng thâwt** (batter-fried shrimp).

## Kung Phat Khing (Prawns Stirfried in Ginger)

Although this quick and easy dish is more Chinese than Thai, it can nicely balance a meal already containing several spicy Thai dishes.

| | | | |
|---|---|---|---|
| 2 | tablespoons vegetable oil | ½ | teaspoon sugar |
| 2 | tablespoons shredded fresh ginger | 8 | large prawns |
| 1 | tablespoon minced garlic | | |
| 3 | tablespoons chicken stock | | |
| 1½ | tablespoons fish sauce | | |
| 1 | tablespoon soy sauce | | |
| 8 | straw mushrooms | | |
| 2 | spring onions, sliced into 6cm lengths | | |

Peel the prawns, cut a shallow slit along their backs and remove the veins. Fry the ginger and garlic in the oil over medium heat until golden, then add the stock, fish sauce, soy sauce and sugar. Stirfry until bubbling, then add the prawns, straw mushrooms and spring onion. Continue stir-frying until the prawns are opaque – no more than three minutes.

One **phrík chíi fáa** (sky pointing chilli), sliced thinly, can be tossed in with the prawns to give this dish more kick.

STAPLES

## Naam Jim (Dipping Sauce)
## & Naam Phrik (Chilli Dip)

The saucer of **phrík náam plaa** – a simple concoction of sliced fresh red and green **phrík khîi nũu** (mouse dropping chillies) floating in **náam plaa** (fish sauce) – is a standard condiment found on nearly every Thai table – as common as salt & pepper shakers in Europe.

Sometimes called náam plaa phrík, this sauce is spooned onto your food whenever you feel the need for more saltiness – much like soy sauce – and for an extra kick that goes far beyond that of black pepper. Although Thai cooks use regular salt in the kitchen for many recipes, you will never see it as a condiment – it's considered a coarse method of salting food.

You may enjoy the marine flavour provided by náam plaa's fermented fish origins. Thailand's fish sauce industry is centred in Rayong, a province about three hours drive east of Bangkok along the Gulf of Thailand coast. A variety of small fishes are used to make náam plaa, including **plaa kà-tàk** (a type of anchovy). Harvested from the gulf, the fish are stored in barrels with an exact ratio of water and salt, and left to ferment – or 'rot' if you will – until a soupy and highly aromatic mixture evolves. The resulting brownish liquid is then carefully filtered to remove all solids, pasteurised and bottled in glass or plastic containers. Bottled fish sauce is sold at every grocery shop and market in Thailand; the most famous and reliable brand is **thiparot** (divine taste).

### ROTTEN FISH, ANYONE?

In North-Eastern Thailand an unpasteurised version of náam plaa known as **plaa ráa** (literally, 'rotten fish') is sold in earthenware jars. Known by its Lao name, *pàa dàek*, in some parts of Isaan, such raw fish sauces are responsible for most of the cases of opisthorchiasis (a parasitic infection of the liver) recorded in Thailand. Why do people eat this? It's because they prefer the home-made flavour of plaa ráa over processed fish sauce.

Most cooks make up a fresh saucer of phrík náam plaa just before a meal is served, so that the chillies retain their bright colour and the separate flavours of chilli and fish sauce are still clearly discernible. Better restaurants will provide an individual saucer of phrík náam plaa for each diner. Restaurants sometimes provide a container of pure náam plaa at the table for those who prefer the amber liquid without chillies.

---

**SPICY SAYINGS**

In Thailand, a man is said to '**kin náam phrík thûay diaw**' (eat chilli paste from a single bowl), if he is faithful to one woman. If he stays with the same woman for a long time, he may be said to '**kin náam phrík thûay kào**' (eat chilli paste from the original bowl).

---

To accompany seafood, phrík náam plaa's flavour palette expands with the addition of minced garlic, lime juice and a little sugar to create **náam jîm aahāan tháleh** (seafood dipping sauce). It is best prepared fresh with the meal.

With fried or grilled chicken, **náam jîm kài** (chicken dipping sauce, a mixture of dried red chilli flakes, honey or sugar and rice vinegar) is a perfect accompaniment. It doesn't need to be freshly prepared and is sold in bottled form. As usual, it arrives at the table in a small saucer. Another favourite sauce, especially for **kài yâang** (Isaan-style grilled chicken), is **náam phrík phāo**, a thicker sauce made with dried chillies which have been roasted together with **kà-pì** (shrimp paste) and then mortar-blended with fish sauce, a little sugar or honey, and possibly roast garlic.

**Thâwt man plaa** (fried fishcakes) come with their own sauce on the side that is very similar to náam jîm kài with the addition of sliced cucumber, chopped shallots, coarse ground roasted peanuts and coriander leaf. This sauce must be spooned onto the fishcakes, as it's too chunky for dipping. **Thâwt man kûng** (fried shrimp cakes) are most commonly dipped in a simple concoction of honey mixed with a few red pepper flakes. Most other náam jîm available are variations on the above.

One genre of sauces central to traditional Thai cuisine, yet which is rarely seen outside of Thailand, is **náam phrík**, a thick chilli and shrimp paste dip usually eaten with fresh raw or steamed vegetables. The most common and most pungent chilli dip of this kind is **náam phrík kà-pì**, made with an extra dose of kà-pì and fresh phrík khîi nūu, the hottest of the Thai chillies. In addition to vegetables, náam phrík kà-pì is usually eaten with **plaa thuu** (mackerel) that has been steamed and fried, or with fried **plaa châwn** (serpent-headed fish, a freshwater variety).

Certain kinds of náam phrík contain **maengdaa naa** (a large flat water beetle commonly found in rice fields). Faràng often mistake this bug for the cockroach, when it is sold in markets. The bugs are thoroughly mashed into the paste, so you're unlikely to know they're there, but if you detect an after-taste reminiscent of menthol the dip probably contains maengdaa naa.

## Naam Phrik Ka-pi (Chilli & Shrimp Paste Dip)

A native of Central Thailand, this is the most classic of all the Thai náam phrík.

3        teaspoons shrimp paste
1        tablespoon minced garlic
5-10    fresh phrík khîi nŭu (mouse-dropping chilli) – depending on how
         hot you want it
6        pea eggplants
½        tablespoon dried shrimp powder
3        teaspoons coconut sugar or palm sugar
         juice of two limes

Roast the shrimp paste in aluminium foil over an open flame or under a broiler until fragrant. Mash the shrimp paste and garlic together with a mortar & pestle until smooth.

Add the chillies and pea eggplants to the mortar and blend until mixed but not quite smooth.

Add the remaining ingredients to the mortar and mix slowly (to avoid splashing).

Scoop into a bowl and serve as a dip, with steamed-fried mackerel or fried serpent-headed fish, fresh cut lengths of green beans, whole **thùa pon** (angle beans), sliced bamboo shoots, sliced gourd, steamed okra, steamed whole Thai eggplant and sliced cucumber. For a more substantial dish, add batter-fried long eggplant slices to the platter.

For a garnish, add a few whole steamed pea eggplants and fresh phrík khîi nŭu.

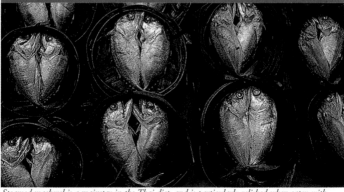

*Steamed mackerel is a mainstay in the Thai diet, and is particularly relished when eaten with fresh-pounded náam phrík (chilli paste)*

## Plaa (Fish)

Thailand boasts 2710km of coastline, much of it fringed with the beaches, islands and coral reefs that attract a massive portion of the country's tourist market. It also provides one of the nation's biggest staples, seafood.

Two completely different marine environments, the Andaman Sea to the west of Thailand's southern reach (part of the Thai-Malay peninsula) and the Gulf of Thailand to the east, offer a huge variety of seafood suitable for the Thai table.

Seafood is much more of a staple in the Thai diet than poultry, beef or pork. To begin with, virtually all Thai dishes are seasoned with shrimp paste or fish sauce, often both. Furthermore, nearly all Thai proverbs linking food and wellbeing mention rice and fish, to the exclusion of all else. So important a role do fish and marine products play in the Thai culinary and mythological spheres that some anthropologists speculate that the Thai race and culture originated not on mainland South-East Asia but in the islands of Austronesia or Oceania.

Seafood used in Thai cooking includes **plaa thuu** (mackerel), **plaa kà-phong** (seabass or ocean perch), **plaa kāo** (grouper or reef cod), **plaa krà-bàwk** (mullet), **plaa jà-lá-mét** (pomfret), **plaa sǎm-lii** (cottonfish), **plaa saa-diin** (sardine), **plaa mèuk kradawng** (cuttlefish), **plaa mèuk klûay** (squid), **puu** (crab), **hǎwy malaeng phùu** (green mussel), **hǎwy naang rom** (oyster), **hǎwy khraeng** (cockle), **plaa lòt** (saltwater eel), **hǎwy phát** (scallop), and a variety of **kûng** (the name given to shrimps, prawns and lobster).

Thailand's numerous rivers, streams, canals, lakes and ponds produce a huge variety of freshwater fish, the Thai favourites being **plaa dùk** (catfish), **plaa châwn** (serpent-headed fish), **plaa nin** (tilapia), **puu naa** (field crabs) and **plaa lāi** (freshwater eel). Although all of these occur naturally in inland waterways, some are also commercially farmed. It's not unusual for rural Thais to dig a fish pond in the back of their homes or near their rice fields for this purpose. Some people even raise fish in ceramic jars, tanks or even plastic buckets beside their houses.

Any gutted and cleaned fish can be wok-fried whole in oil to produce a quick and easy dish served with a simple phrík náam plaa or with a more involved náam phrík paste (see Naam Jim & Naam Phrik earlier in this chapter). Slightly more elaborate dishes call for a whole fish to be steamed or fried and then topped with one of many sauces just before serving. Chillies, Chinese celery, onions, lemongrass, garlic, and preserved Chinese plums are favourite ingredients for such fish toppings. Generally the oilier the fish (such as mackerel and sardine), the more flavourful the sauce needs to be.

STAPLES

One of the healthiest ways to order fresh fish in Thailand is to have it wrapped in banana leaves or foil and roasted over (or covered in) hot coals. Dip the **plaa phão** (roast fish) by the forkful into **náam jîm aahãan tháleh** (seafood dipping sauce) and you'll experience one of the simplest and tastiest seafood dishes you'll find anywhere in the world.

Most **tàlàat thêtsabaan** (municipal markets) in Thailand will feature a large section given over to fish and other seafood. To preserve freshness, some varieties are kept alive in plastic bowls and buckets until purchased. Any fish vendor will clean a purchased fish on your request for no extra charge, or you can do it yourself.

A fish cooked with the head is thought to taste much more flavourful than one without. The 'cheeks' of the fish head – little pockets of flesh in front of the gills – are usually among the tastiest portions. Similarly, large shrimp – such as the **kûng kùlaa dam** (tiger prawn) – are usually cooked with the head on. Cooking shrimp this way maintains much of the crustacean's natural moisture, thus avoiding a dried-out or tough texture. Some recipes call for the head to be removed and stirfried in the wok before adding the body of the shrimp. This releases **man** (fat) from the **hũa** (head), which enhances the flavour and texture of any shrimp dish.

Thais have a particular knack for cooking squid and cuttlefish so that it stays tender. Rarely do they fry or even stirfry it, preferring instead to parboil it quickly – usually for less than a minute. One exception to this is **plaa mèuk phàt phõng kà-rìi** (squid stirfried in curry powder), most likely a dish of Hokkien Chinese origins. Cracked crab, in the shell, is also sometimes prepared this way to produce **puu phàt phõng kà-rìi**.

A favourite night-time street snack is **plaa mèuk pĩng**, dried squid that has been flattened into a sheet via a hand-cranked press and then toasted over hot coals.

Other popular methods of serving seafood include **dìp** (raw), **râat phrík** (smothered in garlic, chillies and onions), **òp** (baked), **nêung** (steamed), **yâang** (grilled), in **yam** (hot & tangy salad) and in spicy **tôm yam** (see Tom Yam & Kaeng Jeut later in this chapter).

*Steamed variety of fish and squid on Khao San Road, Bangkok*

## Phak (Vegetables)

An out-on-the-town Thai meal wouldn't be complete without a plate of vegetables. Both yam and **kàp klâem** (drinking food) always feature lots of vegies, usually either raw or lightly steamed, fulfilling a role similar to crudités in European cuisine.

One of the most omnipresent vegetables in native Thai cuisine is the **má-khēua phráw** (Thai eggplant), a member of the Solanaceae family (like chillies and tomatoes) about the size of a pingpong ball. Unlike its European counterpart, the **má-khēua phráw** has a pale green skin and a rather hard flesh. Thais eat them raw with various chilli dips, and in a variety of kaeng. An even smaller variety, the **má-khēua phuang** (pea eggplant) is also a popular kaeng ingredient, especially for kaeng khīaw-wān (see the boxed text Kaeng of Three earlier in this chapter). Eaten raw or semi-cooked, the má-khēua phuang can be quite bitter, but if cooked longer the flavour smoothes out nicely. Just how long it should be cooked, and how much bitterness should be maintained, is a topic for much debate among kaeng aficionados.

Thais also cook with the **má-khēua yao** (literally, 'long eggplant'). One of the most common dishes using this vegetable is **yam má-khēua yao phāo**, a yam created by tossing a fresh-roasted long eggplant with shrimp, lime juice, ground pork, coriander leaf, chillies, garlic and fish sauce. The smoky taste of the roasted eggplant contrasts well with the bite of the chilli, lime and coriander.

A wide variety of leafy lettuce or cabbage-type vegetables make appearances in everyday Thai cuisine. Among the most common is the dark green and vitamin-filled **phàk kha-náa** (Chinese kale), often stirfried in **tâo jîaw dam** (black bean sauce) to create **phàt phàk kha-náa**, a dish available at just about any Thai or Chinese restaurant in Thailand.

Short lengths of **thùa fàk yao** (long bean) are a favourite raw accompaniment to Isaan dishes like **sômtam** (spicy salad) and **lâap** (spicy minced meat salad). **Thùa phuu** (angle bean) plays a starring role in tangy **yam thùa phuu**.

One of the most common vegetable side orders at any restaurant is **phàt phàk ruam** (literally, 'friendly mixed vegetables'). Quickly stirfried in oyster or soy sauce in a wok over high flame, the selection of vegies often mates such common ingredients as **phàk kàat khīaw** (mustard cabbage), **phàk kàat khāo plii** (long white cabbage), **thùa lan-tao** (snow peas), **khâo phôht àwn** (baby corn), **tôn hāwm** (spring onion), **hèt faang** (straw mushrooms) and **hèt hāwm** (shiitake mushrooms). In the hands of a talented chef, this dish can be an unexpected pleasure, while in the hands of a hack it can be almost flavourless. In our experience some of the best places to eat phàt phàk ruam include vendor stalls in night markets.

## A ROSE IS A ROSE IS A SWAMP CABBAGE

**Phàk bûng**, tagged with more English names than any other vegetable in Thailand, is also known as water spinach, water morning glory, water hyacinth and swamp cabbage. Botanists know it by the even less appetising name, water convolvulus. This ubiquitous, vine-like plant grows copiously wherever there is standing water and seems especially fond of shallow ponds, canals and

*Preparing phàk bûng fai daeng (red fire water spinach)*

drainage ditches, where enterprising locals collect it by the armload.

In the 1970s, when we first began coming to Thailand, phàk bûng could be seen growing along both sides of the roadway between Don Muang airport and downtown Bangkok. Thus its harvesting was one of the first glimpses of Thai agricultural life a newly arrived visitor encountered. Nowadays the drainage ditches along what has become a multi-laned and heavily trafficked freeway are filled with refuse and auto parts rather than the spiky-leafed phàk bûng.

This vegetable, high in iron and vitamin A, tastes delicious whether eaten raw as a cooling accompaniment to spicy dishes or stirfried on its own. To create death-defying **phàk bûng fai daeng** (literally, 'red fire water spinach'), Thais dribble vegetable oil or bacon fat into the wok, turn the gas flame all the way up, toss in handfuls of phàk bûng, sliced chillies, black bean sauce and mashed garlic cloves, and stirfry the lot for less than a minute. The oil that splashes down the sides of wok catches fire and tall flames usually leap over the edge, licking the inside and adding a smoking flavour to the dish.

To add more drama to an already impressive performance, cooks in Chonburi have invented an alternative known as **phàk bûng láwy fáa** (sky-floating water spinach), often advertised in English as 'flying vegetable', which has become popular in night markets across Thailand. In this variation the cook fires up a batch of phàk bûng fai daeng, then by swinging the wok by one handle, flings the phàk bûng across the market area to a waiting server who catches it on a plate. A few food critics have actually suggested that the extra aeration improves the taste of this spicy dish! We advise ducking for cover when the stuff becomes airborne, as the flying phàk bûng doesn't always land on the plate.

The fragrant **hèt faang** (straw mushroom) finds its way into many dishes, including the very popular tôm yam kûng (see the recipe later in this chapter). Fresh **hèt hāwm** (shittake mushroom) is favoured for stirfry dishes, and features in yam hèt hāwm. Yam made from these and other mushrooms are especially popular in cooler mountainous Northern Thailand, where mushrooms grow in abundance for much of the year.

Vegetables primarily used in soups include **buap** (gourd), **fák** (squash), **hūa phà kàat** (giant white radish), **fák nguu** (snake or winter melon), **bùap liam** (sponge gourd), **bùap nguu** (snake gourd), **fák khīaw** (wax gourd) and **náam tâo** (bottle gourd).

*Fresh vegetables at a roadside market*

## Phon-la-mai (Fruit)

In Thailand it sometimes seems as if fresh fruit is everywhere you look, from the orange-hued papaya pyramids piled high on wooden shelves in market stalls, the yellow strings of bananas hanging from the eaves of **ráan cham** (sundries shop), to the panoply of cubed colours carefully stacked behind the glass panes of roaming fruit carts. During festivals and in fancier hotels and restaurants, Thailand's world famous fruit carvers fashion watermelons, papayas, pineapples and mangoes into fantastic floral, animal and even human shapes.

The omnipresent **phōn-lá-mái** (literally, 'fruit of the tree') testifies not only to Thailand's tropical abundance but to the Thais' great fondness for fruit, which they appear to consume at every opportunity. An evening meal is normally followed by a plate of sliced fresh fruit, not pastries or western-style desserts – perhaps this is why Thais tend to avoid obesity so easily.

Available year round, **klûay** (bananas) come in over 20 varieties. The most common is **klûay náam wáa**, a thick-bodied, medium-length banana from which **bai tawng** (banana leaves) are usually harvested for use as cooking wrappers. The long **klûay hăwm** (fragrant banana) is similar to the bananas grown in Latin America. Other varieties are mostly regional, such as the delicate and slender **klûay lép meu naang** (princess fingernail banana), native to Chumphon Province in Southern Thailand, and Kamphaeng Phet's descriptively named **klûay khài** (egg banana) which is, indeed, egg-shaped.

Just about every Thai with some space next to their house grows a few banana plants. Aside from harvesting the banana fruit and leaves, they also make ample culinary use of the **hŭa plii** (banana flower bud) when it appears just after the plant has fruited. The purplish, oval-shaped bud has a tart and astringent taste when eaten raw, typically as an accompaniment to **lâap** in North-Eastern Thailand. Blanching the bud removes most of the bud's astringency and makes it very suitable for use in **yam**. **Tôn klûay** (round cross-sections of the heart of a banana tree trunk or stalk) make an appearance in **kaeng yùak**, a delicious kaeng found in the north.

*Bananas for sale*

Other common year-rounders found throughout the kingdom include **má-phráo** (coconut), **faràng** (guava), **kha-nŭn** (jackfruit), **má-nao** (lime), **ma-krùt** (kaffir lime) **má-khăam** (tamarind), **sôm khĭaw-wăan** (mandarin orange), **málákaw** (papaya), **sôm oh** (pomelo), **taeng moh** (watermelon) and **sàppàrót** (pineapple). All are most commonly eaten fresh, and sometimes dipped in a mixture of salt, sugar and ground chilli.

*Carving papaya*

STAPLES

## MANGOES IN MAY

The watchful visitor could almost fix the calendar month in Thailand by observing the parade of fruits appearing month by month – sweet mangoes in March, mangosteen in April, rambeh in May, custard apple in July, golden-peel oranges in November and so on. Any Thai fruit so distinguished as to be both seasonal and regional will enjoy its own provincial festival, such as Lamphun's annual Lam Yai Festival, which features floats made of **lam yài** (longan), agricultural exhibitions, nightly musical entertainment and, like all agricultural festivals in Thailand, a beauty contest in which the winner will be crowned in the fruit's name – in this case as 'Nang Lam Yai' (Miss Longan).

Common seasonal fruits include the following:

| | |
|---|---|
| **náwy nàa** | custard-apple – July to October |
| **lam yài** | longan – 'dragon's eyes', small, brown, spherical, similar to rambutan; July to October |
| **má-mûang** | mango – several varieties & seasons |
| **mang-khút** | mangosteen – round, purple fruit with juicy white flesh; April to September |
| **má-fai** | rambeh – small, reddish-brown, sweet, similar to an apricot; April to May |
| **ngáw** | rambutan – red, hairy-skinned fruit with grape-like interior; July to September |
| **chom-phûu** | rose-apple – small, apple-like texture, very fragrant; April to July |
| **lámút** | sapodilla – small, brown, oval, sweet but pungent smelling; July to September |

When such fruits are no longer in season, you'll still be able to find them as **phōn-lá-mái cháe im** (preserved fruit), **cháe im** for short. There are numerous ways to make cháe im, including drying, salting, pickling and candying. Chiang Mai's cháe im enjoys a particularly good reputation, and any Thai who visits the city without bringing a bag of cháe im home will seriously disappoint friends and family.

Several fruits can be used as seasoning ingredients in Thai cooking, particularly coconut (desiccated, then pressed with hot water to produce coconut milk), pineapple (fresh, used in kaeng), tamarind (extracted juice, for any dish needing a sour taste), kaffir lime (grated peel and leaves, in kaeng and yam) and lime (extracted juice, in just about everything). Jackfruit has been honoured with its own kaeng, **kaeng kha-nūn**, which is especially favoured in Northern Thailand but also found elsewhere.

Fruit juices of every kind are popular beverages (see the Drinks chapter).

No discussion of Thai fruit is complete without a mention of **thúrian** (durian), dubbed the king of fruits by most South-East Asians yet despised by many visitors to the region. A member of the aptly named Bombacaceae family, this heavy, spiked orb resembles an ancient piece of medieval weaponry. Inside the thick shell lies five sections of plump, buttery and pungent flesh. Legions of connoisseurs as well as detractors have laboured to describe the durian's complex flavouring. Probably the best description is that from 19th century British natural historian and obvious durian devotee Alfred Russell Wallace:

> ... custard flavoured with almonds, intermingled with wafts of flavour that call to mind cream cheese, onion sauce, brown sherry and other incongruities ... neither acid, nor sweet, nor juicy, yet one feels the want of none of these qualities for it is perfect as it is.

*A durian, sliced open to reveal its creamy yellow flesh*

The durian's ammonia-like aroma is so strong that many hotels in Thailand, as well as Thai International Airways, ban the fruit from their premises.

Durian seasons come and go throughout the year depending on the variety. One of the largest and most expensive durians, native to Thailand and widely exported, is the **māwn thawng** (golden pillow).

*Decorative fruit carving*

## Tom Yam & Kaeng Jeut (Soups)

Most Thai soups fall into two broad categories, **tôm yam** and **kaeng jèut**, that are worlds apart in terms of seasonings. With the predominating flavours of chilli and lime, **tôm yam** can be described as a soup-style yam – tôm yam, after all, translates as 'boiled yam'.

Tôm yam is almost always made with seafood, though chicken is also used. **Tôm yam kûng** (tôm yam with shrimp) can be found in all Thai restaurants as well as in many serving non-Thai cuisine. It is often trans-lated on English menus as 'hot and sour Thai soup', although this often

### KA-THI (COCONUT MILK)

Some newcomers to Asian cuisine mistakenly believe 'coconut milk' means the juice contained inside a coconut. Although this juice does make a favourite thirst-quencher in hot weather, it possesses neither the sweetness nor the thickness needed to make a good base for kaeng or any other dish requiring coconut.

To make kà-thí, the fully ripe coconut – which contains little or no juice – is husked, then split open to expose the thick white meat lining the inside of the shell. The coconut grower often removes the husk – by hand, nut by nut – before shipping it to wholesale markets.

Although pre-grated coconut is available in all markets, the traditional method of grating a coconut is still widely practised. This is done with a wooden **krà-tàai khùut má-phráo** (literally, 'coconut-digging rabbit'), so-named for the shape of the device's carved wooden body. Protruding from the rabbit's 'mouth' is a steel or iron rod with a sharp-ened, flanged tip. The cook sits astride the wooden base and the inside of a half coconut is forcibly rotated against the tip to grate the meat into a bowl placed on the floor below. Some krà-tàay khùut má-phráo are further carved to resemble cats, rabbits and other animals, and in Northern Thailand some krà-tàay khùut have a built-in receptacle to catch the grated coconut meat. If you grate coconut yourself, note that the older and riper the nut, the richer the milk will taste – but avoid using coconut with any 'off' smells as this will affect the taste more than you might expect.

Whether grated at home or purchased from a market, the next step is to soak the coconut meat in very hot water for around 15 minutes until the water is lukewarm. The meat is then strained through a muslin cloth to produce the kà-thí. The first straining is considered 'thick coconut milk' while the second is 'thin coconut milk'. One cup of grated coconut soaked in 3¾ cups of hot water will produce approximately 2½ cups of coconut milk.

misleads non-Thais to relate the dish to Chinese hot and sour soup, which is thinner in texture, milder and includes vinegar.

Lemongrass, kaffir lime peel and lime juice give tôm yam its characteristic tang. Fuelling the fire beneath tôm yam's often velvety surface are fresh phrík khîi nũu and sometimes a half teaspoonful of **náam phrík phão** (a paste of dried chillies roasted with shrimp paste). Improvisation comes into play with this dish more than most, as cooks try to out-do one another in providing a savoury soup with at least one or two 'mystery' ingredients.

Many cooks add galangal for extra fragrance, or back up the lime and

After the coconut milk sits for an hour or so, it will separate (put it in the refrigerator to speed up the process). The thicker section of coconut cream at the top is called **hũa kà-thí** (coconut cream) while the rest of the milk below is **hãang kà-thí** (coconut milk). Most kaeng recipes begin with the cooking of the khrêuang kaeng in coconut cream, after which the kaeng's other ingredients, including the coconut milk, are added to the pot.

Some Thai markets now offer a free soaking/squeezing/straining service on the spot if you buy grated coconut from the vendors.

Canned Thai coconut milk is exported all over the world and makes a reasonable substitute for fresh kà-thí. Read the ingredients first; some cheaper canned coconut milk is adulterated with palm oil. *Chao Koh* is the best brand and comes in UHT-processed boxes. Coconut powder, mixed with water to produce coconut milk, is usually inferior to both canned and fresh kà-thí.

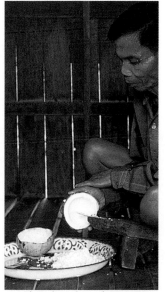

*The traditional way of grating coconut using a krà-tàai khùut mǎ-phráo or 'coconut-grating rabbit'*

kaffir lime with a little tamarind juice. If enough tamarind is added, the name of the dish should be altered to **tôm prîaw** (literally, 'boiled sour'). For colour and flavour, halved cherry tomatoes can be added. Aside from lemongrass and galangal resting on the bottom of the bowl, solids in this soup are usually limited to shrimp and straw mushrooms. Coriander is an important garnish for both appearance and fragrance.

The result should be a rich broth with lime and chilli overtones but also a balance of salty and smooth – rather than acidic – textures. Tôm yam is meant to be eaten with rice, not sipped alone. The first swallow of this soup often leaves the uninitiated gasping for breath. It's not that the soup is so hot, but the chilli oils that provide the spice tend to float on top.

Of the several variations on tôm yam that exist, probably the most popular with westerners is the milder **tôm khàa kài** (literally, 'boiled galangal chicken', but often translated as 'chicken coconut soup'). The lime and chilli are considerably muted by the addition of coconut milk. Another soup, **pó tàek** (broken fishtrap soup), uses much the same seasonings as tôm yam with the addition of either sweet or holy basil, but brings in a melange of seafood, including squid, crab, fish, mussels and shrimp.

## Tom Yam Kung (Chilli & Lemongrass Soup with Shrimp)

One of the most well-known Thai dishes, tôm yam kûng is quick and easy to prepare. Reduce the number of fresh chillies in this simple, classic recipe if you're chilli-shy.

6     large whole shrimp
1½   tablespoons fresh chopped galangal
1     lemongrass stalk, thinly sliced
2     kaffir lime leaves, thinly sliced
15    phrík khîi nǔu (mouse-dropping chillies)
10    fresh straw mushrooms
3     tablespoons lime juice
2     tablespoons fish sauce

Remove the heads from the shrimp and make a stock by simmering them in 3¾ cups of boiling water for about 10 minutes. Strain the stock into a saucepan.

Add the shrimp, galangal and lemongrass to the stock and simmer for five minutes.

Stir in the remaining ingredients, remove from the heat and serve with plenty of white rice.

## Kaeng Jeut Wun Sen (Mung Bean Noodle Soup)

Kaeng jèut brings a good balance to a meal already including several spicy Thai dishes.

| | | | |
|---|---|---|---|
| 2 | tablespoons vegetable oil | 4 | coriander roots |
| ⅓ | cup mouse-ear mushrooms | ⅓ | cup lily buds |
| 1 | cup ground or minced pork | 2 | teaspoons fish sauce |
| ½ | cup soft tofu, cut into cubes | | |
| ½ | teaspoon fresh ground black pepper | | |
| 2 | garlic cloves, minced or sliced thinly | | |
| 4 | cups (1l) chicken stock | | |
| 1 | teaspoon salt | | |
| 1 | cup soaked mung bean noodles, cut into short lengths | | |

Using a mortar & pestle, pound the coriander root, garlic and black pepper into a paste. Heat the oil in a large saucepan and fry the pounded mixture until very fragrant. Add the pork and stirfry on medium heat until it's cooked through.

Add the chicken stock and bring to a boil. Lower heat, add remaining ingredients and simmer until warm. Remove from the heat and serve.

**STAPLES**

If you're looking for a shortcut to making tôm yam broth, soup stock-cubes are available at just about any grocery store, supermarket or **ráan cham** (sundries market) – even Thais use them at home with some frequency.

At the other end of the soup spectrum is **kaeng jèut** (bland soup), a soothing broth seasoned with little more than fish sauce and black pepper. Although the number of variations on kaeng jèut are seemingly endless, common ingredients include **wún sên** (mung bean starch noodles), **tâo-hûu** (tofu), **hūa chai tháo** (Chinese radish) and **mǔu sàp** (ground pork).

Spicier than kaeng jèut, **kaeng liang** gets its kick from green or black peppercorns rather than chillies and is probably one of the oldest recipes in Thailand. A good kaeng liang will be rich with sponge gourd, baby corn, cauliflower and various greens, substantiated with pieces of chicken, shrimp or ground pork.

The cooler north favours stewed meat soups such as **pèt tǔn** (steamed duck soup), **néua tǔn** (steamed beef soup) and **kài tǔn** (steamed chicken soup), which are usually eaten with noodles. These soups generally feature a broth darkened by the addition of soy sauce and spices such as cinnamon, star anise or Chinese five-spice mixtures. Cabbage or bean sprouts give the soup some crunch, while Chinese celery provides fragrance.

## SOME LIKE IT HOT

Schools throughout Thailand celebrate a yearly event called Wai Khru, a special day when students honour and pay respect to their teachers. During a year I spent teaching English at a secondary school in Yala, I was invited by two friends, a Thai English teacher named Siriwan, and Bill, another American English teacher, to attend a special luncheon at the nearby Yala Teachers College as part of Wai Khru.

Yala, the capital of the southern province of the same name, sits near the end of the long, dangling elephant trunk part of Thailand that reaches down past the Isthmus of Kra and latches onto Malaysia. Before arriving in Yala, I'd heard two persistent rumours about the south: that the people there spoke a rapid-fire, elliptical dialect, and that the food was the hottest in Thailand. As it turned out, I didn't encounter the infamous fast-and-furious dialect in Yala. Southern food, however, was another story.

Arriving at the college for Wai Khru at midday, and managing to miss the battery of speeches that typically serve as prelude to the real purpose of such events – eating – I was auspiciously ushered into an airy room with a long table set for a meal. Actually airy is not a very accurate description, for although the room was wide open to the free circulation of air, the air inside was astonishingly inert. Several large rotating fans were in evidence, but they clearly had their work cut out. The room was so hot that, considering why we were there, I began to sweat more copiously in anticipation of the minimal movement and effort that would be required to eat anything. Only the glasses of ice water, beading and dripping on the table before us, appeared to be sweating more than we were.

For their part, the dozen or so Thai teachers, despite a few prototypically earnest exchanges – '**ráwn mái?**' (hot, no?),' answered by '**ráwn!**' (hot!) – seemed less fazed by the intense heat, neat and crisply dressed as they were in pressed government uniforms.

We were invited to sit around the table. Though not particularly territorial under ordinary circumstances, I was perhaps compelled by a sudden twinge of social Darwinism to selfishly position myself as closely as possible to one of the rotating fans, hoping to remain at least partially conscious through the coming meal.

Several large, silver tureens appeared, each wreathed in swirls of pungent steam. The first one was filled with scalding **tôm yam kûng**, stocked with large succulent shrimp, and studded with generous quantities of tiny but potent red and green chillies. The soup was followed by a few Thai curries. I don't recall them clearly though, due to the heat in the room and the peculiar intensity of what I can only describe in retrospect as a seriously devastating soup that took no prisoners.

The **tôm yam kûng** was ladled out into smaller bowls, and we were invited by the **ajaan yài** (head teacher) to begin eating. It began innocuously enough: a subtle sniffle or two from a teacher here, the occasional slight sigh of another there, even the odd gasp or cough.

I quickly found myself ahead of the reaction curve, urgently reaching for one of the rolls of toilet paper which, when typically placed inside a decorative cylindrical container so that you pull the paper out through a hole in the top, serve as napkins at dinner tables in Thailand. My eyes were streaming and my nose was running. I wondered if I would ever regain the full use of my tongue.

As the realisation that this was clearly the hottest food I'd yet encountered on planet Earth began to dawn on me, I abandoned all pretence of bravery and decorum, and, tearing off long streamers of toilet paper, flagrantly honked away into it, unabashed. Between honks and eye daubs, I noted that Bill was exhibiting similar symptoms and behaviour.

Having already lived several months in Thailand, I was used to seeing faràng like Bill and I struggle against the unforgiving intensity of Thai cuisine. What was new and surprising to me, though, was witnessing a group of Thais undergoing a similar struggle. As minutes passed, and more soup was consumed, the teachers became increasingly more distressed, as evidenced both in sight and sound. Handkerchiefs were produced, noses were blown, eyeglasses removed, brows, foreheads – then entire faces—daubed, wiped and mopped. Sniffling, sighing and gasping became more frequent and pronounced, and seemed now to be completely contagious.

When the head teacher, Ajaan Suchart, – a reserved, well-mannered, genial man, not given to discernible outbursts of any kind – began, suddenly and loudly, to suck in air and then utter a definitive, 'Oh-hoh!' I took this as a solemn declaration that our soup was indeed an exemplar of its kind. As if on cue, his cry served to trigger a series of similar choral responses and affirmations from around the table. One teacher, the diminutive Ajaan Lek, summed up the experience perfectly, uttering a most declarative, '**phèt** (spicy)…' stopping just a hair's breadth from adding a well-known curse.

At the height of our collective gasping, crying, sighing, blowing, wiping, and mopping, it occurred to me that if a group of outside observers were called upon to witness our little party, they might well conclude that we were undergoing some grave and agonising torture. In fact, we were enjoying ourselves, and the food, immensely – our temporary discomfort a small price to pay for an uncompromisingly delicious meal.

– Bill Preston

*Bill Preston lived and worked in Thailand for three years. He is now an editor at Pearson Education in White Plains, New York.*

STAPLES

## Phrik (Chillies)

Much of Thai cuisine's colour and fire comes from **phrík** (chillies), which, like eggplants, tomatoes and potatoes, were unknown to Siam before the 16th century.

*Bagging up sky pointing chillies*

Portuguese and Spanish seafaring traders first introduced the plant to Europe, then Africa and Asia, and by the mid-16th century the Javanese were using chillies as food, spice and medicine. Portuguese mariners visited the Ayuthaya kingdom as early as 1511, but it's more likely that it was during the 17th century reign of Ayuthaya's King Narai, the first Thai king to welcome trade with Europe (and the only king in Thai history to allow a non-Asian – Constantine Phaulkon, a Greek – to become a court minister) that the chilli began to flourish in the Thai kitchen. Although it is generally thought that the chilli reached Thailand via Europe and India, there is some evidence suggesting it may have arrived from the east – across the Pacific – via the Manila galleon trade between Spanish-controlled Acapulco and South-East Asia.

Whatever route the chilli took, it found a very receptive culinary climate in Thailand. Previous to its arrival, the Thais spiced their food with black pepper blended with strong aromatics such as garlic, galangal and ginger. Chillies so thoroughly supplanted black pepper as the main source of spicy heat that they took on the Thai word, **phrík**, while the indigenous variety came to be referred to as **phrík thai** (Thai pepper). The latter, usually in its young green form, remains an important ingredient in Thai cooking and still finds its way into many types of **khrêuang kaeng** (curry paste). But for most of the last 400 years, the backbone of all spicy Thai cuisine has come from the chilli.

The chilli has become so integral to Thai cuisine that when they aren't available, the Thais may exclaim 'phrík kheu thai; thai kheu phrík' (chilli is Thai; Thai is chilli).

Surprisingly Thailand doesn't cultivate a great variety of chillies. While Mexico boasts up to 90 different varieties, Thailand restricts itself to a dozen or so, of which three predominate.

The most commonly used of all Thai chillies, **phrík chíi fáa** (literally, 'sky pointing chilli'), is long and slender (measuring about 6-10cm) and is grown in red, green and yellow versions. In markets overseas it is sometimes sold as 'Thai chilli' or 'Japanese chilli'. Thais prize the phrík chíi fáa highly, and often the seeds are removed from this chilli before it's added to the mortar or wok in order to leave more room for its revered texture, colour and flavour. By Thai aesthetic standards, the seeds of this variety also tend to be a little hard to chew. Red phrík chíi fáa is the main chilli ingredient in most khrêuang kaeng, and for this purpose the dried version of the chilli is typically used. Drying the chilli reduces its heat significantly since the sole heat-producing ingredient, capsaicin, abides primarily in the oils of the chilli's seeds and in the white flesh around the seeds. Fresh sliced phrík chíi fáa goes well in certain yam dishes and in **phàt bai kà-phrao** (chicken or shrimp stirfried with holy basil).

The second most commonly seen chilli in Thailand is the infamous **phrík khîi nǔu**, (literally, 'mouse dropping chilli'), meant as a description of its tiny torpedo-like shape. In English it is often known as 'bird's eye chilli', of which there are several varieties. Measuring only 1-2cm, this little devil is the hottest chilli you'll find in Thailand. Although only twice as hot as the phrík chíi fáa if measured in Scoville units (see the boxed text Keeping Up with the Heat), the phrík khîi nǔu tends to be eaten fresh and whole, which means you experience all the capsaicin-containing seeds and placenta.

You'll see sliced phrík khîi nǔu floating in phrík náam plaa and in any authentic tôm yam kûng. In Thailand there are two main varieties, regular phrík khîi nǔu and the hotter **phrík khîi nǔu sǔan** ('farm' phrík khîi nǔu). If you put them side by side, you'll notice that the 'farm' version is a little squatter or fatter. The seeds are also noticeably smaller.

A larger chilli, **phrík yùak** (banana-stalk chilli) averages about 10-15cm and has a wider 'shoulder' than the two previously mentioned chillies. When young it's yellow-green in colour and just barely spicy, but when ripe it turns a deep red and increases in strength. The seeds are largish, and the skin is rather thick and waxy. Thais prefer to cook this chilli – either boiling or grilling it – before adding it to most dishes. Young phrík yùak are also sometimes pickled in vinegar to make **phrík náam sôm**, a condiment popular with noodle dishes and Chinese food. You'll also find phrík yùak in a few yam.

Carrying no heat charge at all, **phrík wǎan** ('sweet', green bell pepper), is not commonly used, apart from in Chinese restaurants.

---

## KEEPING UP WITH THE HEAT

American, Wilbur Scoville, came up with the first empirical test for chilli hotness in 1912 at Texas A&M University. In what has come to be known as the Scoville test, **phrík wǎan** (green bell pepper) measures zero Scoville units, a Mexican jalapeño 3500 to 4500 Scoville units. Thailand's long and slender **phrík chíi fáa** (sky pointing chilli) scores 35,000 to 45,000 units, about the same as North America's Tabasco chilli. The **phrík khîi nǔu** (mouse-dropping chilli) increases the ante to 60,000 to 80,000 units, not quite up to India's bird's eye chilli (100,000 to 125,000 units) but at these levels few tasters can tell them apart. Hottest chilli in the world? The habanero or scotch bonnet, native to Mexico's Yucatán Peninsula, scores a thermonuclear 300,000 Scoville units.

## Herbs, Spices & Other Seasonings

Stroll down the aisles of any Thai market and you'll immediately be enveloped in all the aromas that give Thai cuisine its distinctive quality. The smells can be so overwhelming at times that you wonder whether the exquisite balance of flavours extolled by lovers of Thai cuisine truly exists. Could anything stand up against the salty funk of shrimp paste, the wet sourness of pickled cabbage, the intense perfume of ginger or the nostril-searing clouds of powdered chilli? It is as if the Thais were attempting to create olfactory versions of the ocean, the jungle, the deltas and mountain slopes which make up their homeland, beneath the one market roof. Won't the gustatory powers of these many stalwarts overwhelm? The answer is yes. And no. If you were to eat any of these ingredients separately, their strength would be too much, but combined in small amounts, and eaten with rice, the balance created is potentially perfect. Thai cuisine is all about finding that balance without sacrificing the power of the individual elements.

At the base of all Thai cooking is the salt that spurs the eating of rice, and the main source of culinary salt for the Thais is **náam plaa** (fish sauce). **Kà-pì** (shrimp paste), which comes in a variety of grades and colours, from fresh to heavily fermented, from salmon pink to chocolate brown, is valued primarily for its deep marine flavours and sauce-thickening power more than for its saltiness. Crystallised salt is never used as a table condiment, but is often added during cooking. A touch of salt is also added to some fruit juices and to most Thai sweets.

The juice of **má-nao** (lime) and the peel or leaves of **ma-krùt** (kaffir lime) impart a citrus tartness to Thai dishes often mis-described as 'sour'. Further tartness may be achieved through the use of **má-khăam pìak**, the flesh and seeds of the husked tamarind fruit pressed into red-brown clumps. These clumps are soaked in water and the pulp strained away to produce a dark red juice with a flavour that is both tangy and savoury. Taking tart yet a step further, the less well-known **ma-kàwk** (ambarella), a South-East Asian native, resembles a small mango but has a very clean and astringent flavour that goes well in certain yam.

Thais rarely use prepared vinegar, even for pickling vegetables. Instead they use **phàk dawng**, made by taking the leftover starch-filled water used to rinse white rice, filling a bucket with this milky water and soaking cabbage leaves in the bucket for a few days. An interaction between the rice starch and the fresh vegetables invokes a yeasting process. The resulting pickled vegies are slightly sour and used to perk up noodle soups of all kinds.

STAPLES

Wherever a Thai dish contains a noticeable tartness or spiciness, these tonalities must be balanced – some might say enhanced – with a sweet flavour. Thai food may be sweetened with cane sugar, coconut sugar or palm sugar (see Khawng Waan later in this chapter).

Any English-language Thai cookbook will explain how a terrific Thai dish blends themes of hot, salty, sour and sweet. What's missing from the standard four-way formula is the important role of aroma. While many cooks rarely consider smell when putting cooking ingredients together, Thai recipe books and cookery magazines always cite certain ingredients that are added for fragrance or aroma, as distinct from flavour. For example, the recipe for a North-Eastern Thai dish, in *Khrua* magazine, reads:

> Take fresh bird's eye chilli, shallot, lemongrass and make a paste in a mortar. Put in a curry pot and adjust saltiness with fish sauce. Thicken with roast ground rice. Add coriander leaf and mint basil to achieve fragrance.

Westerners often lump such herbs in with spices, but here they belong to a separate category of aromatics. To retain the highest degree of fragrance, such ingredients should be added to a dish last, and they should not be cooked very long, if at all. Often a quick wilting in the heat of the dish is more than sufficient to make such herbs palatable.

Chief among the **samūn phrai** (culinary and/or medicinal herbs) found in the Thai kitchen is **phàk chii** (coriander leaf) – known to many North Americans by its Spanish name, cilantro. Although in many dishes phàk chii may appear to be nothing more than a last-minute garnish, the perfume exuded by this leaf can be an essential element. Phàk chii is especially valued for its role in countering the 'fishy' smell in seafood, and so is liberally used in dishes of that genre. **Náam jîm aahāan tháleh**, the table dipping sauce commonly served with seafood, always contains phàk chii.

In the preparation of a kaeng or in sauces meant for fish, **râak phàk chii** (the roots of the coriander plant) are often pounded into a paste along with garlic and other ingredients. Several standard **khrêuang kaeng** (curry pastes) include crushed **mét phàk chii** (coriander seeds).

For many faràng, basil is synonymous with Thai cuisine, and although not as widely used as coriander it is often more visible. Three kinds of basil are commonly used, the large leafed **bai hōhráphaa** (sweet basil) appears in certain kaeng, seafood dishes and especially **phàt phèt**, a stirfry that uses khrêuang kaeng without coconut milk to produce a sort of dry curry. The second type, **bai maeng-lák** (Thai basil, lemon basil or mint basil – take your pick) has smaller, smoother leaves and more delicate stems than those of bai hōhráphaa. Bai maeng-lák is popular in soups and as a side to **khanōm jiin náam yaa** (thin rice noodles with ground fish curry) and **lâap** (spicy minced meat salad). Some cooks prefer to use bai maeng-lák over bai hōhráphaa for everything that requires basil. A third type of basil, **bai kà-phrao** (holy basil) is most prominent in **phàt bai kà-phrao**, a delicious stirfry of bai kà-phrao, garlic, chillies and chicken or shrimp. It is also used in some seafood dishes and occasionally substitutes for bai hōhráphaa, even though the two basils taste completely different.

**Bai sá-rá-nàe** (spearmint leaves) appear in many kinds of yam and lâap. In North-Eastern Thailand they're also eaten raw as an accompaniment to lâap and rice noodle soups.

A pointed, blade-like leaf called **bai toey** (pandan leaf), from the indigenous pandan plant is primarily used to add a vanilla-like flavour to Thai sweets. The well-known **kài hàw bai toey** (chicken wrapped in pandan leaves) uses individual pandan leaves as wrappers for chunks of chicken marinated in soy sauce, sesame oil, garlic and coriander root. The resulting packets are fried or grilled and served with a dipping sauce similar to the marinade.

**Tà-khrái** (lemongrass) is almost as popular a name for Thai restaurants as it is an ingredient. Virtually all khrêuang kaeng contain tà-khrái and it also looms large in tôm yam, yam and certain kinds of lâap. It grows easily in warm climates, spreading in long, bladed clumps. If you buy tà-khrái at a grocery store or market, use only the lower 10-12cm of the plant and discard any woody outer leaves.

*Cutting fresh lemongrass from a backyard garden*

Three aromatic roots or rhizomes, belonging to the ginger family and indigenous to mainland South-East Asia, have played an important role in Thai cuisine for a very long time. Like black pepper and dried chillies, **khǐng** (ginger) is cultivated in huge amounts and exported to other countries. Thais tend to cook using only young, pinkish ginger rather than the older brown-skinned root found in most western markets. Minced or sliced ginger is found in innumerable dishes from kaeng to soups to stirfries, as it's used in both Thai and Chinese cookery. Thin-sliced flower buds from a wild ginger known as **kà-lāa** (torch ginger) are sometimes used in **khâo yam** (Southern Thailand rice salad).

**Khàa** (galangal) has a similar appearance to khǐng but the interior of the root is harder and has a deeper, more savoury, less spicy flavour. Although it's found in numerous Northern and Central Thai dishes, khàa's most famous appearance is in **tôm khàa kài**, a soup with chicken, galangal, chillies and coconut milk. The third member of the ginger fraternity, **kha-mîn** (turmeric), contains a bright yellow-orange interior and is especially popular in Southern Thai cooking. Here, whole fish is usually rubbed with kha-mîn before frying in the belief that it counters bad fish aromas.

Both **krà-thiam** (garlic) and **hāwm daeng** (shallots) can be found throughout Thai cuisine and are essential to most khrêuang kaeng. The krà-thiam here tends to yield smaller cloves than the garlic varieties of Europe. The skins are also thinner, and many Thais leave part of the skin on when cooking with garlic, believing that much of the bulb's aroma resides in the peel. Although many English-language Thai cookbooks say it's OK to substitute onions for hāwm daeng, the two have completely different flavours. **Tôn hāwm** (spring onions or scallions) appear in many stirfries and are also used as a garnish for most fried noodle dishes. **Lûuk hāwm** (bulb onion) is much less commonly used except in Chinese-influenced dishes.

From the Indian spice cupboard come **yîiràa** (cumin), **òp choei** (cinnamon) and **lûuk krà-waan** (cardamom). All three spices may be found in such Indian-inspired kaeng as kaeng kàrìi kài or kaeng mátsàman, but Thai cooks often leave out the cardamom, whose aroma they tend not to appreciate.

Soy seasonings, introduced to Thailand by Chinese immigrants, are used almost exclusively in Chinese-influenced stirfries. **Sii-íw khǎo** (white soy) corresponds to the kind of common soy sauce found on the tables of Japanese and Chinese restaurants around the world, while **sii-íw dam** (black soy or dark soy) sauce is a thicker, slightly sweet preparation. **Tâo jîaw** (paste of fermented, salted soybeans) is a mandatory ingredient for phàk bûng fai daeng and phàt phàk kha-náa. To give the latter dish more of a salty bite, **plaa khem** (preserved salted fish) is occasionally used instead.

STAPLES

## Sangkhayaa Fak Thawng (Pumpkin Custard)

One of the most traditional of Thai sweets, sāngkhayāa fák thawng shows how east-west fusion experiments are nothing new. This recipe probably dates from the 17th century, when Thai chefs learned how to make egg custards from visiting Portuguese merchants. Although not exactly light on calories, sāngkhayāa fák thawng is stocked with protein, phosphorous, minerals and vitamins.

The fák thawng (golden squash) is similar to the bright orange pumpkin popular in the UK and US, except that it's smaller and has a mottled, slightly striped shell. Some supermarkets outside Thailand sell the fák thawng as 'pumpkin squash' but all pumpkins are, of course, a variety of squash.

Many cooks prefer to use the richer duck egg, but chicken eggs work fine and international palates may prefer the lighter texture. Remember, the fresher the egg, the better the custard. Thai cooks will strain the custard mixture through a muslin cloth before steaming. This process removes any egg or palm sugar solids that might mar the custard's texture.

| | |
|---|---|
| 1 | fák thawng (or small ripe pumpkin) weighing about 500g |
| 4 | eggs |
| ½ | cup (125ml) coconut cream |
| ¾ | cup palm sugar or ½ cup raw cane sugar |

Beat the eggs thoroughly in a medium-sized mixing bowl. Add the coconut cream and palm sugar and mix slowly until the colour and texture are even.

Wash the outside of the pumpkin, then cut a circular line a 5cm radius from the stem. Scoop out the centre of the pumpkin containing seeds and stringy matter and discard. Rinse the inside and dry with a cloth or paper towel.

Fill the cavity with the custard mixture. Place the pumpkin in the top of a double-boiler if you have one the right size, or make your own with a heat-proof bowl placed in the bottom of a large saucepan containing about 6cm of water. Cover and steam on medium heat until you see that the custard has begun to set – shake the saucepan a little; when you can no longer make little 'waves' on the surface of the custard, it's beginning to set. Lower the heat and steam for 25-30 minutes.

Remove the pumpkin and let cool to room temperature. To serve, slice into thick cross-section wedges, shell and all.

## Khawng Waan (Sweet Stuff)

Many English-language Thai cookbooks contain a 'Thai desserts' chapter even though the concept doesn't exist, nor is there a translation for the word. The closest equivalent, **khǎwng wǎan**, simply means 'sweet stuff'. Cookbooks written for the Thai public contain sections on kaeng, phàt, yam, tôm yam, kàp klâem and jaan diaw (one-plate dishes), but never a section for Thai sweets, which are relegated to separate cookbooks, perhaps with the recognition that they hold no place in the traditional Thai meal.

Khǎwng wǎan mostly works itself into the daily Thai diet in the form of a snack, hence you won't find khǎwng wǎan in a traditional Thai restaurant. Rather they are prepared and sold by market vendors or by a shop specialising in regional khǎwng wǎan. For example, in the city of Phetburi, long famous for **khanǒm mâw kaeng** (a rich Thai custard), several shops in the vicinity of Khao Wang – a hill mounted by a historic ex-royal palace – sell packaged khanǒm mâw kaeng and other sweets to Thai tourists.

Few Thais make khǎwng wǎan at home. The typical sweets supplier – most are women – is someone trained in the art, since khǎwng wǎan preparation techniques tend to require more skill than other dishes. The **mâe khrua** (female chef), spends the morning making up khǎwng wǎan which are bundled into banana leaves, poured into pandan leaf cups or cut into colourful squares. These are then arranged onto large trays and sold by the **chín** (piece) at local markets or from street carts.

Prime ingredients for many Thai sweets include grated coconut, coconut milk, rice flour (from white rice or sticky rice), cooked sticky rice (whole grains), tapioca, tapioca flour, mung bean starch (whole or pureed mung beans), boiled taro and various fruits. For added texture and crunch, certain sweets also contain fresh corn kernels, sugar palm kernels, lotus seeds, cooked black beans and chopped water chestnuts. Egg yolks are a popular ingredient for khǎwng wǎan – including the ubiquitous **fǎwy thawng** (literally, 'golden threads') – probably influenced by Portuguese desserts and pastries introduced during the early Ayuthaya era. Thai history says that Marie Guimar, the French Catholic wife of Constantine Phaulkon – the Greek who was a minister in the court of King Narai – was the first to make egg-based sweets for the Ayuthaya court.

The fast-growing sugar cane is the main sweetening source for khǎwng wǎan although **tôn taan** (sugar palm), whose cultivation today is mostly restricted to Phetburi Province, is still preferred for certain dishes, usually in the form of a soft, light brown paste called **náamtaan pìip**. Coconut sugar, though similar in colour, usually comes in a stiffer paste, often formed into balls, and bears a faint taste of coconut. Visitors to Thai markets often mistake náamtaan pìip with a raw, lumpy cane sugar called **náam âwy** (also the word for cane sugar juice).

*Akha tribeswoman, Northern Thailand*

Thai sweets similar to the European concept of 'sweet pastry' are known as **khanōm**. Here again the kitchen-astute Portuguese were influential. The word itself may be a contraction of khâo nom (literally, 'milk rice') even though Thai khanōm is rarely made with cow's milk (until recently the odour of cow's milk was offensive to most Thais) but rather coconut milk or water thickened with rice flour.

Probably the most popular type of khanōm are the bite-size items wrapped in banana or pandan leaves, especially **khâo tôm kà-thí** and **khâo tôm mát**. Both consist of sticky rice grains steamed with **kà-thí** (coconut milk) inside a banana-leaf wrapper to form a solid almost toffee-like mass. Khâo tôm kà-thí also contains fresh grated coconut, while khâo tôm mát usually contains a few black beans or banana. In **khanōm thian** (candle

*Refreshing náam khǎeng kòt*

pastry, named for its shape), a mixture of rice or corn flour, sweetened coconut milk and sesame seeds are steamed in a tall slender banana leaf packet. A very simple and popular steamed sweet, **tà-kôh**, is made from tapioca flour and coconut milk over a layer of sweetened seaweed gelatine. It comes in small cups made from pandan leaves. A similar blend, minus the gelatine and steamed in tiny porcelain cups, is called **khanōm thûay** (cup pastry).

Coconut milk also features prominently in several soupier sweets with colourful names. In the enormously popular **klûay bùat chii** (bananas ordaining as nuns), banana chunks float in a white syrup of sweetened and slightly salted coconut milk. **Bua láwy** (floating lotus), consists of boiled sticky rice dumplings in a similar coconut sauce. Substitute red-dyed chunks of fresh water chestnut and you have **tháp thim kràwp** (crisp rubies). As at a modern ice cream parlour, you can often order extra ingredients, such as black beans, sugar palm kernels or kernels of corn, to the mix. Crushed ice is often added to cool the mixture.

# drinks

You won't go thirsty in Thailand. For starters the incredible array of fruit that grows abundantly here ensures that you have a myriad of flavoursome and healthy juices to choose from. Trang's coffee houses will impress caffeine fiends, and for those looking for something with more kick, the Thais produce a fine range of beers, whiskies and even some promising wines. There's also the local wild liquor, the taste of which can be as memorable as its effect.

## Alcoholic Drinks

In a society where any degree of intoxication violates the most basic of Theravada Buddhist tenets, it may come as a surprise that Thailand ranks fifth worldwide in per-capita alcohol consumption.

These days most Thais indulge, though women are more discreet than men in their consumption, most preferring not to drink in public. This is changing in big cities like Bangkok and Khorat, where it's not so unusual to see groups of younger women enjoying an after-work beer. Another exception is in North-Eastern Thailand, where Isaan women appear to be much less reserved when it comes to downing a glass of **lâo khǎo** (white liquor). Due to the influence of Islam, Southerners – men and women – drink far less than their compatriots in other regions.

Most Thais drink only domestically produced beers and liquors, primarily for reasons of expense. During the economic boom of the 1980s and early 1990s, the importation of foreign whiskies and wine grew feverishly among the moneyed classes. After the Thai economy began to stumble in 1997, even the 'tuppies' (Thai yuppies) returned to local tipples in large numbers.

Whether sticking to home-grown or sampling imports, drinking in Thailand can be expensive. The Thai government has placed increasingly heavy taxes on liquor and beer, so nearly half the price of a large beer, for example, is tax. One large bottle (660ml) of Thai-owned and Thai-brewed Singha beer costs about half the minimum daily wage of a Bangkok worker.

## Drinking Customs

Thais harbour no inhibitions about there being a 'proper' time of day when they can drink, in fact alcoholic beverages may be consumed with any meal. Although certainly not customary among working people, it's not unusual to see a Thai male drinking a large bottle of beer with breakfast in a restaurant.

As in most parts of the world, drinking is seen as a way of 'unwinding', hence evenings, weekends and holidays are when most people hit the bottle. Although public drunkenness, especially among males, is rarely chastised, many Thais view inebriation with disdain. Because of this, men often form cliques which meet periodically away from the disapproving eyes of their families. The venues for these drinking cliques vary tremendously according to class.

Any type of festival or wedding is an excuse for drinks to be shared. Even at a funeral, it's not unusual to see a few bottles of Mekong or lâo khǎo around, as a funeral is meant to celebrate the living as well as commemorate the deceased. Despite its acceptance, alcohol is never permitted inside shrine buildings or monastic quarters within a wát compound. During the annual three-month **phansāa** (rains retreat) season, roughly from late July to late October, many Thai Buddhists give up drinking temporarily as a show of Buddhist faith.

---

### PLACES TO DRINK

Close to my house in Chiang Mai, stands a wood and corrugated iron shelter where the neighbourhood **samlor** (pedicab) drivers meet every afternoon to share **lâo khǎo** (white liquor) or, when the fares have been good, Mekong rice whisky. A little further along the same street is a night market where lower middle-class men gather around bottles of beer, Mekong whisky and soda water. At either location, politics, women and sports are favourite topics of discussion. More upscale venues in the neighbourhood such as clubs, karaoke bars and discos attract a more well-heeled clientele who prefer imported beers and liquors. Here the chat tends to revolve around money, business and cars.

In venues like these, Thais often invite passing foreign visitors to sit and drink with them. There is no 'typical' experience of this nature, but it's not unusual to be pressed to drink more than you'd like. When you've had enough, leave your glass full, smile and keep repeating **phaw láew** (enough). It's doubtful your Thai drinking companions will allow you to pay for a round of drinks, but it's certainly worth trying.

Thais do not have a toast corresponding to 'cheers', but sometimes they will raise glasses in a celebratory manner. More rarely, they will intone **chaiyoh** (victory), although this is generally reserved for formal occasions. In such instances, you should raise your glass and repeat the toast.

*Singha, Thailand's premier beer*

DRINKS

DRINKS

## Bia (Beer)

Only a few brands of beer are readily available all over Thailand. Advertised with such slogans as 'pràthêht rao, bia rao' (our Land, our Beer) and 'pràthêht thai, bia thai' (Thailand, Thai beer), the Singha (Lion) label is considered the quintessential 'Thai' beer by faràng and locals alike. Pronounced sĭng, it claims an enviable 66% of the domestic market.

Singha's original recipe was formulated in 1934 by Thai nobleman Phya Bhirom Bhakdi and his son Prachuap, the first Thai to earn a brewmaster's diploma from Munich's Doemens Institute. Many international beer critics have declared the strong, hop-tasting brew to be the best beer produced in Asia. The barley for Singha is grown in Thailand, the hops are imported from Germany and the alcohol content is a heady 6%. The beer is brewed in Bangkok, and comes in brown glass bottles with a shiny gold lion on the label. Singha also comes in cans, and is available on tap as bia sòt (draught beer) in many pubs and restaurants.

Kloster, similarly inspired by German brewing recipes and also brewed in Bangkok, is a notch smoother and lighter than Singha, has an alcohol content of 4.7% and generally costs about 5B to 10B more per bottle. Tuppies and faràng often favour the clean tasting brew as something of a status symbol. Kloster claims only about 5% of Thailand's beer consumption and, like Singha, it is available in cans as well as bottles. Look for a straight-sided green bottle with a label that looks like it was designed in 18th or 19th century Germany.

Both Kloster and Singha were available only in 660ml bottles until the mid 1970s, when an expanding tourist market demanded the smaller 330ml bottles common in other countries. Cans didn't appear until the 1980s, when Thailand's growing affluence meant that some beer drinkers could afford the higher price of non-returnable containers (which was unfortunate for the environment).

Around that same time, Bangkok's Boon Rawd Breweries – makers of Singha – began producing a lighter beer called Singha Gold to compete with Kloster. Most drinkers seem to prefer either Kloster or regular Singha to Singha Gold, which is pretty bland.

Carlsberg, jointly owned by Danish and Thai interests, waded into the market in the early 1990s and proved to be a strong contender. As elsewhere in South-East Asia, Carlsberg used an aggressive promotion campaign and when market research found that Thais thought the brew was too weak, the company adjusted its recipe to come closer to Singha's 6% alcohol content. In its first two years in business, Carlsberg managed to grab around 25% of the Thai market. Like Kloster, it has a smoother flavour than Singha, and is preferred by some drinkers during hot spells.

## WAYLAID AGAIN

When the man finally emerged from the ditch, supported by two of his workmates, it was clear he had lost all use of his legs. With an uncoordinated heave, his companions sat him on the back of a readied motorcycle, locked his arms around the driver and gave him a farewell slap as the driver sped off into the sunset, toward the victim's home.

I'd watched all this from the comfort of my car. My house was only another minute's drive away, it had been a hot and exhausting day, and the prospect of taking a long, cool shower was supremely inviting. But I pulled over onto the verge amongst a dozen motorcycles and pick-ups clustered around an open-sided, wood and corrugated-iron whisky stall. Obviously there was fun to be had here.

Smoke rose from an oil-barrel grill in the centre of the bar, carrying to me the sweet, burnt smell of barbecued meats. The place was abuzz with conversation and laughter. Above the hum I caught shouted approximations of my name, appended with invitations to drink. Even after three years I was still regarded as something of a novelty.

It was the last day of the month, payday, and people were making the most of their hard-earned cash. As I tentatively moved towards some familiar faces, the **phûu yài bâan** (village headman) jumped up and came over to me. Simultaneously grasping my hand and evicting the two men who had been sitting opposite him, he sat me down, poured a glass, and banged it down in front of me. 'Mekong?' It was a simple question, but I hesitated, partly out of weary sobriety, partly out of deja vu.

'In a moment. I'll have a cold beer first. It's been a hot day, and I'm really thirsty.' My peculiar foreign perception that beer was the most refreshing of tipples was already known, so was no cause for surprise.

'Bring a bottle of Beer Chang for the faràng.' And so it began. Within moments my glass had been filled with ice and beer, and those around raised their glasses in unison. Experience told me that this salutation, followed by the obligatory swig, would be maniacally repeated every couple of minutes for the first hour or so, then gradually regulated as the evening wore on. One way or another, the locals always made sure I didn't go home sober.

Just as the final glimmer of sun dipped below the mountains, the motorcyclist-turned-taxi-driver returned from delivering his incapacitated colleague home. 'How's Ai Long?' the labourers at the next table laughingly inquired. The predictable reply came: '**mao khanàat!**' (very drunk!). It turned out, Ai Long had fallen into the ditch while relieving himself. His barely concerned drinking partners were members of a construction team, on their way home after a day toiling in the March heat. Their drink of choice was **lâo khão** (white liquor), drunk neat with occasional chasers of water.

DRINKS

I'd already finished a couple of bottles of beer, and was helping the villagers I was sitting with drain their fourth **baen** (375ml bottle) of Mekong. So when the high-spirited construction workers thrust a glass of lâo khão in my direction, any claim that I was intent on staying sober wouldn't have held much sway. I downed the stinging brew, and answered questions regarding my nationality, my ability to eat spicy food, and whether I had a girlfriend yet. My answers earned me a couple more shots of the increasingly palatable firewater.

By now the table was dripping with condensation from the glasses, and the inevitable spilled liquor. Set like islands in this sea of chaos, plates of **kài yâang** (grilled chicken), **sâi ùa** (spicy Northern Thai sausage), and a wide array of fresh herbs and vegetables provided tasty sustenance for the drinkers. Every now and then someone would break into song, usually chants of slighted lovers or bawdy ditties, momentarily interrupting the innuendo-laden banter and friendly laughter.

From time to time conversation turned to more serious topics – the state of the economy, the latest trouble on the Burmese border, what snow was really like, and whether Norway was always dark. I contributed what I could to the raised subjects, but all the talk was really with one aim, to re-affirm the comfort and congeniality of the present moment. Whatever the troubles of other times or places, right now things couldn't be better.

With the bar rapidly running out of supplies, people started to drift away. Not willing to let circumstance end the fun so early, four of our party moved on to a nearby house to join up with another group of revellers. The setting now a kitchen, but the activity the same.

I did eventually make it home that night, and may even have had that long, cool shower. To the best of my knowledge, I didn't fall into any ditches.

*– Simon Robson*
*Simon, a freelance editor, lives in Mae Rim.*

As the beer wars heated up, Singha retaliated with advertisements suggesting that drinking a Danish beer was unpatriotic. Carlsberg responded by creating Beer Chang (Elephant Beer), which matches the hoppy taste of Singha but has a higher alcohol content. Beer Chang has managed to gain an impressive following mainly because it retails at a significantly lower price than Singha. Predictably, the next offensive in the war was launched with the marketing of Boon Rawd's new cheaper brand, Leo. Sporting a black and red leopard label, Leo costs only slightly more than Beer Chang but is similarly high in alcohol. To differentiate itself from the flavour of the competition, Boon Rawd gave Leo a maltier taste.

Dutch giant Heineken, which opened a plant in Nonthaburi in 1995, comes third after Singha and Carlsberg to most national palates, and holds a similar ranking in sales.

Most likely, we can look forward to more variation in Thai beer brands in the coming years, as the manufacturers scramble to command the market by offering a variety of flavours and prices.

Thai beers, particularly Singha and Kloster, make fine accompaniments to virtually all Thai dishes.

### Rice Whisky

Long-time favourites, and more affordable than beer, are Thailand's 'whiskies', which are made from sticky rice. The two major rice whisky distillers – Suramaharas Co and the Surathip Group – are locked into a two-way battle for the Thai whisky market in much the same way Singha and Carlsberg vie for the beer market. The first produces the famous Mekong brand, a world-famous spirit named for South-East Asia's longest river. The second company makes the slightly pricier and slightly classier (by image, if nothing else) Sang Thip.

Known simply by their brand names, both liquors have a light, slightly sweet, rum-like flavour and an alcohol content of 35%. Although Thais consume more beer by volume than they do any other alcoholic beverage, Mekong and Sang Thip run a very close second, and when the sun sets over sidewalk eateries all over Thailand you'll see table after table cluttered with the amber-coloured whisky bottles.

More expensive Thai whiskies appealing to the can't-afford-Johnnie-Walker-yet set include Blue Eagle and Spey Royal, each with 40% alcohol. Both brands come dressed up in shiny boxes, much like the far more expensive imported whiskies they're imitating.

Thais typically purchase spirits by the bottle, not by the glass. Two bottle sizes are widely available, the traditional **klom** (750ml) and the **baen** (a 375ml, flask-sized bottle). An even smaller bottle, the **kák** (188ml), seems to have disappeared from shelves in recent years. Although spirits may be purchased at grocery and liquor stores, most modest Thai restaurants and night markets will have Mekong and Sang Thip on hand, possibly the other more expensive labels as well. A chilled tumbler of Mekong, ice and water with a squeeze of lime goes very well with yam.

### Other Spirits

With an alcohol content of 40% and a supposedly aged stock, Sang Som is the only true rum (made from sugar cane) made in the country. All other spirits, such as vodka and brandy, are imported.

**DRINKS**

## COUNTRY SPIRITS

I once attended a friend's wedding in a small village south of Chiang Mai. Fon was as excited and busy as any young bride-to-be, so I was pretty much left on my own to walk the minefield that is social custom in rural Thailand. I had known the family for many years, and their warm acceptance assuaged my shyness, while giving my curiosity free reign.

My nose and love of cooking led me to the kitchen, where most of the activity took place on the floor as there wasn't a table in sight. Women sat cross-legged in front of circular chopping blocks and baskets of fresh vegetables, talking loudly and laughing, as cleavers flashed in the mid-morning light. On charcoal braziers near the kitchen walls, woks as big as washtubs were smoking and spitting, and the rhythmic *thwok* of pestles in mortars indicated they were preparing pastes for an array of curries and soups.

Crushed garlic, pounded lemongrass, fresh chillies and bowls heaped with shrimp paste were arranged on cutting boards near the woks. I watched as the ingredients were added to the hot fat, and soon I was enveloped in a cloud of vapour as acrid as any tear gas attack at a student protest. My sputtering and coughing brought peals of laughter, the tears streaming from their eyes almost as copiously as from my own.

One of the cooks grabbed hold of my outstretched arms and guided me staggering to the door and into sweet, fresh air. From there she led me to another room inside the house where I was plopped onto the floor, much to the amusement of the menfolk occupying the same space. After a few minutes, my wheezing had subsided and my eyes had cleared enough to see one of the uncles offering me a glass of what I assumed to be water. I was glad to know that there was a commonality between our cultures on this point. I took a big gulp of 80 percent white lightning, then the sour smell of it registered.

Almost instantly, the liquor's effect had me listing to one side. I passed the glass on then slid into a foetal position on the floor. I've had home brews of many kinds, but never have they hit me so hard. After the men's chuckling died down, I overheard them saying the kitchen was not the proper place for me, and that it was much better to be drinking lâo khão with the men. From my prone position, my argument that the ranks of the world's great chefs were disproportionately male, was greeted with good-natured derision. The glass was coming my way again and knowing that I couldn't drink this stinky liquor and last the day, I asked for a glass of water. My sleight-of-hand between the glasses went unnoticed and they all made agreeable noises as I seemingly took another manly swig of whisky.

After what seemed to be a polite tenure in the drinking circle, I wobbled unsteadily over to where tables were set up for the arriving guests. On the tables, more food was being prepared. Mounds of garlic cloves were surrounded by cackling aunties and cousins, and I took my seat to finally witness a successful technique for separating the husk from the bulb without pulping it. With a few flicks of the fingers they moved on to the next one as I was still trying to decide which one to begin with. With my hands cramping and little progress being made, someone began singing a simple song that reminded me of a sea shanty. All the garlic huskers joined in, as others began clapping along.

After a few songs, they turned to me and asked me to sing something from my own country. I was trapped. My singing sounds like a cat fight, and I didn't think they would appreciate 'Stairway to Heaven' in any case. In sheer desperation, I started singing 'Mama's little baby loves shortnin' bread'. Within three beats, all at the table were clapping in time and howling their approval for my choice of song. I sang the only verse I knew several times and ended with a cracking, baritone 'shortnin' breeeead' just as a terrified bellow came from the concrete slab behind me.

I spun around to see a hobbled water buffalo being bled from the neck into a succession of large metal bowls. As the beast collapsed, first onto its forelegs and then to its side, the butchers tried to keep a bowl under the incision so as not to waste a drop. The carcass was then set upon by men wielding razor sharp machetes. The entrails were separated and taken away amidst clouds of houseflies, to be cleaned and prepared. The hide was peeled off the flesh and taken away to be scraped and salted, and the remaining carcass was quartered in a way that bore no resemblance to the cuts of meat I know. As grisly as it was, I was struck by the thought that this was how humans had eaten for aeons, a world away from the plastic-wrapped foam trays of supermarkets.

Some of the haunches and ribs were quickly claimed and the rest were carried to the kitchen, where the singing sounds of steel blades being sharpened against stone filled the room. Being shooed from the kitchen yet again, I went to watch the wedding ceremony, a tender affair in which bridge and groom knelt with their elbows propped on embroidered cushions, a sacred string encircling the tops of their heads and joining the two in matrimony.

In the revelry that followed, the bride asked me if I wanted some of my favourite dish, **lâap** (spicy minced meat salad). She placed before me a bowl of raw meat and some kind of grass floating in a bowl of fresh blood. This decidedly did not look like the lâap I knew and loved. Someone passed me a basket of sticky rice and encouraged me to dig in. I had resigned myself to 'go native', and here was my moment of truth.

In my broken Thai, I politely asked the father of the bride to pass the moonshine.

*– Gordon Morton, Jr*
*Gordon, a graphic design consultant married to a Chiang Mai Thai,*
*spends much of his spare time exploring Northern Thailand.*

**DRINKS**

## Lao Khao (White Liquor)

Deep in the rural countryside – areas that the Thais call **chonábòt** – where farming is the main activity and incomes are meagre, a colourless liquid called **lâo khão** (white liquor) is the beverage of choice. Lâo khão comes in two broad genres, legal and contraband. The legal kind, distilled from sticky rice and distributed nationwide, is commissioned by the Thai government and could almost be said to represent a subsidised general anaesthetic for the pains of the working poor. It's sold in 750ml bottles with a rather crude label bearing Thai script and a drawing of rice ears. Like Mekong or Sang Thip (see Rice Whisky earlier in this chapter), lâo khão is 35% alcohol, but sells for roughly half the price. Sweet, raw-tasting and much more aromatic than the amber stuff, it's usually drunk neat, or less commonly mixed with soft drinks such as Sprite or Coke (although no amount of mixer will disguise the distinctive taste).

Over on the untaxed, illegal side of the bar, you'll find a more interesting selection of liquors distilled from various agricultural products including sugar palm sap, coconut milk, coconut sap, sugar cane, taro, as well as sticky rice. Alcohol content varies from as little as 10% to as much as 95%. Such **lâo thèuan** (wild liquor) tends to be weaker in Southern Thailand and stronger in North and North-Eastern Thailand. Perhaps the warming effect of alcohol is more appreciated in the northern regions, where there is a distinct cool season. These types of home-brew or moonshine are generally taken straight, with water as a chaser. In smaller towns, almost every no-frills restaurant keeps some lâo thèuan under the counter for sale.

Thais take regional pride in the quality of local moonshine, and often invent names for the liquor. In Loei Province's Tha Li district, for example, the local lâo thèuan may be referred to as 'Mae Heuang', named after a river that runs through the area, and an intentional pun on Mekong rice whisky. The intensity with which lâo thèuan connoisseurs in neighbouring provinces will compare the attributes of their respective spirits – seeing which one maintains a bubble the longest when shaken, for example – would be familiar to anyone who has dabbled in home-brewing and moonshine making. The illegality of lâo thèuan does not seem to be much of an issue in Thailand. Thais drink it quite openly.

To be frank, most lâo thèuan tastes little better than rubbing alcohol and it not uncommonly contains impurities that can turn the stomach. The sugar cane version found in Kanchanaburi Province is perhaps the most palatable. Experiment with caution; if nothing else, the high alcohol content can lead to especially nasty hangovers.

Lâo khão isn't usually drunk with meals, but rather before as an aperitif. Sometimes it is drunk with such **kàp klâem** (drinking food) as **mǔu yâang** (grilled strips of pork eaten with spicy dipping sauces).

*Making lâo khão (white liquor) with a home still*

## DRINKING OUT

When dining out, you'll notice that rice liquors are never drunk neat. Instead they are ordered by the **chút** (set), that is, accompanied by ice, mixers (soda water, plain water, cola) and halved limes. Some restaurants feature a special price for a chút, making it more attractive.

Once ordered, the bottle and mixers are placed on a small, shelved table that stands alongside one of the dining table's narrow ends. Throughout the meal, the chút is attended to by a server, usually a teenage boy or girl referred to simply as **dèk** (child). Seldom do the diners mix their own drinks; instead the vigilant dèk tops them up whenever they drop to half full or less. You choose a mixer at the beginning of the meal, and then leave the drink-strength up to the server. Typically the dèk goes light, pouring perhaps only one or two fingers of rice whisky in the glass before filling it with ice and mixer. This makes a shared bottle last longer and, according to locals, a light drink always tastes better (and digests better) than a strong one.

Beer service undergoes a similar treatment, ending up on the bar table for the server to handle refills. Empty bottles are shuttled below the bar so that they can be counted when the bill is totalled.

### Lâo Yaa Dawng (Herbal Liquor)

Add herbs, roots, seeds, fruit or bark to lâo khão, allow it to steep for a few days or weeks and you get **lâo yaa dawng** (pickled herb liquor). The yaa dawng additives can do much to enhance the flavour and colour of lâo khão, turning it amber and imbuing the liquid with a variety of fragrances. Many of the lâo yaa dawng preparations are purported to have specific health-enhancing qualities. In rural areas, people have long believed in the medicinal qualities imparted by these concoctions. One particular root, for example, is said to banish the aches and pains of a day's manual labour.

Herbal liquors have become fashionable throughout the country with the blue-jeaned, long-haired crowd who listen to and play **phlaeng phêua chiiwít** ('songs for life', a genre of modern Thai folk music based on traditional melodies and rhythms). Perhaps they feel that drinking locally brewed lâo yaa dawng rather than mass-produced whisky and beer is a way of returning to their Thai roots – literally and figuratively. Lâo yaa dawng can be found at roadside vendor stalls, small pubs and in a few guesthouses catering to backpackers. Some of them taste fabulous while others are a chore to get down.

## Wain (Wine)

Unlike Cambodia and Laos, who as part of French Indochina shared close ties with Europe, Thai society has had little historical contact with grape wine. Imported wines were available in Bangkok for much of the 20th century, but they tended to be scarce and expensive, and their enjoyment was mostly limited to the small European expatriate community. Local knowledge of wine has been limited to a small, well-to-do clique. This includes His Serene Highness Prince Subhadris Diskul, a grandson of King Rama IV and today one of Thailand's foremost art historians, whose knowledge of French wines is as extensive as his knowledge of Khmer temple ruins – a legacy of his many years of university study in France and the United Kingdom.

A Thai whisky producer experimented with wine-making in the 1960s and 70s, in part to tempt the military 'rest & recreation' market during the Indochina War. The resulting 'Thai Red Wine' and 'Thai White Wine' were barely suitable for cooking purposes, much less for drinking and thankfully they've since disappeared.

During the 1980s and early 90s, as Thailand enjoyed steady double-digit economic growth, a whole new generation of young working Thais became enthralled with imported wines. Wine bars and wine cellars popped up all around Bangkok, Italian and French restaurants expanded their wine lists to keep up with the trend and even some of the higher-end Thai restaurants began maintaining small wine collections. Although the baht devaluation of the late 1990s made imported wines too expensive for many Thais – and dozens of wine shops closed as a result – wine now seems to have found a permanent place in the Thai epicurean psyche, at least among more sophisticated urban-dwellers. Imported wines from France, Chile, Australia, South Africa, Spain and the US are still widely available in western restaurants and supermarkets.

Given the current interest in wine, coupled with the baht's disadvantaged exchange rate on the global market, the time is ripe for local enterprises to start creating wines on Thai soil once again. The latest attempt is a winery called Chateau de Loei, located on the cool, high plains of the Khorat Plateau in Loei Province. Dr Chaijudh Karnasuta, the owner of the winery (and chairman of the Oriental Hotel), has spent a considerable amount of money and time studying wine-making methods. His first vintage, a chenin blanc, is quite drinkable and the syrah/shiraz shows promise. Both are available at finer restaurants in Bangkok, Chiang Mai and Phuket, as well as in many wine shops for around 500B per bottle. Chateau de Loei's management is currently experimenting with 21 other grape varieties from the US, as well as three from France.

DRINKS

It's possible to visit Chateau de Loei Vineyards by contacting the adjacent Rangyen Resort (tel 042-891089), off Route 203 near the town of Dan Sai. Because of the travel time required to reach here, you should plan on spending the night at the resort.

Kasetsart University in Bangkok, Thailand's main centre for agricultural experimentation, has several projects in progress trying to produce sparkling wines from tamarind, mayom (star gooseberry) and pineapple.

Matching wine with Thai food is always rather tricky, especially since grape wine is not a traditional Thai beverage. Chateau de Loei's chenin blanc goes well with almost any Thai dish except for **kaeng phèt** (hot kaeng), which overpowers just about any wine. Chilled light German or Alsatian wines seem like a natural choice for spicier fare, and if you really want to take on a curry with a bottle of wine, we suggest you splash out on a good Gewürztraminer.

---

### KAP KLAEM (DRINKING FOOD)

Dishes known as **kàp klâem** are meant to be eaten with alcoholic beverages. Some English menus list them as 'snacks' or 'appetisers'.

| | |
|---|---|
| fried peanuts | **thùa thâwt** |
| fried cashews | **mét má-mûang hìmáphaan thâwt** |
| fried potatoes | **man faràng thâwt** |
| fried fishcakes | **thâwt man plaa** |
| fried shrimp cakes | **thâwt man kûng** |
| shrimp chips | **khâo krìap kûng** |
| 'three kinds of chicken' (chopped ginger, peanuts, chilli peppers and bits of lime, mixed | **kài sãam yàang** |
| fried spring rolls | **paw pía thâwt** |
| fresh spring rolls | **paw pía sòt** |
| toasted pork | **mŭu pîng yam** |
| Yam (hot & tangy salad) with: | |
|   mung bean starch noodles | **yam wún sên** |
|   grilled beef | **yam néua** |
|   squid | **yam plaa mèuk** |
|   grilled eggplant | **yam mákhĕua yao** |
|   cashew nuts | **yam mét má-mûang hìmáphaan** |
|   fried eggs | **yam khài dao** |
|   pomelo | **yam sôm-oh** |
|   mango | **yam má-mûang** |
|   fried, shredded catfish & peanuts | **yam plaa dùk fuu** |

## Non-Alcoholic Drinks
### Fruit Drinks & Soft Drinks

The variety of juice and shakes available in markets, street stalls and restaurants is seemingly endless. The all-purpose term for fruit juice is **náam phŏn-lá-mái**. Put **náam** (water or juice) together with the name of any fruit and you have a fruit drink.

When a blender or extractor is used, it's called **náam khán** (squeezed juice). Saying **náam sàp-pàrót khán**, for example, emphasises that the pineapple juice is freshly squeezed. Thais prefer to drink most fruit juice with a little salt mixed in. Unless a vendor or restaurant is used to serving unsalted drinks for tourists, yours will come slightly salted. If you prefer plain fruit juice, specify **mâi sài kleua** (without salt).

A Thai favourite, **náam âwy** (sugar cane juice) is a very refreshing accompaniment to kaeng dishes. Many small restaurants, food stalls and **ráan kŭaytĭaw** (noodle shops) that don't offer any other juice will have a supply of náam âwy on hand. A similar juice from the sugar palm, **náam taan sòt**, is also very good and both are full of vitamins and minerals.

*One of the many uses for bamboo*

Two fruit extracts found in many traditional Thai restaurants include the delicious **náam má-tuum** (an amber drink made from bale fruit) and **náam krà-jìap** (a red-tinted beverage made from roselle fruit). Both boast a long list of health-enhancing properties, and can be rendered as **chaa** (tea) if brewed with hot water. **Chaa khĭng** (an infusion of ginger and hot water sweetened with sugar or honey) is a popular herbal tea.

DRINKS

Fruit blended with ice to make a smoothie is called **náam pon** (literally, 'mixed juice') as in **náam málákaw pon** (papaya smoothie). Fresh juice is widely available, while smoothies are more restricted to tourist areas.

On a hot day, **má-phráo àwn** (young green coconut juice) is particularly refreshing, and because coconuts are so plentiful, this is one of the least expensive drinks. You will see street vendors specialising in má-phráo àwn, and it is also available in many restaurants.

Both Coca Cola and Pepsi have long been established in Thailand, along with Sprite and the multicoloured Fanta family.

## Kaafae (Coffee)

Since the 1980s, Nescafé and other instant coffees have made deep inroads into Thai coffee culture, at the expense of freshly ground beans. Most restaurants – especially those in hotels, guesthouses and other tourist establishments – serve instant coffee with packets of non-dairy creamer on the side. Upmarket hotels and coffee shops sometimes offer filtered and espresso coffees at premium prices.

Traditionally, coffee in Thailand is grown in the hilly areas of Northern and Southern Thailand, roasted by wholesalers, ground by vendors and filtered just before serving. The filtering system consists of nothing more than a narrow cloth bag attached to a steel handle. Ground coffee is placed in the bag and hot water is poured through it to produce a thick black beverage. Thai-grown coffee may not be as full and rich-tasting as gourmet Sumatran or Jamaican beans but it's still considerably tastier than instant. The hill-tribe communities of Northern Thailand's mountainous slopes produce the nation's best coffee. One wholesaler in Chiang Mai specialises in beans organically grown by hill-tribe cooperatives. Another good coffee-growing area is the hilly central Trang Province of Southern Thailand, which supplies many of the **ráan kopíi** (coffee shops) for which Trang is famous.

Sometimes restaurants or vendors with the proper accoutrements for making traditional filtered coffee keep a supply of Nescafé just for faràng (or moneyed Thais, since instant always costs a few baht more). To get real Thai coffee ask for **kaafae thŭng** (bag coffee), which refers to the traditional method of preparation. Trang's Hokkien cafes are best for this. Elsewhere in Thailand you'll find it at outdoor morning markets. Some Thais also refer to such coffee as **kaafae tôm** (boiled coffee) although this can mean coffee run through a modern coffeemaker.

The usual kaafae thŭng is served in a glass, mixed with sugar and sweetened condensed milk. If you don't want either, be sure to specify **kaafae dam** (black coffee) followed with **mâi sài náamtaan** (without sugar).

In the 1990s Thailand underwent something of a coffee revolution. The number of places serving European-style coffees multiplied quickly,

*Drinks made from bale fruit and roselle fruit*

especially in Bangkok. A Thai chain called Black Canyon opened inexpensive espresso cafes in shopping malls all over the country. More recently, two Thais who had lived in Australia opened a place called Kuppa in an abandoned Bangkok warehouse and began roasting coffee there in a French roasting machine. They now supply the prestigious Oriental and Peninsula Hotels. Later the same year, Bangkok's first Starbucks (a Seattle-based US chain) opened and was an immediate success.

## Tea

Both Indian-style (black) and Chinese-style (green or semi-cured) teas are common. The latter predominates in Chinese restaurants and is the usual ingredient in **náam chaa**, the weak, often lukewarm tea-water traditionally served free in aluminium teapots. Ask for a **kâew plào** (plain glass) and you can drink as much as you like. For iced náam chaa, ask for a glass of **náam khǎeng** (ice) and pour your own. For fresh, undiluted Chinese tea request **chaa jiin**.

Black tea, both imported and locally grown, is usually available in the same restaurants or food stalls that serve real coffee. **Chaa thai** (Thai tea) derives its characteristic orange-red colour from ground tamarind seed added after curing. Like Thai coffee, the traditional way to make chaa thai is to pour hot water through a filter 'sock' filled with dried tea. An order of **chaa ráwn** (hot tea) almost always results in a serving of chaa thai with sugar and condensed milk. Specify whether you want milk and sugar.

A favourite both in Thailand and abroad is **chaa yen**, a tall glass of Thai iced tea sweetened with sugar and condensed milk in which the milk is added last to create a thick, cloud-like layer on top of the tea. Without the milk it's **chaa dam yen** (chilled black tea), which will come with sugar and sometimes a squeeze of lime. If you want this, ask for **chaa dam yen sài má-nao**.

## Water

At meal times, plain water is the most popular beverage. Purified drinking water is simply called **náam dèum** (drinking water), whether boiled or filtered. All water offered to customers in restaurants or to guests in an office or home in Thailand will be purified, so you needn't fret about safety.

In restaurants you can ask for **náam plào** (plain water) which is always either boiled or taken from a purified source. It's served by the glass at no charge, or you can order by the bottle. A bottle of **náam sohdaa** (soda) costs about the same as a bottle of náam plào but the bottles are smaller.

# home cooking
# & traditions

The amount of food that can be produced on a single charcoal-fuelled firepot would have the appliance-mad chefs of the world reeling. In fact, cooking a multi-course meal with nothing more than a wok, spatula and a few pots is an everyday occurrence in Thailand. Furthermore, Thai kitchens remain predominately an outdoor facility, the escaping aromas being proof to what can be created without the help of a cupboard of gadgetry.

Until the reign of King Mongkut (Rama IV, 1851-68), virtually all Thai cooking was done outdoors. Because the original **meuang** (city states) preferred river valleys for settlement, traditional houses were raised high on stilts to keep the living area above the fertile flood plains, and to protect the inhabitants from wild animals. Domestic animals were kept tethered to the stilts or in a nearby pen, and the space below the house was used for chores such as cooking, chopping firewood and weaving textiles.

Although stilted wooden houses can still be seen in rural areas and small towns, a shortage of lumber meant houses began to be built of cement or bricks, and without stilts. Consequently, cooking moved to the

---

### FAMILY FEAST

Five aunts, two uncles and nine cousins live in different areas of the country, and a couple of times a year we all converge at my grandfather's house to the north of Bangkok. Like anywhere, large family gatherings can be an emotionally stressful time, even if everyone is pampered with good home cooking. Coming from the gentle mountains of the north for a family reunion in Bangkok – a city of over seven million people, with traffic jams lasting for hours – only adds to the stress. Yet it's surprising how weeks of dread always yield to pleasant surprises.

Vying to be the most devoted child or grandchild, everyone rises at the crack of dawn on the day of the reunion. Added to the desire to impress is the Bangkokian tendency to be incredibly picky about what is served. One aunt will drive two hours to Bangkhen to buy the best **pèt yâang râat phrík** (roast duck covered in chillies) in town; another, an hour to Lat Phrao for the 'most original' **mìi yòk** (jade noodles); and yet another, two and a half hours, to Pak Chong, for out of season **lam yài** (longan) and sticky rice in coconut milk. Frantic mobile phone conversations ensue while a cousin is stuck in traffic and may not get to the shop selling **mǔu daeng** (marinated red pork) which goes with the jade noodles, or the duck has run out, or someone can't find the lam yài vendor. Just when you think the chaos has reached fever pitch, everything miraculously falls into line. Durian is found instead of lam yài, the duck shop has marinated pork and there are luckily a few ducks in reserve.

Finally around 1pm the gathering of the clan commences. Young cousins run from car to kitchen carrying plastic bags full of food, aunts swiftly untangle rubber bands and place the food in dishes, and uncles supervise the maids while they fuss around with tables and chairs.

There will inevitably be some last minute hysteria when someone realises that we had too many meat dishes and not enough vegetable

side or back of the house. To protect the cooks from sun and rain, house-owners added shelters of thatched palm or corrugated metal, supported by beams of various materials.

These days the outdoor kitchen is still the norm. What you will find in these kitchens in the way of tools and utensils may vary greatly, as the **hâwng khrua** (kitchen) is an appropriation of certain things western, blended with certain things Thai. A simple kitchen will feature little more than a charcoal firepot, a few pots and pans, ladles, spatulas and shelves for dry goods. A more elaborate set-up would include a gas cooker, refrigerator and a greater variety of utensils.

---

dishes. So a young cousin will be sent off on his bicycle, pedalling madly in search of **phàk bûng** (water spinach), **phàk khà-náa** (Chinese kale) or other vegetables. The wok, glowing red, will be ready for the chopped garlic, copious amounts of oyster sauce and vegetables. As flames lick the side of the wok, the kitchen crackles with energy and becomes engulfed in the aromas of garlic and fish sauce that are so distinctly Thai, and finally we are exhausted, but ready to enjoy the multifarious collection of dishes we've amassed.

As the family patriarch, grandfather is served first, and will be given something from every dish on the table, all of which he must taste so that no cousin or aunt feels slighted. Then we all dig into the **kài phàt khǐng** (chicken stirfried with ginger), **khanǒm pang nâa mǔu** (bread topped with coriander and minced pork, then fried), **sà-té kài** (chicken satay with peanut sauce), **khàep mǔu** (fried pork rind) with **náam phrík kà-pì** (chilli and shrimp paste dip) and an array of gorgeous food carefully selected from Bangkok's finest food vendors, restaurants and market stalls.

Once completely stuffed, everyone starts arguing about who will take the food home. In Thai culture, it's bad form for anyone to accept all this terrific food, as it appears self-indulgent. Consequently my grandmother ends up with a fridge full of food which she will give to a less fortunate neighbour the next day.

Sitting back in his old armchair after the dishes have been cleared away, my grandfather will beam with happiness at the presence of his family, not caring one bit how special each dish was, or where it came from. By allowing us to fuss unnecessarily, he gives us all a sense of importance and accomplishment.

*by Pim Kemasingki Shaw*
*Born in Chiang Mai to an English father and Thai mother, and educated in Thailand, Switzerland, Canada and Great Britain, Pim is managing editor of Chiang Mai Newsletter (www.chiangmainews.com).*

Urban dwellers with more disposable income may have indoor kitchens, although even the middle class often prefer at least one wall open. This is so the powerful aromas from cooking chillies, shrimp paste and garlic can escape quickly. Wealthier Thais living in walled compounds – not uncommon in Bangkok – may have a separate building for the kitchen which is tended to by servants. Most upper-middle class households have at least one servant who does most or all of the cooking.

Home cooking is traditionally considered a woman's task, so any woman with a job outside the home usually has a **mâe khrua** (female cook) or **dèk khrua** (child cook) who assumes these duties. Aside from hired help, the extended family – grandparents, aunts and sisters – often lend a hand in the kitchen. In some homes, granny's sole function seems to be to prepare the meals.

As is customary in the west, if a male in the home has a particular interest in taking over these duties, he is usually welcome to do so. Thai culinary culture, however, does not have an equivalent to the 'weekend barbecue' enjoyed by some western males. The closest thing, in rural Thailand, is the custom wherein temple festival food is prepared by men, reportedly because the task of stirring and ladling enough food to cater for so many people requires greater physical strength.

When the novelty of home cooking wears off, there's always

*The Northern Thai method for steaming sticky rice*

the option of takeaway food. Such fare may be picked up at a local market where prepared dishes are displayed in big bowls or on large, flat trays, or from neighbourhood restaurants. Everything, including hot curry and soups, goes into small plastic bags. More traditionally, takeaway food is wrapped in banana leaves. Because the profit margin at markets and small restaurants tends to be very thin, dishes cost only marginally more than they would to make at home.

*Souvenir paintings promote an idyllic vision of Thailand's river and canal life*

## Utensils

In the traditional outdoor kitchen, the **tao fai** (firepot) is still the most common heat source. It consists of a thick-walled pot made from clay mixed with sand, rice husk and ashes. Tao fai come in different sizes, the most common measuring about 24cm in diameter at the mouth, tapering inward to the flat base. Along the lip are three flanges or 'feet' that support a pot or wok while allowing the circulation of air into the fire cavity.

Inside the tao fai, a **tà-kràp** (clay grate) holds the charcoal fuel or, less commonly, short pieces of wood. Near the bottom of the tao fai, a rectangular hole allows cooling air in so the stove doesn't burn a hole in the floor, and allows access to ashes that have fallen through the grate. Another rectangular hole near the top of the tao fai has an adjustable door so that heat can be adjusted by controlling the ventilation. A tao fai always sits on the ground or floor – often on an asbestos mat – so the cook must squat or sit on a low stool to fan the flames with a bamboo or palmleaf fan while tending the pan.

Although some gourmets emphatically state that food prepared on a tao fai tastes superior, a Thai household with a little more money may upgrade to a **tao káet** (gas burner). One burner suffices for some homes, yet upper-middle class households have up to four. Even so, what a Thai cook can produce with just one tao fai or tao káet would amaze anyone used to a four-burner stove.

Full Thai meals can be prepared over one burner, whether charcoal or gas, with just three types of cookware. First and foremost is the **krà-thá**, a shallow, wide-mouthed round-bottomed pan most people know as the 'wok'. The most popular krà-thá – and the easiest to use – has one long, sturdy wooden handle. Although they may be made from a variety of metals, krà-thá are usually made from tempered steel, which needs careful attention when cleaning and storing as it's prone to rust.

Krà-thá are primarily used for stirfries although some cooks also use them for kaeng. Whatever the dish, Thais use a **phai** (spatula with a curved edge) to move ingredients in the wok.

As essential as the wok are two **mâw** (pots), one for boiling rice and another for making kaeng. The traditional mâw is made of fired clay or other earthenware, but aluminium or porcelain-laminated steel versions have become commonplace. The shape of the mâw varies, the more traditional ones having curved sides, a flat bottom, a **hŭu** (handle) on each side and a tight-fitting lid. A **mâw khàek** (rounded, narrow-necked pot) and **hùat** (steamer) are necessary for preparing sticky rice.

Since Thai dishes do not have to reach the tabletop steaming hot (see Etiquette in The Culture of Thai Cuisine chapter), the cook can prepare a

*A kitchen in Baw Sang*

meal in sequence, sitting one pot aside – lid in place to keep it warm – while cooking the next dish. Rice is usually boiled first, then the kaeng or another dish requiring a pot is prepared, and lastly any stirfries. Nowadays, in urban kitchens, rice is mostly prepared in an electric rice cooker rather than in a pot.

Many other utensils are used throughout the country, two of the more important being the **khrók** (mortar) and **sàak** (pestle), which come in various sizes. A smaller stone set is used to grind spices and make **khrêuang kaeng** (curry paste), while a larger earthenware khrók and **sàak mái** (large pestle) are used for salads such as **sômtam** (tart & spicy salad).

---

### KIN LIANG BAAN THAI (Being Hosted in a Thai Home)

If you're invited to eat at someone's home, consider yourself blessed, as Thais do not freely dispense home invitations – most food celebrating is done at festivals or restaurants. If you've been invited for an evening meal, you'll probably be asked to arrive sometime between 6 and 7pm. An exception to this popular dining hour might be in Bangkok, where your hosts' work commute necessitates a later hour. Whatever the invitation, arrive on time if you can.

In Thailand it is not customary for invitees to bring along a gift for the hosts, but the men in the household will almost always appreciate a bottle of foreign liquor, especially Scotch whisky. Do not bring Mekong or other Thai liquor as it's not perceived as 'special' enough to be gift material. A tin of imported tea or coffee will also be appreciated.

If the home you're visiting has a separate dining room, you'll probably be led there as soon as you arrive. If there is no dining room, a table may be set up outdoors. In rural areas you may dine in the main living area, possibly sitting on the floor. I once was invited to the home of a family who lived above their **ráan cham** (sundries shop) in Phrakhanong, a busy district in southeast Bangkok. Because their upstairs living area was rather small, they set a table up in the middle of their shop downstairs, where we dined while neighbourhood children crowded around the doorway to peek at the faràng guest.

Although a pre-dinner cocktail hour per se isn't observed, many Thais will offer guests a drink before the meal. **Kàp klâem** (drinking food) such as a spicy yam or a plate of cashews fried with chillies will almost always be served to accompany the drinks. Most Thai men drink alcohol and male guests will be offered beer, Mekong whisky or possibly something imported. Thai women don't customarily drink in public, but a foreign woman will usually be offered an alcoholic beverage. If you're a female guest, and you notice none of the Thai women present are

Thais slice and mince vegetables, herbs, meats and other ingredients on the **khĭang**, a flat, circular cutting board made of dense tamarind wood about 5cm thick.

The slicing itself is carried out using knives of varying length and sizes. For jointing chickens or cutting through harder, tougher items such as galangal root, Thais use a Chinese-style cleaver known as a **mîit mŭu** (pig knife) or **bang taw** (cleaver). Thinner, sharper knives known as **mîit** are used for peeling and carving fruit and vegetables. More rustic kitchens usually have an **ii-tôh** (a hardy, hatchet-like utility knife) for splitting coconut shells or chopping kindling for the firepot.

---

drinking, they'll appreciate your solidarity if you accept tea, water or a soft drink instead of alcohol. Despite the 'division of beverages', men and women will sit together throughout the evening. In some Thai households – particularly those that are devoutly Buddhist – no alcohol is served. If you happened to have brought a bottle of booze as a gift, don't worry, your hosts will not be offended; non-drinking Thais are not puritanical about their habits and are happy for others to enjoy bacchanalia. They will most likely pass your gift on to drinking friends.

Except among close friends, Thai kitchens are considered 'private' zones, much like bathrooms, so helping out in the kitchen, whether in the cooking, serving or cleaning up stages, isn't usually done. Still, the offering of assistance is an appreciated gesture. '**Chûay tham a-rai dâi mǎi?**' means (Can I help you do anything?).

The meal will usually be served shortly after your arrival. You may notice that your hosts, including any children present, will eat very sparingly at first. In a very traditional household, the family will eat only token amounts of the food they've prepared until it is obvious that you have stopped eating. Then they will dig in with gusto! This underscores the notion that the meal was prepared for your enjoyment, rather than theirs. If you notice this is happening, once they begin eating in earnest, it's time for you to sit back and let them eat. In more modern Bangkok households you won't see as much of this reticence on the part of either hosts or guests.

In some households, don't be surprised if a television is set up near the table and turned on, to provide entertainment for all present. That TV might distract from the meal is an idea for the most part reserved to upper-class Thais.

More drinks typically arrive during and after the meal, though hot Chinese tea is often served immediately afterwards as well. Lingering on for an hour or two after a meal is not the usual custom, so once everyone has had their tea or a couple of final drinks, it's usually time to go.

*Mortars & pestles, and ingredients for kaeng khĩaw-wăan*

The **maew khùut má-phráo** (traditional coconut grater) is also part of the traditional kitchen kit, especially in rural areas where people still grate their own coconut rather than buying it pre-grated in the local markets. The **krà-chawn** (sieve) is useful for straining liquids such as coconut milk from soaked, grated coconut meat. Very traditional households may fashion their own krà-chawn by piercing a halved coconut shell with small holes. The double-handled **krà-chawn má-nao** (lime sieve) used for squeezing lime juice also gets a lot of use.

For steaming fish, dumplings, sweets or other dishes, the cook uses a **rang thĕung** (a round flat steamer made of steel or bamboo). This is fitted into the top of a pot containing several centimetres of water to produce a double boiler or steamer.

# celebrating
## with food

Religious, regional and national festivals are so numerous in Thailand, it often feels as if there's no room for a normal day. Each celebration, from a house blessing to Nan Province's chilli festival, comes with its own particular ceremonies, activities and, of course, food. No celebration is complete until all participants – including the spirits – have had their fill.

## SPIRIT DINING

 Every Thai house, office building, rice field or other place heavily used by humans has to have a spirit house to go with it – a place for the **phrá phum** (earth spirits) native to the site to live in. Without this structure you're likely to have the spirits living in the house with you, interfering with your daily activities, causing all sorts of trouble. A typical spirit house looks like a miniature Thai temple mounted on a pedestal – at least your average spirit house does. A large hotel may have a shrine covering 100 sq metres, while off the highway to Hua Hin stands an artificial spirit mountain built to accommodate the earth spirits displaced by an adjacent quarry.

How do you ensure that the spirits take up residence in your spirit house rather than in the main house with you? Mainly by making the spirit house the more auspicious place to live in, through daily offerings of flowers, candles, incense and food. The spirit house must enjoy a prominent location, not shaded by the main house or building. Thus its position has to be planned from the very beginning and installed with due ceremony. If your own house is improved or enlarged, then the spirit house should be as well. The local **phâw khruu** (father guru) or **mâe khruu** (mother guru) usually presides over the initial installation as well as later improvements.

The interior of a spirit house is typically decorated with ceramic or plastic figurines representing the property's guardian spirits. The most important figurine, the **jâo thîi** (place lord), embodies a phrá phum who reigns over a specific part of the property. More elaborate spirit houses may also contain figurines that serve as family or servants for the resident spirits. Thai believers purchase these figurines – as well as the bowls, dishes and other accoutrements necessary for making daily offerings – at rural temples or, in larger cities, at supermarkets and department stores.

A scale veranda attached to the front of each spirit house will hold the daily food offerings, which typically consist of small portions of rice – phrá phum are said to be especially fond of sticky rice – fresh fruit, sweets, and cups of water or tea. On special occasions, such as when the building owner wants to placate the resident spirits (either to thank them for an unexpected piece of luck or to ward off expected misfortune), much more ample food offerings – a boiled chicken, a platter of fish, even a whole pig's head studded with sticks of incense – may be presented.

## Animist & Buddhist Occasions

In a land where Buddhism and animism mix freely, feeding the household also means feeding the spirits (see the boxed text opposite).

Many towns in Thailand feature a **làk meuang** (city pillar), which is associated with the founding of the city and is where its guardian spirit is thought to reside. The townsfolk will leave daily offerings of food, liquor, flowers and incense at a shrine built around the làk meuang. In Bangkok the làk meuang is a wooden pillar erected by Rama I in 1782, that stands opposite the magnificent Wat Phra Kaew (Temple of the Emerald Buddha).

The làk meuang spirit – Phra Sayam Thewathirat (Venerable Siam Deity of the State) – receives daily supplications from countless worshippers, some of whom commission costumed dancers to perform a type of classical dance known as **lákhawn kae bon** at the shrine. Other offerings include steamed pigs' heads, thought to be especially pleasing to such deities.

Once the **phǐi** (spirits) are taken care of, the worshippers' next spiritual obligation is to Buddhism. It is said that the phǐi are feared, but the Buddha is loved, and in the Buddha's honour, innumerable pots of rice, curry and other delights are regularly offered to the Buddha's direct disciples, the monks. Beyond this daily obligation (see the boxed text Making Nutritional Merit in The Culture of Thai Cuisine chapter), there are other occasions when cuisine intersects with Buddhist life, such as local religious ceremonies and national festivals.

Monks perform a variety of ceremonies on behalf of the Thai Buddhist laity. Among the most important is the consecration of a new house (or re-consecration of an older house when deemed necessary), whereby a quorum of monks comes to perform a series of rituals to 'guard' the house and its inhabitants from evil influences. Such a **phí-thii mongkhon** (blessing ceremony) involves tying sacred string around significant locations in the house – such as the entrance – and painting occult runes on an upper panel of the front door. Afterwards, the group of monks – nine is considered an auspicious number – will sit in the house's main living space and chant Buddhist scriptures and blessing prayers for an hour or more.

When the chanting is finished, the household lays out a sumptuous feast of rice and side dishes for the monks. No expense is spared, as to economise unduly would be tantamount to compromising the blessing ceremony. The ceremonies always take place in the morning so that the monks can eat before noon (their monastic vows require they fast from noon until dawn the following day). Similar phí-thii mongkhon are carried out for weddings, funerals and other Buddhist ceremonies.

Weddings can be particularly elaborate occasions when it comes to food, and once the monks and attending laity have been fed there may even

be another banquet held at a wedding reception. When this is the case, a wide variety of delicacies will be prepared, including the auspicious **lûuk chúp** (dipped fruit), sweets made of soybean paste, sugar and coconut milk that are boiled, coloured and fashioned to look exactly like miniature fruit and vegetables – chillies, carrots, eggplants, apples, grapes and so on.

One event in which food is brought to the **wát** (temple) rather than served to the monks at home is the **ngaan bùat** or **banpaja**, a ceremony in which a young male is inducted into the **sangha** (Buddhist monastic community). Once the supplicant has shaved his head and eyebrows, repeated the necessary vows, donned the saffron robes and slung the black alms bowl over his shoulder, he will join the resident monks in a feast usually provided by his parents. As with all events where monks are invited to dine, they sit on the floor, never on chairs, so as to demonstrate their ascetic devotion to Buddhist practice. The **bun** (religious merit) earned at such an event accrues not only to the monk and his parents, but to everyone present. When you eat food prepared for such merit-making events, you are said to **kin bun** (eat merit).

Another rung up on the scale of celebratory events involving food is the **ngaan wát** (temple fair). Usually keyed to auspicious dates on the Buddhist lunar calendar, and often related to fund-raising efforts for the wát, the ngaan wát has the atmosphere of a rural carnival. Along with carnival games such as air-gun target shooting, ring toss and roulette-style wheels, there is music, dancing and lots of food-stalls serving dishes including the popular **kǔaytǐaw phàt** (fried rice noodles). These stalls may be staffed by volunteers or vendors who tithe a certain percentage of their profits to the wát.

## National Holidays

National holidays involve plenty of feasting, and the biggest is mid April's **songkran** (Water Festival), which celebrates the zodiac passage of the sun from Pisces to Aries. Taking place at the height of the dry, hot season, Songkran is celebrated in a raucous manner – by throwing buckets of cold water at anyone who dares to venture into the streets. On a spiritual level, the more animistic Thais believe that during this three-day period the king of the heavenly beings, Indra, visits the human world to tally his annual record of the good deeds and misdeeds humans have performed. Villagers and shop-owners garland their doorways with flowers, banana tree fronds and sacred leaves to welcome the god. Indra's departure on the morning of the third day marks the beginning of the new year, when young people wash the hair of their elder kin. Buddha images are also ceremonially washed and monks are offered particularly appetising almsfood, such as extra rich coconut milk curries or sesame-peanut-rice candies.

*Lûuk chúp, miniature fruits made of soybean paste, sugar and coconut*

## SPOOKY FOOD

If you see Thais carefully exhibiting eight different foods – all black – you won't be invited to a mournful Goth wake or some kind of colour-matching, Gucci-black feast inspired by Bangkok yuppies. No, this is worse. Evil is going on. The imaginative Thais have a bizarre way of stopping a potentially apocalyptic event. They throw black food at it, until safety returns.

Thais offer the black food to a green-headed god who threatens to eat the sun, and thus plunge earth into a nuclear winter. If Rahu loves you, however, he will only nibble at the edge of the sun's solar-plexus, which you would see as a partial eclipse.

Rahu may swallow the sun entirely, causing a total eclipse forever and an end to the supply of food. But after considering how polite the Thais are to feed him his favourite swarthy morsels, Rahu will gently push the sun out of his mouth and bring the eclipse to a shining finale.

The list is well-known by many Thais, and includes interesting choices for a people who finally decided that the only way to beg Rahu not to 'swallow the sun' was to create an entire meal just from food coloured black. What eight black foods would you choose? The Thais decided:

- black chicken, burnt to perfection
- black coffee
- black alcohol, which probably tastes quite fierce
  sticky rice blackened by fire
- two different black desserts
- a black egg, not rotten, just embalmed in a special salted
  formula designed to preserve eggs before refrigerators were
  invented, and then buried in earth for a while
- black beans.

*– Richard Ehrlich*

*Richard, a freelance writer living in Bangkok, served as Leonardo DiCaprio's media consultant during the filming of The Beach in Thailand.*

*Phra Nang Bay*

## Regional Festivals

During **trùt jiin** (Chinese New Year), Chinese all over Thailand celebrate with a week of house-cleaning, lion dances, fireworks and restaurant feasting. The most impressive festivities take place in the Chinese-dominated province capital of Nakhon Sawan. Favourite foods eaten during trùt jiin include mooncakes (thick, circular pastries filled with sweetened bean paste or salted pork) and lots of noodles.

During December and January in the northern province of Nan, **thêhtsakaan sôm sĭo thawng** (the Golden Orange Festival) is held to celebrate the peak harvest of Nan's golden-skinned oranges. Among the festival events are a parade of floats decorated with the highly prized oranges and the coronation of an Orange Queen. In years when there's a bumper crop of **phrík yài** (a large chilli native to Nan) and the chilli-growers have some extra income to spend, Nan province also celebrates **thêhtsakaan phrík** (the Chilli Festival), which includes pepper-festooned floats, chilli-eating contests and the coronation of, what else, a Chilli Queen.

*Carving fruit for a Northern Thai Festival*

In May, Chiang Mai's Intakin Festival takes place at Wat Chedi Luang and around the city's làk meuang. This festival propitiates the city's guardian deity with bowls of sticky rice, pig's heads, boiled chickens, bananas and coconuts, in hope that the annual monsoon will arrive on time. Also in May – when the mango crop is ripe – **thêhtsakaan má-mûang** (the Mango Fair) is celebrated in Buak Hat Park with lots of mango eating and the coronation of...the Mango Queen.

On the last weekend in September, when Utaradit Province's langsat crop is fully ripe, a Langsat Festival is held to promote Utaradit's favourite fruit. Activities include food-stalls, agricultural exhibitions and a beauty contest. Nightly entertainment ranges from singing contests to traditional dances.

At least two festivals in Thailand are associated with vegetarianism. The first, held late February or early March at Pattani's San Jao Lim Ko Niaw (a shrine to a local Chinese woman who tried to persuade her brother not to build a local mosque, then hanged herself from a local cashew-nut tree), brings together Chinese and Muslim residents. During the festival a wooden image of Lim Ko Niaw is carried through the streets, fire-walking rites are held and followers pledge seven days of vegetarianism, all to appease the woman's powerful spirit. The more famous Vegetarian Festival, **thêhtsakaan kin jeh**, is held in several locations around the country.

---

## UNCLE KAM'S PARTY

The first evening we were in Chiang Mai, we left our guesthouse in search of something to eat. Susie decided to lead the pack, and soon we heard her shout 'party!'. Rows and rows of motorbikes, pickup trucks and bicycles were parked outside what appeared to be a large residential compound. Loud Thai music was blaring and at least 100 people were seated at long tables, drinking and eating.

Feeling slightly intrusive, I was about to tell everyone that this looked private when a red-faced man came stumbling up and shouted, 'welcome to amazing Thailand!'. I realised it was too late to back out when a group of people insisted we take their seats. Soon, all 18 of us had glasses of Mekong and Coke and were sitting at a table piled high with home-cooked Thai dishes. Then came baskets of warm sticky rice, and an old woman brought a pestle and mortar to a bench next to the table, where she sat down and began pounding tomatoes, grated raw papaya, fish sauce, dried shrimp, chillies, lime and pickled crab to make a **sômtam** for us to taste.

One of the girls was dragged off to the kitchen by a local teenage girl who wanted to show off the **thâwt man plaa** (fried fishcakes) that were being deep-fried in what looked like a metre of oil. Dish after dish was brought to the table as one villager after another teased us into eating rare local delights such as fried chicken feet and deep-fried winged ants. Soon we were split up amongst the tables as more people wanted to meet the faràngs.

Despite having grown up in Thailand, I couldn't believe the hospitality. We wandered in with nothing and were given the best of everything. I was so busy translating for my various friends that I didn't have time to find out what the festivities were all about. So we drank, ate and soon the drums and guitars were brought out for a dance. Local

## Vegetarian Festival

One of Thailand's most unique food festivals is the annual **thêhtsakaan kin jeh** (Vegetarian Festival), which takes place during the first nine days of the ninth lunar month of the Chinese calendar (usually late September or October). This festival occurs only in Thailand, and only among the Chinese community here. Basically, the festival celebrates the beginning of the month of 'Taoist Lent', when devout Chinese abstain from eating all meat products. In Phuket, the festival activities are centred around five Chinese temples, with the Jui Tui temple on Thanong Ranong being the most important, followed by the Bang Niaw and Sui Boon Tong temples.

---

women joked about the fresh-faced visitors, while old men staggered up to invite young blondes to do a Thai **ram wong** (circle dance). Children clapped their hands and giggled at the awkward rhythm and styles of those only used to funk and rave.

Exhausted, we collapsed onto our chairs as another round of food was brought to our tables. This time mangosteen, durian, and lychee were handed around.

Soon, stuffed with food and dizzy from Mekong, we decided to call it a day and offer to contribute towards the occasion. We went to find the person in charge. And there, standing alone at the far end of the living room surrounded by an array of delicious dishes, was the most beautifully ornate coffin I had ever seen.

Absolutely mortified, it dawned on us that we had just managed to gatecrash a funeral. I felt sick.

Then we realised that the deceased's immediate family were behind us, ushering us inside. We were all given joss sticks, flowers and candles and told to crawl up on our hands and knees to the coffin and say a little prayer of blessing to the spirit of the dead.

Afterwards I tried to apologise, but no one took any notice. 'Don't be silly, no other villager around here has had a faràng bless their spirit before; everyone should envy my father. He died last week of a heart attack', explained a woman pleasantly.

Still feeling terrible, we tried to leave but they wouldn't hear of it. So we stayed on into the small hours of the morning as the villagers continued feeding us, dancing with us and drinking toast after toast in honour of Lung Kam, the old man in the coffin.

*– Pim Kemasingki Shaw*
*Born in Chiang Mai to an English father and Thai mother, and educated in Thailand, Switzerland, Canada and Great Britain, Pim is managing editor of Chiang Mai Newsletter (www.chiangmainews.com).*

Besides abstention from meat, the festival involves various processions, temple offerings and cultural performances, and culminates with incredible acts of self-mortification. Community members participating as 'mediums' bring nine emperor gods to earth for the festival by entering into a trance state and piercing their cheeks with all manner of objects – sharpened tree branches (with leaves still attached!), spears, trombones (really), daggers; some even hack their tongues continuously with saw or axe blades.

During the processions, these mediums stop at shop-front altars along Phuket's central streets where incense, fruit, candles, flowers and nine tiny cups of tea are placed as offerings to the nine emperor gods. Here the mediums pick up the offered fruit and either add it to the objects piercing their cheeks or pass it on to bystanders as a blessing. They also drink one of the nine cups of tea and grab some flowers to stick in their waistbands. The shop-owners and their families stand by with their hands together in a prayer-like wâi gesture, out of respect for the mediums and the deities temporarily possessing them.

The entire atmosphere is one of religious frenzy, with deafening firecrackers, ritual dancing and bloody shirt fronts. Oddly enough, there is no record of this kind of activity associated with Taoist Lent in China. Some historians assume that the Chinese here were somehow influenced by the Hindu festival of Thaipusam in nearby Malaysia, which features similar acts of self-mortification. The local Chinese claim, however, that the festival was started by a theatre troupe from China who stopped off in nearby Kathu around 150 years ago. The story goes that the troupe was struck seriously ill and that they decided the illness had befallen them because they had failed to propitiate the nine emperor gods of Taoism. The nine day penance they performed included self-piercing, meditation and a strict vegetarian diet.

The Tourism Authority office in Phuket prints a helpful schedule of events for the Vegetarian Festival each year. If you plan to attend the street processions, consider bringing earplugs. The festival also takes place in Trang, Krabi, Phang-Nga and other southern towns, as well as in Bangkok's Chinatown.

# foreign
**infusion**

Thai food is a melange of the indigenous and the imported. In fact, many foods synonymous with Thailand originated well beyond the kingdom's borders. It seems Thais have taken the best produce and cuisine that traders and travellers had to offer, and turned it into a finely balanced cuisine. At the same time, Thailand's cuisine continues to spread its own influence, turning up in kitchens and restaurants right across the globe.

If we could re-visit North-Eastern Thailand about 5000 years ago, when the people of Ban Chiang were cultivating Asia's first domesticated rice, we might have been served a simple meal of freshwater fish, vegetables and rice, spiced with local herbs and rhizomes. Reports made by Chinese visitors in the 12th century and Thai records from the following century make mention of a similar menu.

Fish, rice and vegetables still play a major role in Thai cuisine, and the main seasoning base for most Thai dishes is still made from indigenous roots and herbs such as ginger, galangal and lemongrass. It's reasonable to assume that the native inhabitants of Thailand's Northern and North-Eastern river valleys had a well-developed cuisine long before significant international trade began. To expand this native base, however, Thai cooks have been borrowing ingredients and adapting foreign cooking methods for a very long time.

Contact with India and Sri Lanka early in the last millennium introduced rich spices to the Thai kitchen. Although **kaeng** (curry) may very well be an indigenous culinary form, the curries of South Asia clearly had an impact. Even more important was the arrival of the chilli pepper in the 16th or 17th century. By 1855 the chilli was so omnipresent in Thai cooking that Sir John Bowring wrote "the Siamese prepare considerable quantities of curry as their habitual food. These are generally so hot that they burn the mouth of a European". So established was the chilli by this time that Bowring seems to have missed the irony that it was European traders who introduced this spicy fruit to Thailand. Europeans, particularly the Portuguese, also had an influence on the preparation of sweets using egg yolk and flour (the Thais, of course, using rice flour).

Another great culinary infusion came from China. Dating from at least the 15th century, Chinese Muslim caravans from Yunnan Province used Chiang Mai as a 'back door' for commodities transported between China and the seaport of Mawlamyaing in Myanmar. These caravans first introduced Chinese tea to Thailand, as well as a variety of fruit and possibly the techniques for making **cháe im** (preserved fruit), now so popular in Northern Thailand.

Later Chinese immigration in the 19th and 20th centuries brought more significant influences into the Thai kitchen. Thailand may very well owe the entire genre of **phàt** (stirfried) dishes, as well as noodles, to Chinese influence. One of the classic fusion dishes in Thai cuisine is **phàt thai**, which takes Chinese stirfried rice noodles and makes it Thai by adding ground peanuts, lime juice, fish sauce and powdered chilli. Most other noodle dishes found in Thailand today are still recognisably southern Chinese.

Smaller historic influences less apparent to the outsider made their way into Thai kitchens via the country's fluid borders. **Isaan** (North-Eastern) cuisine is at heart a Lao cuisine with minor adjustments, while **Pak Tai** (Southern) food holds Malay and Hokkien Chinese origins. In Northern Thailand the Burmese, the Shan and the Yunnanese have each left their mark on the local cuisine.

Other influences, such as the transition from eating with fingers to using cutlery have influenced the way Thais eat more than the way they cook. The move from sitting on the floor around low round tables – still practised in much of the North – to the use of chairs and tables also belongs in this category. It could be argued that such watersheds in Thai eating behaviour were motivated more by a perception of Europe as a great power than by any genuine affinity for cutlery, chairs and high tables. Whatever the motivation, it's easy to surmise that such transitions in setting may have made Thais more psychologically receptive to other western influences.

Although Thai cuisine has been imbibing foreign influences for centuries, the reality is that the increasing efficiency of transport and communications since the Industrial Revolution has brought Thailand into even closer contact with the outside world. The first known restaurants (as opposed to rice & curry shops, which are much older), which appeared in the late 19th and early 20th centuries were Chinese, although in Bangkok a number of European establishments served the diplomatic corps and their families.

The number of foreign restaurants increased exponentially with the post-WWII expansion of diplomatic, commercial and military ties with such countries as Germany, the UK, the US, France, Italy, Belgium and the Netherlands. Although the cuisine from these countries was primarily confined to expatriate households, certain recipes – particularly from French, German, Italian and American kitchens – started turning up in local restaurants.

Thai food began fusing with western cuisine following Thailand's first tourism boom of the early 1960s, when some kitchens adjusted their recipes to please faràng palates. For the Thais, such experiments almost always compromised rather than enhanced their national cuisine, so such adaptations never caught on outside the hotels. Thankfully many hotels began to cater more to those seeking authenticity, so the trend moved toward avoiding foreign influences. Now fashion has come full circle at Anna's Café in the Silom district, where an ex-Los Angeles resident of Thai nationality boasts of his mission to introduce Thai-American cuisine to Bangkok.

## THE COLUMBIAN EXCHANGE

Just like chillies, many everyday fruits, flowers and spices which we accept as being indigenous to South-East Asia are, in fact, newcomers to the region. Until the late 16th century, spicy heat in regional cooking depended chiefly on ginger and black pepper. In contrast, chillies of many shapes and sizes had been cultivated in Mexico and Peru for millennia – yet the inhabitants of the pre-Columbian 'New World' had never seen a black pepper vine.

This exclusive two worlds system broke down swiftly and irretrievably following the Old World's 'discovery' and rapid exploitation of the New. Christopher Columbus first made landfall in the Americas in 1492. Within six years, Vasco Da Gama had rounded the Cape of Good Hope and discovered the sea route to India and South-East Asia. A link between the Spanish and Portuguese empires was completed when Spanish voyagers, sailing west across the Pacific, reached the Philippines, and Portuguese voyagers, sailing east across the Bay of Bengal, reached Indonesia, Malaysia and Thailand.

By the 16th century, regular traffic between Europe and South-East Asia had been established. In this way many strange and exotic products of the New World first came to South-East Asia, sometimes with an en route stop in Europe. Chillies made the journey across the Pacific early on, and by the end of the 16th century they were already widespread in Java. According to reports at that time, chillies were used by the Governor of Banten in place of black pepper. A similar process took place in Thailand, where the indigenous black pepper eventually became known as **phrík thai** (Thai pepper) to differentiate it from the brightly-coloured, instantly popular South American newcomers.

Dietary introductions to South-East Asia from the New World include such fruits as papaya, pineapple, custard apple and guava. This latter fruit is known in Thai as **faràng**, a familiar generic term for Europeans, perhaps applied in recognition of the intrepid sailors who first brought the refreshing green fruit from half-way round the world.

Many other foods considered standard fare in today's South-East Asian menus are also New World imports. These include potatoes, sweet potatoes, tomatoes, peanuts, kidney beans and – more recently – avocados.

Among the most important of these migrants from the Americas was maize – long the main staple of the Aztecs and Incas. The wonderful thing about maize was that it supplemented the South-East Asian diet without competing with the indigenous wetland rice crop. Maize – like chilli – flourishes best in semi-arid soil, and consequently flourished in the drier northern parts of Thailand. By the late 20th century it had been refined and cross-bred to produce new strains of baby corn, which are now re-exported to stock the supermarket shelves of Europe and America.

Of course, this fascinating and profitable transplanting of new crops was a two-way process. At about the same time as Thais were taking their first tentative taste of chilli or bite of pineapple, the inhabitants of the New World were discovering the delights of sugar cane, banana, yam, okra, lemon, lime, orange, grapefruit, grapes, wheat and barley.

Other, less pleasing exchanges are also thought to have taken place, such as syphilis for the black plague.

*– Andrew Forbes*
*Andrew is director of Crescent Press Agency in Thailand.*

*Fresh grapes*

## Pineapple Vinaigrette Salad

Mating tropical pineapple with Italian parmesan, this easy-to-prepare salad is a classic example of east-meets-west cuisine.

1   cup mung bean sprouts
1   cup grated carrot
¾   cup cubed pineapple
½   cup grated parmesan cheese
2   tablespoons rice vinegar
½   cup (125ml) pineapple juice
½   teaspoon salt
¼   teaspoon black pepper

Mix together the rice vinegar, salt, black pepper and pineapple juice to make a dressing. Slice the 'heads' off the bean sprouts and mix the sprout 'tails' with the carrot, parmesan and pineapple cubes. Serve chilled with the dressing on a lettuce-covered plate.

The goal of 'authenticity' has also been paralleled by the growing popularity of east-west or 'Pacific Rim' cuisine, which began in 1980s California and has spread vigorously throughout parts of Europe, Australia and South-East Asia. Thai cuisine has probably played a greater role in this trend than any other South-East Asian cuisine. It has almost become *de rigueur* for western chefs to pay a visit to Thailand to sample the native cuisine, collect a few recipes and perhaps take a few Thai cooking classes. Armed with a repertoire of Thai flavours and techniques, these chefs then return home and create new recipes (or adapt original Thai recipes) for the western kitchen.

In Thailand it works in reverse, with Thai chefs travelling abroad – often at the invitation of hotels or restaurants in the west – to gather new ideas. Some Thai cooks also learn by apprenticing themselves to western chefs in Bangkok or Phuket, where they pick up new techniques and ingredients which they then transfer to the Thai kitchen. Yet another source of creative influx are the increasing number of younger Thais – not necessarily in the restaurant profession – who study abroad, learn to appreciate other cuisines, and then return to Thailand and share their acquired perceptions with friends and family. Several of the most experimental cafes and restaurants to open in Bangkok have been started by Thais with little previous culinary experience but lots of foreign exposure. These conceptual experiments are risky except where the entrepreneurs are fortunate enough to find a chef with considerable improvisational talents.

*Nàw mái fàrang (foreign bamboo shoot or asparagus), native to Europe*

## ART, WINE & PHAT CHAA

*Bangkok native Theerada Suphaphong, age 24, stays busy teaching at Vajiravudh College and doing freelance design work for the city's art community. Having spent seven years studying in the US, Theerada is typical of a new generation of young Thais who bring a global orientation to their daily lives in Thailand, yet continue to nourish their Thai cultural roots.*

While studying in the San Francisco area for three years I must have tried around 50 Thai restaurants. Most places didn't use enough curry or shrimp paste, but I thought Manohra on Folsom St was one of the better ones.

Later, while studying at the University of Oregon, I became involved with the Thai Students Association. Cooking Thai food together was probably one of our most substantial activities!

With my family here in Bangkok I love to drive out to Paknam (Samut Prakan) on the weekends to sit down for long, slow, seafood meals at Bang Pu restaurant overlooking the Gulf of Thailand. Their **kaeng khûa sôm sàpàrót** (pan-roasted pineapple curry with sea crab) and **phàt chàa** (seafood stirfry with chillies and ginger) are delicious, with a real country flavour you don't find anywhere else.

My family's favourite traditional Thai restaurant is Kalapaphreuk (on Thanon Pramuan in the Silom district of Bangkok), but my friends and I like some of the more modern places with a mix of traditional and nouvelle Thai. The Pickle Factory on Soi Phra At is good at combining Thai and Italian dishes, and also serves traditional dishes like **yam sãam kràwp** (fried squid, fish bladder and cashew nuts mixed with náam plaa, sugar, lime juice and chilli). The atmosphere is unlike anywhere else in Bangkok – lots of sofas, coffee tables, comfortable chairs, candles and a nice garden, so you feel like staying all evening. And it's not expensive. For classic Thai cuisine I like Tamnan, which makes outstanding **yam thùa phuu** (angle bean yam) and **kaeng sôm** (spicy, tangy fish & vegetable stew). The restaurant is in the owner's home, and is decorated with antiques from Nepal and Burma. Decor means a lot to me and my friends, and I think many younger Bangkok Thais feel the same way.

Mall restaurants are also popular with young Thais since they can combine shopping, movie-going and dining in one place, without having to face the traffic more than once an evening. The cafe on the 2nd floor of The Emporium (Soi 24, Sukhumvit) is always full of couples on dates. Myself, I prefer places that combine art exhibitions with eating, like About Studio/About Café on Thanon Maitrichit. I often run into friends from the art community there.

In Phuket my favourite spot is Krajok Si, and in Chiang Mai I like to eat at the Anusan night market. I love Chiang Mai's **náam phrík nùm** (eggplant & chilli dip), which you just can't find in Bangkok, not the real thing anyway.

The Thai dishes I like most are **yam plaa dùk fuu** (catfish yam) – Vijit restaurant on the Democracy Circle has the best – and pungent fish dishes like **kaeng tai plaa** (a very spicy Southern Thai fish curry). My grandparents live in Pak Kret; I'm half Mon, and really like Mon dishes like **khâo châe** (soupy rice eaten with small bowls of assorted foods). I can take a lot of chilli, so I also like **náam phrík taa daeng** (red eye chilli dip).

I think Italian-Thai works well because both cuisines use garlic and basil. I love to drink red wine. The best place to hang out and try different wines is Chim Wine in the Chatuchak Weekend Market, where you can get wines by the glass or by the bottle.

*Theerada Suphaphong at the Fabb Fashion Café*

FOREIGN INFUSION

## McTHAILAND

By the 1980s the global success of US-style franchise restaurants had reached Thailand, and today McDonald's, Burger King and Pizza Hut are no longer an unusual sight in the nation's larger cities. For the most part these establishments provide a somewhat trendy, slightly exotic alternative for young Thais with disposable income while having little or no effect on mainstream Thai cuisine. If anything, the influence runs in the other direction. McDonald's outlets in Thailand recently added a 'Thai taste' hamburger to their menu, substituting pork for beef and spicing the burger with plenty of chilli and holy basil. One of Pizza Hut's most popular pizzas is the tôm yam version, topped with red curry paste, kaffir lime leaves and shrimp.

Bangkok and Phuket are the crucibles for fusion cuisine in Thailand and mixing Italian and Thai has been the most common avenue of exploration so far. At Sara-Jane's in Bangkok, they prefer to keep the Italian and Thai sections of the menu separate, allowing customers to mix and match their orders at the table. The kitchen at the Fabb Fashion Café takes matters several steps further, producing 'Ink Pasta with Spicy Seafood' (written on the Thai column of the menu as **pasta mèuk khîi mao seafood**), which perfectly blends the basil and chilli of **kŭaytĭaw phàt khîi mao** (drunkard's fried noodles) with fresh fettuccine, squid, mussels and shrimp cooked in squid ink. In an old Sino-Portuguese-style shop house in Phuket, a restaurant called Krajok Si puts together a relatively traditional Thai menu that nevertheless makes use of cooking techniques and presentation familiar to anyone acquainted with France's nouvelle cuisine.

Kuppa, one of the trendiest cafes to open in Bangkok, combines an enviable coffee menu and industrial decor with such Thai-western dishes as sirloin steak served with sômtam, sticky rice and **jàew** (a thick and spicy Isaan chilli sauce).

Other experiments continue to emerge, including the blending of Mediterranean Spanish and Thai, but few sustain a strong following. Nevertheless Thai cuisine has proved its ability to exist alongside outside influences, and will continue to weave together old and new culinary threads for the enjoyment of the country's discerning diners.

# regional
## variations

As Thailand did not become a true nation until 1238, with some areas remaining autonomous into the 1920s, it is not surprising that each area of Thailand has its own distinct cuisine. Geography, climate, ethnology and even politics have all played a part in what food is served in each region. Water beetles may be considered a delicacy in one town, yet in another they would be considered, well, water beetles.

**REGIONS**

Northern
North Eastern
Central
Southern

REGIONAL VARIATIONS

Thailand's topography, peoples and cuisines vary immensely from north to south, east to west, and from mountain plateau to sea coast. Thai kingdoms alternated between occupying their neighbours' lands and being subsumed by them, and it is primarily these historical connections which account for regional differences today.

About 75% of citizens are ethnic Thais, divided into the **thai phâak klaang** of Central Thailand; the **thai lao** of North-Eastern Thailand; the **thai pak tâi** of Southern Thailand; and the **chao nĕua** of Northern Thailand. Each group speaks its own Thai dialect and practises unique customs. Politically and economically the thai phâak klaang dominate, although they barely outnumber the thai lao.

People of Chinese ancestry make up 11% of the population, most of whom are second or third generation Hokkien (or Hakka, from Fujian), Tae Jiu (from the Chaozhou district of Guangdong), Hailam (from Hainan Island) or Cantonese (from Guangzhou). In Northern Thailand live a substantial number of Hui – Chinese Muslims who emigrated from Yunnan in the late 19th century to avoid religious and ethnic persecution.

The third largest group are the Malays (about 4%), mainly in the provinces of Southern Thailand. The remaining 10% is divided among smaller non Thai-speaking groups like the Vietnamese, Khmer, Mon, Semang (Sakai), Moken (sea gypsies), Htin, Mabri, Khamu and various hill tribes concentrated in Northern Thailand.

Each enjoys its own unique cuisine and some can claim origin to a number of nationally available dishes. However the cuisines of many smaller groups rarely leave the local village.

Broad geo-cultural characteristics thus divide the country into the four main zones of Central, Northern, North-Eastern and Southern Thailand, which correspond to the four major regional cuisines recognised throughout the country today.

# Central
## Background
Many of Thailand's rain-fed rivers flow southward and converge in the central plains, which fan out as a flat delta dominated by the Mae Nam Chao Phraya (River of Kings). Rich silt brought downriver by the Chao Phraya and its tributaries provide an extremely fertile base for the country's 'rice bowl'. In addition to riziculture, the central delta supports major crops of sugar cane, cassava and fruit. The rivers that feed into the delta are linked by an extensive network of hand-dug canals that supply farm irrigation, freshwater fisheries and an important means of transport. Many Thais live alongside these rivers and canals in stilted houses or floating homes, unperturbed by the rise and fall of the waterways.

Life in the delta has proved so attractive over the years that today this area is more densely populated than any other region in the country. Central Thais share a common dialect which is considered 'standard' Thai simply because Bangkok, the cultural epicentre, happens to be in the middle of the region. Central Thais tend to carry an air of self importance, and often look upon their compatriots from the kingdom's other three regions as rather unsophisticated at best. Many Chinese are found throughout the region, descendants of those who settled here and became farmers and merchants in the 19th century. Significant numbers of Mon – possibly the original inhabitants of Central Thailand – also make their home here, particularly in Pathum Thani and Kanchanaburi Provinces. The Mon have integrated themselves so well in Thai culture that today it's very difficult to tell Mon from Thai; very few have maintained the language.

## Flavours & Influences
Just as the Central Thai dialect has become 'Standard Thai' in schools and government offices throughout the country, so Central Thai cooking is today considered 'classic Thai' cuisine. The region's central position, and more importantly its relative wealth, mean that spices, seasonings and produce hailing from any corner of the kingdom are easily available. Coconuts from the South, bamboo shoots from the North, **maeng daa** (water beetle) from the North-East – all find their way into Central Thai markets.

Despite the diversity of ingredients, there are common themes in Central Thai cooking. The curry triumvirate of **kaeng phèt** (hot curry), **kaeng khĭaw-wăan** (green curry) and **kaeng phánaeng** (similar to kaeng phèt but thicker and milder) – all brimming with coconut milk and fragrant with spices – exemplify the Central Thai preference for strong, rich flavours (see the boxed text Kaeng of Three in the Staples & Specialities chapter). Other classic **aahăan phâak klaang** (Central Thai foods) that support this preference include **phàt phèt** (stirfry with basil and curry paste), **tôm yam** (chilli & lemongrass soup), **tôm khàa kài** (chicken coconut soup), **náam phrík kà-pì** (chilli and shrimp paste dip), **yam** (hot & tangy salad) and **hàw mòk** (a souffle-like dish with red curry paste, beaten eggs, coconut milk and seafood).

The Chinese community has also had an influence on aahāan phâak klaang. Aside from kŭaytĭaw and bà-mìi – found all over Thailand – you'll find a steady interest in delicately spiced **kaeng jèut** (bland soup), in which cubes of soft tofu, green squash, bitter gourd, ground pork and mung bean starch noodles are common ingredients. Also popular are the equally Chinese influenced **phàt krà-tiam phrík thai** (dishes fried with garlic and black pepper) and **òp mâw din** (dishes baked in a clay pot).

The Central Thais have a preference for what they perceive to be a balance of hot, salty, sour and sweet. Of course such a balance exists only

## CHINOISERIE

Ethnic Chinese probably enjoy better relations with the population in Thailand than in any other country in South-East Asia. Although this is partly due to the traditional Thai tolerance of other cultures (despite a brief spell of anti-Chinese sentiment during the reign of Rama VI), it has much to do with the practical nature of early Thai rulers, who recognised that the hardworking Chinese could bolster the national wealth.

The Chinese served Thailand well. Rama V used Chinese business-people to infiltrate European trading houses, a manoeuvre that helped defeat European colonial designs on Siam. Wealthy Chinese introduced their daughters to the royal court as consorts, developing royal connections and adding a Chinese bloodline that extends to the current king.

The government encourages the teaching of Chinese languages and the establishment of Chinese schools, cultural centres and businesses. In 1909 a royal decree required the adoption of Thai surnames for all citizens so Chinese had to take on a Thai surname. Often these are fabricated from an original Chinese name by dressing it up with Sanskrit prefixes or suffixes, or by finding a similar sounding Thai-Sanskrit name. For example, the common Thai name suffix -wong, from the Sanskrit *vamsa* (family), works perfectly for the common Cantonese surname, Wong. Tack on a Sanskrit prefix like *phatta*, from the Sanskrit *bhatta* (wealth) and you have the perfectly Thai Phattawong.

This spirit of tolerance combined with easy nationalisation has proved conducive to a Chinese presence in the delta heartland, where Chinese count for one quarter of the population.

in their minds, as every aahǎan phâak klaang dish emphasises one or two over the others. With regard to sweetness, in particular, the Central Thai prefer a higher degree than the people of any other region.

## Foods

The popular **khài jiaw** (Thai omelette), is offered as a side dish or part of a multi-dish meal. The Central Thai method of cooking khài jiaw is to mix eggs with a little water and lime juice, then drop the mixture into a wok containing 2cm of very hot cooking oil. The omelette puffs up, and is turned once so both sides are flecked with golden brown, before being served with **náam phrík sǐi raachaa**, a thick, salty-sweet orange-coloured chilli sauce from the coastal town of Si Racha (see the boxed text 'Sauce it!'). A more elaborate omelette called **khài yát sài** comes with a filling of fried ground pork, tomatoes, onions and chillies. Another popular Central

### Sauce it!

Although its use in Thailand is limited to only a few dishes, Si Racha chilli sauce seems to have spread all over the globe over the last decade. We've seen it in noodle restaurants in Vietnam as well as at taco stands in Mexico. The heavy sweet tones of this sauce clearly expose the Central Thai's sweet tooth.

If you run out of Si Racha chilli sauce (the most famous brand is Phu Khao Thawng – look for a drawing of Bangkok's Golden Mount in the seal), don't despair, you can make your own!

| | |
|---|---|
| 10 | phrík chǐi fáa (sky pointing chillies) |
| 10 | cloves of garlic, sliced |
| 5 | ripe tomatoes |
| ¼ | cup (60ml) vinegar |
| ¼ | cup sugar |
| 1 | tablespoon salt |

Slice open the dried chillies, shake out and discard the seeds and soak the chillies in warm water until soft and flexible. Boil the tomatoes in water until the skins begin to split, then remove from the pot and peel.

Drain the chillies, then blend with tomatoes and garlic in a mortar & pestle. Transfer the mixture to a blender and add half the vinegar, half the sugar and half the salt. Blend well, taste the mixture, and keep adding vinegar, sugar and salt until you achieve an even balance of flavours.

Thai dish often served with náam phrík sǐi raachaa is **hǎwy thâwt**, fresh oysters quickly fried with beaten eggs, mung bean sprouts and sliced spring onions to produce a sort of oyster omelette.

Even though most kǔaytǐaw dishes are inherently Chinese, there is one, **kǔaytǐaw reua** (literally, 'boat noodles'), that originated just north of Bangkok. This concoction of dark beef broth and rice noodles was originally sold on the boats of Rangsit's canals. Later, when the **mâe khrua** (female cooks) moved their business to dry land, they used their boats as props, often dishing up the noodles from big pots resting inside the beached vessels. The original recipe for kǔaytǐaw reua included leaves of **kanchaa** (marijuana), for flavour rather than any intoxicating effect, but with the price of pot in Thailand having skyrocketed, the cooks no longer use it. **Kǔaytǐaw râat nâa** (kǔaytǐaw with gravy) is another popular dish in Central Thailand, where you'll often hear it referred to as **lâat nâa**.

Other Central Thai specialities are tied to one or more locations within the region. Nakhon Pathom, 56km west of Bangkok, is famous for **khâo lǎam** (sticky rice and coconut steamed in a bamboo joint). Anyone getting off the train in Nakhon Pathom to see Phra Pathom Chedi – the largest Buddhist monument in the world – is confronted by stacks of khâo lǎam for sale along both sides of the road leading to the stupa. After paying their respects to Phra Pathom Chedi, Thai visitors stop and buy a few joints of fresh khâo lǎam on their way back to the train station for their friends or relatives back home. Children strip away sections of the bamboo immediately and pull the globs of sweetened sticky rice out with their fingers.

Further west, in Kanchanaburi Province, the Mon population cooks up a greater variety of curries than any other ethnic group in Thailand. A typical Mon **ráan khâo kaeng** (rice & curry shop) proffers eight or more **kaeng mawn** (Mon curries). One ráan khâo kaeng in the small town of Thong Pha Phum carries the boastful name, Rawy Maw (Hundred Pots). Few – whether tourists or truck drivers – can drive through without stopping for a plate of rice topped with as many different curries as will fit.

In the eastern town of Chanthaburi, head for the Vietnamese quarter, along the Chanthaburi River, where you'll find a range of **kǔaytǐaw sên jan** (local name for rice noodle) dishes, including delicious **kǔaytǐaw phàt puu** (crab-fried noodles). Further east in Trat, bordering Cambodia, sample **khanǒm bêuang**, a Vietnamese vegetable crepe prepared in a wok. Trat contains more outdoor food markets than any other provincial capital, so it's especially good for sampling inexpensive and varied Central Thai cooking.

Phetburi, a couple of hours southwest of Bangkok, is famous for **khanǒm jiin thâwt man** (thin rice noodles with fried fish cake) and a Mon dish called **khâo châe phêtburii** (moist chilled rice served with sweetmeats,

*Khâo sùay (beautiful rice)*

a hot season speciality). But the dish for which Phetburi is most known throughout the kingdom is **khanōm mâw kaeng**, a double-layer baked custard made with pureed mung beans, eggs, coconut milk and sugar. There are many local variations on this popular sweet, some of which use fresh durian or lotus seeds. It verges on sacrilege for a Thai to visit Phetburi without sampling a slice or two of khanōm mâw kaeng.

Hua Hin and Prachuap Khiri Khan, further south along the Gulf coast, have well-deserved reputations for seafood. One local speciality not to be missed is **plaa sāmlii tàet dìaw**, whole cottonfish sliced lengthways, dried in the sun for half a day, fried quickly in a wok and served with spicy mango salad. The sun-drying evaporates excess water and oil, and firms up the flesh to produce a toothsome texture.

One peculiar Thai-Japanese hybrid that's extremely popular in Central Thailand is **sukiyaki** (hotpot), usually shortened into the more Thai-sounding **sùkîi**. This dish is only served in restaurants that have the proper set up, usually consisting of booths or round tables that contain a large stationary pot sitting on a gas burner. The pot is filled with a rather bland broth, and once it's boiling, diners add raw ingredients – mung bean starch noodles, egg, water spinach and cabbage – to the hot broth using chopsticks. Thin-sliced beef and shrimp are cooked above the pot on a metal dome. As the ingredients cook, they are removed from the pot with chopsticks and eaten with Chinese-style sauces, while more raw ingredients are added to the pot. This is not a meal for people in a hurry.

Central Thais prefer **khâo jào** (white rice) with multi-dish meals. Per capita consumption of expensive **khâo hāwm málí** (jasmine rice) is high in Central Thailand, perhaps an expression of greater disposable incomes or a more discerning nose for rice than in other parts of the country.

## DON'T MISS

- The curry triumvirate of kaeng phèt, kaeng khīaw-wāan and kaeng phánaeng
- The delicately spiced soup, kaeng jèut
- Si Racha's own chilli sauce, náam phrík sīi raachaa
- Boat noodles served from beached vessels
- The multitude of Mon curries of Kanchanaburi Province
- Some of the best kŭaytīaw dishes Thailand has to offer

# North
## Background
The first substantial Thai city-states – Lanna, Chiang Mai and Chiang Saen – arose in what is now Northern Thailand, an important historical, cultural and commercial crossroads between Thailand, Myanmar, Laos and China. The north's early **jâo meuang** (city-state chieftains) were fiercely independent, and it was their rankling against Lao and later Cambodian rule that brought about the 12th century founding of Sukhothai, considered the first united Thai kingdom.

Although the Thai capital was moved south, the North remained linked to the monarchy via an important vassal status. It wasn't until 1927 that King Rama VII and Queen Rambaibani rode into Chiang Mai (Northern Thailand's unofficial capital) at the head of an 84-elephant caravan, becoming the first Central Thai monarchs to visit Northern Thailand. The remote nature of the relationship between Northern and Central Thailand over the centuries allowed the **chao nēua** (Northerners) – locally called **khon meuang** – to retain a strong regional identity that shows up in their language, dress, food and architecture, including the country's most majestic Thai temple ruins. These days, the chao nēua take much pride in their local customs, and consider them to be part of Thailand's 'original' tradition and culture. To Thais from other parts of the country, chao nēua often appear to be friendlier and more laid-back than the people from other regions.

Because Northern Thailand is so mountainous, there are few lowland areas suitable for agriculture. Hill-tribes, who are used to ploughing the slopes to raise corn and mountain rice, carry out much of the cultivation in the highlands, while the lowland Thais are engaged in commerce or less land-dependent farming, such as fruit growing. In spite of a high poverty level and rapid modernisation, the hill-tribe cultures are arguably stronger now than at any time in the last half century.

Hospitality in Northern Thailand is renowned throughout the country. Traditionally, in front of every northern home stands a **háan náam** (small roofed platform holding clay water jars) from which visitors or passers-by are welcome to quench their thirst. Other cultural hallmarks of Northern Thailand include the **kalae** (an elaborately carved wooden 'X' motif which decorates house gables), simple woven cloth shoulder bags and the ubiquitous **sêua mâw hâwm** (cotton tunic) worn on Fridays by employees at many banks, universities and other institutions.

In traditional Northern homes, families take meals sitting on the floor around a **tòhk** (low, round table made of lacquered wood or woven bamboo). The rim of the tòhk is usually raised a few centimetres to prevent items from sliding off.

## CULTURE INVENTED

The **khăn tòhk** dinner – a presentation in which guests sit on the floor around a low, round table, eating Northern Thai dishes from small plates and bowls while watching cultural performances – has become a staple of the tourist industry in Chiang Mai. Visitors sometimes ask to see a traditional khăn tòhk, not realising that they are a recent invention.

A **khăn** is a small serving bowl, while a **tòhk** is a footed table or tray; **khăn tòhk** thus simply refers to a meal eaten in this style. Although Northerners have long shared family meals in this way (and many still do), the first khăn tòhk dinner performance as we know it today was devised and arranged in 1953. It was organised by Professor Kraisi Nimanhaemin, a Chiang Mai resident of partial Indian descent (from the same family as Thailand's finance minister during the late 1990s). Kraisi wanted to host a special event in honour of two friends departing Chiang Mai: the US consul, George Whitney, and a Chiang Mai magistrate who was moving to Bangkok to assume a position at the Ministry of Justice. With advice from the Fine Arts faculty at Chiang Mai University, Kraisi organised a programme of Chiang Mai-style cuisine, music and dance – the first time anyone had consciously put all these elements together in one event. Kraisi hosted the dinner at his own home, and sent out invitations requesting people to dress as **khon meuang** (meuang people, a euphemism for Chiang Mai natives).

At the time, many Chiang Mai residents chastised Kraisi for promoting 'backward' (ie non-European, non-Central Thai) culture. Despite such criticism, Kraisi held two more khăn tòhk dinners, the second in 1953 for a group of World Bank representatives considering a loan to Thailand, and a third for the International Monetary Fund in 1956. Attended by scholars and foreign ambassadors, these events helped to revive pride in Chiang Mai history and renewed interest in Northern Thai culture.

Essentially created as a tool of diplomacy, the khăn tòhk dinner soon developed into a cultural showcase for Chiang Mai. This new regional pride inspired the 1972 opening of the Chiang Mai Cultural Center (modelled on the Polynesian Cultural Center in Hawaii). To support itself, the CCC charged admission, thus becoming the first to collect money for a khăn tòhk dinner. After the CCC became a standard component of many Chiang Mai tour itineraries in the 1970s and early 1980s, several other entities – including hotels – began offering khăn tòhk dinners to tourists. Although the event has become a tired cliche for many, for new arrivals to Chiang Mai it can still be a pleasant introduction to traditional Northern cuisine, music and dance. But don't go looking for an 'authentic' performance, considering that it was an event designed for non-Thai consumption in the first place.

REGIONAL VARIATIONS

*A traditional Northern Thai village meal, served on a thòk (footed table)*

## CHIANG MAI

**Si Phen**
A simple daytime-only restaurant with Northern and North-Eastern Thai food.

**Aroon Rai**
A casual and inexpensive spot for Northern Thai food plus good **kaeng kàrìi kài** (Indian-style curry).

**Warorot Market**
The city's oldest market, stocks everything you will need.

**Heuan Phen Restaurant**
Superb Northern Thai dishes served in antique-decorated wooden house.

**Vegetarian Centre of Chiang Mai**
A big open-air pavillion with all Thai, all vegetarian fare.

**Khao Sawy**
For this Yunnanese noodle dish, check out Islam and Feuang Fah restaurants.

**Anusarn Night Market**
A variety of vendor stalls serving everything from **kài phàt bai kàphrao** to **tôm yam kûng**.

Food served on a tòhk arrives in **khǎn** (small lidded bowls), while slightly larger **kawng khâo** (cylindrical woven baskets) hold the sticky rice. These meals are known as **khǎn tòhk**, named for the bowls and table used. Nowadays only rural chao nēua and a few culture revivalists in Chiang Mai still eat khǎn tòhk style. Tour companies and tourist hotels in Chiang Mai and Chiang Rai often arrange 'khǎn tòhk dinners' (see the boxed text Culture Invented on previous page).

## Flavours & Influences

Because Northern Thailand's cooler climate is conducive to vegetable cultivation, **aahǎan nēua** (Northern Thai cuisine) features a larger variety of vegetables than other regional cuisines. As in North-Eastern Thailand and Laos, sticky rice – **khâo nêung** in Northern Thai – is preferred over **khâo jâo** (white rice), and is eaten with the hands. Also popular here is **sômtam**, a tart and spicy salad usually made with green papaya. However, unlike North-Eastern Thais, the chao nēua tend to eat it as a between-meal snack rather than as part of a meal.

The chao nēua make use of many roots and herbs seldom seen elsewhere in the country, especially culinary herbs with a bitter flavour. For example, spicy **kaeng khae** soup contains **cha-om** (bitter acacia leaf) along with **phàk chii faràng** (sawtooth coriander), plus two types of eggplant known for their bitterness, **mákhēua práw** (Thai eggplant) and **mákhēua phuang** (pea eggplant).

Sour tones are enjoyed in other soups, such as **kaeng phàk hèuat** (soup with tamarind juice) and **kaeng hó** (soup with pickled bamboo shoots).

## Foods

At rural weddings and funerals in Northern Thailand you will find rich and fragrant **kaeng hangleh**, a Burmese curry made with no coconut milk (see boxed text Kaeng Hangleh). Two other popular Northern Thai curries are **kaeng yùak** (banana palm heart curry) and **kaeng kha-nūn** (jackfruit curry). Thais from other parts of the country often refer to curries from this region as **náam kaeng** (literally, 'curry water') because they tend to be thinner and more watery than curries further south.

Northern Thailand is famous for a variety of sausages, especially **sâi ùa**, one of the most popular food items requested by Thais visiting from other regions. To make sâi ùa, take a typical Thai curry paste of dried chillies, garlic, shallots, lemongrass and kaffir lime peel, blend it with ground pork, stuff it into pork intestine and then fry it to produce a spicy red sausage.

Another sausage, **nāem mâw** (pot sausage) requires no cooking. Instead ground pork, pork rind and pre-prepared sticky rice are mixed with salt, garlic and chilli, pressed into a clay pot, then left to stand exactly three days. The nāem mâw is then wrapped in banana leaves and served or sold. The fermenting effects of the garlic and chilli 'cook' the mixture into a sour-tasting sausage, which must be eaten on the third day, before it spoils. Another sausage, **mūu yâw**, has a look and texture resembling that of a large German frankfurter.

Three chilli pastes are considered quintessentially Northern. The first, **náam phrík nùm** (literally, 'young chilli paste') is made by pounding together young fresh green chillies with roast eggplant to make a thick green paste. This dip if often used to accompany steamed vegetables and fried pork rinds.

For **náam phrík àwng**, dried red chillies, ground pork, tomatoes, lemongrass and various other herbs are pounded together then cooked until the pork is done. Raw vegetables go best with this chilli dip.

The third, **náam phrík náam puu**, makes liberal use of **náam puu**, a condiment made by pounding small field crabs into a paste and then cooking the paste in water until it becomes a slightly sticky black liquid. Many faràng visitors mistakenly believe that náam puu is uncooked and therefore unsafe to eat; whether they'll find it appetising even knowing it's cooked is another story. Mixed with shallots, garlic and dried chillies, náam phrík náam puu makes a good chilli dip to eat with hot sticky rice and bamboo shoots.

A less well-known chilli dip from Northern Thailand is **náam phrík khàa**, a bright red concoction redolent with galangal. It is often served with steamed or roasted fresh mushrooms, which are found in abundance just after the rainy season in October and November. Around this time, fresh mushrooms also crop up on many menus as tasty **yam hèt hǎwm**

## Kaeng Hangleh (Burmese-style Curry)

This delicious curry came to Northern Thailand in the late 19th century with Burmese immigrants who worked in Chiang Mai's thriving teak business. Unlike most Thai curries, kaeng hangleh contains no coconut milk. The meat content is almost always pork, though a few restaurants in Chiang Mai serve hangleh with chicken. Hangleh curry paste is also sometimes used as a component for the curry broth in khâo sawy (egg noodles with chicken or beef curry).

Rural Northerners consider hangleh the perfect dish for celebratory occasions. It's often served at Buddhist weddings and funerals since it's a dish that everyone seems to enjoy, while the killing of a pig suggests wealth and status. The name is a Thai-Shan corruption of the Burmese hin-leh (literally, 'small curry') and refers to an improvised dish in which a hotchpotch of available ingredients is combined to make a curry. In Northern Thailand there are almost as many hangleh recipes floating around as there are villages, and each cook often takes great pride in their personal formula. In cities like Chiang Mai, the recipe is more standardised and you will even see bags of 'hinleh powder' for sale. When prepared for celebratory events, men are responsible for cooking the curry in big pots, stirring the contents with coconut fronds.

This recipe contains three different aromatic roots from the ginger family, making it especially fragrant. Even with all these ingredients, many cooks will still add a redundant bag of Chiang Mai hangleh powder (Makheua Praw brand is popular) to make sure the colouring is consistent. This recipe also represents a more 'citified', low-fat version of hangleh, as you might find in a Chiang Mai restaurant. In a village version of kaeng hangleh, the use of cooking oil isn't necessary as villagers use mǔu sǎam chán, meaning cuts of pork that include meat, fat and skin. When we asked the villagers of Mae Raem, Chiang Mai Province, for a recipe to feed four, they laughed at the idea that anyone would make hangleh for fewer than 20 people!

(shiitake mushroom yam) and **khài phàt hèt hŭu nŭu** (eggs stirfried with mouse-ear mushrooms).

Although noodle dishes are popular all over the country, Northern Thailand is considered the noodle crossroads, since the region's ethnic mix of Yunnanese, Shan and Burmese has produced a variety of kŭaytĭaw and khanŏm jiin unparalleled elsewhere in the kingdom. In Chiang Mai, the most well-known noodle speciality is **khâo sawy,** a delicious bowl of flat egg-noodles with chicken or beef curry. It's served with small saucers of shallot wedges, sweet-spicy pickled cabbage, lime and a thick red chilli sauce.

Kaeng hangleh can be served with white rice, but to make it authentically northern, serve it with sticky rice.

**khrêuang kaeng hangleh (hangleh curry paste):**
5-10   dried phrík chíi fáa (sky pointing chilli)
10     cloves garlic, peeled and roasted
5      shallots, peeled and roasted
1      teaspoon minced galangal
1      teaspoon minced ginger
1      teaspoon minced turmeric
1      teaspoon sliced lemongrass
1      teaspoon shrimp paste
1      teaspoon salt

Slice open the dried chillies, shake out and discard the seeds and soak the chillies in warm water until they are soft and flexible. Mash all the ingredients together with a mortar & pestle until a thick orange-brown paste is formed.

**kaeng hangleh mŭu (pork hangleh curry)**
1½   tablespoons vegetable oil
3     tablespoons hangleh curry paste
400g pork, cut into 4cm cubes
1     cup (250ml) meat stock

In a wok or large skillet, fry the curry paste in the vegetable oil on medium heat until well blended and fragrant.
    Add the pork and stirfry for about five minutes.
    Add the stock, lower the heat and simmer for 20-30 minutes, stirring frequently. If the curry becomes too thick, add more stock or if it's too thin, cook longer. Serve with sticky rice.

Noodle historians argue about whether **khâo sawy** is of Shan or Yunnanese origin. Although the name may have come from a similar Shan noodle dish, known in Myanmar as hkauk swe, Yunnanese Muslims seem to have been the original khâo sawy vendors in Chiang Mai. The Yunnanese still command two of the best khâo sawy shops in town, near the Ban Haw Mosque, where the Yunnanese mule caravans of yore used to tie up.

Those in the mood for more historical food debate can contemplate the origins of **khanŏm jiin náam ngíaw**. The name suggests Shan origins (ngíaw is a Northern Thai word referring to people of Shan descent) but once again it seems to be the Yunnanese who pride themselves most on this dish, particularly those in Mae Salong, a mountain village in Chiang Rai Province. Recipes vary, but khanŏm jiin náam ngíaw commonly consists of pork rib meat, tomatoes and black-bean sauce, fried with a curry paste of chillies, coriander root, lemongrass, galangal, turmeric, shallots, garlic and shrimp paste. The resulting melange is served over fresh thin rice noodles.

For 'Chinese' noodles, **wún sên** (mung bean starch noodles) find their way into a surprising number of dishes in Northern Thailand, including **kaeng phàk wǎan** (a soup with 'sweet greens'), **kaeng yùak** (banana palm heart curry), **kaeng hó** (curry/soup with pickled bamboo shoots) and **phàt wún sên** (stirfried with fermented sausage and eggs).

In the small Utaradit district of Laplae, restaurants specialise in **mìi pan**, a spicy mix of thin rice noodles, bean sprouts and coriander leaves wrapped into a rice paper roll. Mìi pan typifies the cultural mix of Northern Thailand, as it's reminiscent of Vietnamese spring rolls, and popular in a Thai town where the majority is of Lao descent. Slightly more common throughout the middle north is **kŭaytǐaw hâeng sùkhŏthai** (Sukhothai dry rice noodles), thin rice noodles served in a bowl with peanuts, barbecued pork, ground dried chilli, green beans and bean sprouts.

**DON'T MISS**

- A khān tòhk meal, for a unique culinary experience
- Rich and fragrant Burmese-style kaeng hangleh
- Sâi ùa, and other spicy sausages
- Yunnanese-style khâo sawy
- The quintessentially northern 'young chilli paste'
- The ethnographically spicy noodle dish, mìi pan

# Isaan (North-East)
## Background

North-Eastern Thailand is dominated by the Khorat Plateau, rising some 300m above the central plains. The plateau extends across most of North-Eastern Thailand but is divided by the Phu Phan mountain range into two wide drainage basins, the Sakon Nakhon Basin in the upper region (fed by the Mekong River and its tributaries) and the Khorat Basin in the lower region (fed by the Chi and Mun rivers). Unlike the Chao Phraya and other rivers of Central Thailand, which flow into the Gulf of Thailand, the rivers of North-Eastern Thailand empty into the South China Sea via Laos, Cambodia and Vietnam. This means only the small portion of the region on the Mekong border with Laos and Cambodia can take advantage of the watershed feeding these rivers. This, combined with relatively low rainfall and thin soil, has made it Thailand's poorest region.

In contrast, the region has had a long and glorious history, which began with the 4000-year bronze age of Ban Chiang, predateing both Mesopotamia and China as a metallurgical and agricultural site. Thais use the term **isāan** to classify the region, **khon isāan** for the people, and **aahāan isāan** for their food. The name comes from *Isana*, a Sanskrit name which means 'flowing with wealth', and is also an early epithet for the Hindu deity, Shiva.

Solidly aligned with the Lao kingdoms to the north and north-west, Isaan remained more or less autonomous from early Thai kingdoms until, in the 1800s, the French created the Indochinese state of Laos, forcing Thailand to define its boundaries. Rama V divided Isaan into the four **monthon** (semi-autonomous satellite states) of Lao Phuan (north-eastern), Roi-Et (central), Lao Klang (south-western) and Ubon (south-eastern). The monthon system was abolished in favour of the Bangkok-ruled **jangwàat** (province) system only in 1933.

Isaan's poverty has made it fertile ground for the communist movement, and Ho Chi Minh spent 1928-29 proselytising here. In the 1940s a number of Indochinese Communist Party leaders fled to Isaan from Laos and helped strengthen the Communist Party of Thailand. From the 1960s until 1982, Isaan was a hotbed of guerrilla activity. Almost immediately following the 1982 amnesty on all armed resistance to the Thai government, the Communist Party's North-Eastern strongholds began a rapid dissolution, hastened by a decade of economic growth which drew large numbers of Isaan peasants to various provincial capitals and to Bangkok.

Isaan culture and language are marked by strong Lao and Khmer influences. The Khmer left behind hundreds of Angkor-period monuments,

## Kai Yaang (Isaan-style Grilled Chicken)

1      whole chicken, halved
½      cup fresh lemongrass, sliced into threads
10    cloves of garlic, sliced
3      coriander roots
1      tablespoon fresh ground or cracked black peppercorn
1      teaspoon salt
1      teaspoon fish sauce

In a mortar, grind the lemongrass, garlic, coriander root, black pepper
and salt into a paste. Add the fish sauce and mix until well blended.

Rub the chicken pieces with the paste and let marinate in a refrigerator for two hours.

Cook slowly over hot coals, turning frequently to prevent burning.
When the chicken is done, cut into smaller pieces with a Chinese
cleaver (leave whole if you prefer). Serve with sticky rice and **náam
jàew** (a thick, jam-like sauce made by pounding dried red chilli flakes
with shallots, shrimp paste and a little tamarind juice).

and along the Mekong River stand many Lao-style temples, including the most important religious pilgrimage point in Isaan, Wat Phra That Phanom. Many Isaan people speak Lao or Thai dialects that are very close to those spoken in Laos – in fact there are more people of Lao heritage in North-Eastern Thailand than in all of Laos. In certain areas of the lower North-East, Khmer is the most common language.

Partly due to the region's lack of development, older customs remain more intact here than elsewhere in the country. Isaan music, for example, is highly distinctive and uses traditional instruments such as the **khaen**, a reed instrument with two long rows of bamboo pipes strung together. A very rhythmic Isaan song form called **lûuk thûng** (literally, 'children of the fields') is the most popular of all contemporary music styles throughout Thailand.

The best Thai silk comes from North-Eastern Thailand, and cotton fabrics are also highly regarded, especially those woven using the **mát-mii** (yarn-dyeing) method.

Despite its many inherent attractions – especially for people seeking cultural authenticity – Isaan hosts fewer tourists than any other region. In a typical year only 2% of the country's international tourists venture into North-Eastern Thailand.

## Flavours & Influences

Isaan cuisine is famous outside the region. Dishes emphasise the bright clean flavours of herbs along with the savoury tones imparted by grilling and roasting. Economic necessity and a short rainy season also mandates the use of many preserved ingredients and sauces; hence pickled bamboo shoot is more common than fresh.

Not surprisingly Lao and Isaan cooking overlap in many ways, although the many small differences make it clear that they are distinct cuisines. In Laos, for example, the meat, poultry or fish ingredients for **lâap** (spicy minced-meat salad) are minced to a paste, while the khon isăan prefer a more coarse cut. Both cuisines share a preference for a raw, unpasteurised fish sauce known as **plaa ráa** or **plaa dàek**, but the Isaan version has a finer texture.

## Foods

Most well known of the Isaan foods is the classic triumvirate of **kài yâang**, **sômtam** and **khâo nĭaw**, often spoken as one set phrase to represent the essence of Isaan cuisine. **Kài yâang** – or as it's more commonly called in Isaan dialect, **pîng kai** or **kai pîng** – simply means 'grilled chicken' and refers to the Isaan method of rubbing a chicken in a marinade of garlic, coriander root, black pepper and fish sauce before cooking it slowly over

## A VILLAGE REPAST

A few years ago a Thai friend in Bangkok extended an open invitation to visit his family home in a very small village in Loei Province, not far from the Lao border. Sometime later I happened to find myself travelling in Loei, and decided to visit my friend's family. Once I found the village, it took some time and some explaining to find his house, as I didn't even know my friend's surname (not unusual since Thais rarely use their surnames socially).

The house I was directed to was a simple one-storey affair built of brick and plaster, with a cement roof and unglazed windows. When no one answered my knock at the door, or my loud calls of 'mii phai yuu baw' (North-Eastern Thai for 'Anyone home?'), I tested the door and found it unlocked. In Thailand an unlocked door is as good as an invitation to enter, and feeling I had no other recourse, I went inside.

There wasn't a stick of furniture in the lower rooms, only rice mats spread here and there, an obvious sign that this was a family of simple means. Seeing there truly was no one at home, I turned around to leave, and bumped into a short, dark man in well-worn shirt and trousers, a phâakhamãa (short sarong) knotted around his waist and a dàap (machete) in one hand. A quick prayer-like wâi gesture brought a big smile to his face, and in a few minutes we'd sorted out that I was a friend of his son and he was the father, Chan.

Chan took me on a tour of the village, an activity which took only 10 minutes because it was so small, introducing me to everyone we met along the way. Along the one dirt street that ran through the village, we met the phûu yài bâan (village headman), who warmly invited us to dinner that night. Back at Chan's house, my village tour ended, and we could hear the chickens being killed for the evening's repast.

When we arrived at the headman's house at sunset, it looked like the whole village had turned out. As at Chan's, the headman's place was mainly one big room, furnished with rice mats plus a few rustic cabinets along the walls. In the middle of the floor were two large porcelain-covered metal bowls filled with clumps of **khâo nĭaw** (sticky rice). We were immediately invited to sit down, and once seated on the floor, everyone else sat, forming a large rough circle around the bowls.

Several men brought out tall, unlabelled bottles of a clear liquid – half were filled with drinking water, the others with **lâo khăo** (white liquor). Everyone took a few gulps of the liquor, chased with water. By his side, the headman had a bottle filled with an amber-coloured liquid. This was **lâo dawng**, the same liquor into which various roots and herbs had been added to mellow the taste and enhance the health of the drinkers. He shared this bottle with a few of his cronies sitting nearby.

The food began arriving shortly thereafter. The chickens had ended up in **tôm kài**, a tart and spicy soup containing lots of lemongrass and chilli, plus young tamarind leaves. Freshwater fish from the nearby Mae Heuang river were used to make **lâap plaa**, a hot & tangy salad of minced fish, chillies, mint, garlic and lime juice. A dried, sweetened beef, which they called **néua săwan** (literally, 'heaven meat') was passed around, and there was a big bowl of greens in an oily sauce, possibly **kaeng phàk wăan** (literally, 'sweet greens'). We picked up clumps of sticky rice with our hands, compressed it into golfball-sized orbs, and dipped it into the foods.

The lâo khăo continued to flow, and soon a **khaen** (Isaan pan pipe), **pin** (Isaan lute) and a hand drum appeared. The ensemble played standard Isaan favourites, mostly **măw lam** (bawdy courting music), and many of the villagers sang and danced. I was pulled onto my feet for a couple of rounds of **ram wong**, a folk dance in which you move your hands and arms in circular motions while dancing clockwise around your partner. Pairs move around the room in a circular motion with the other dancers – a dance of smaller circles within larger ones.

The eating continued amidst the music and dancing, in the traditional spirit of **kin lên** (eat play). No matter that the soup and lâap had gone tepid, as this was spontaneity and there were no set party hours.

Being the sole faràng in a roomful of partying North-Eastern Thais can become trying, but I knew my visit was a good excuse for everyone to enjoy themselves at the headman's expense, and that tomorrow many of those present would be hard at work in the rice and corn fields I'd seen outside the village. Determined to give them the most for their money, I rallied on until midnight, when Chan and his wife mercifully led me back to their house. As I fell asleep on a rice mat beneath a mosquito net, I could still hear the music churning away.

**REGIONAL VARIATIONS**

hot coals (see the recipe Kai Yaang). Recipes for the marinade vary widely; lemongrass is often substituted for coriander root, for example. Nowadays you'll find kài yâang anywhere, but the town of Si Saket enjoys the best grilled chicken reputation. When street vendors cook kài yâang they usually cut the chicken into halves or quarters, flatten the pieces with the back of a cleaver and tie them to a simple split bamboo frame for ease of grilling. Flattening the pieces also makes them cook a little faster.

An Isaan restaurant specialising in kài yâang will provide a variety of **náam jîm** (dipping sauces) to go with the chicken. An authentically Isaan náam jîm is **náam jàew**, made by pounding dried red chilli flakes with shallots, shrimp paste and a little tamarind juice to make a thick, jam-like sauce. Another, **náam phrík chíi fáa**, features dried chilli, garlic oil, salt and sugar, often cooked briefly to blend all the flavours and darken the chilli.

Any vendor or restaurant that features kài yâang will also offer **sômtam**, in which grated green papaya is pounded in a large earthen mortar with lime juice, garlic, fish sauce, fresh chillies and a number of other ingredients depending on the recipe or the customer's request. The resulting salad is slightly soupy, although the unripe papaya remains crisp.

Although there are many ways of making sômtam, two main styles hold sway. Thai-style sômtam adds to the basic recipe a handful of small dried shrimp, a few cherry tomatoes, roasted peanuts and **náam plaa** (fish sauce). Lao-style sômtam adds pickled field crab legs and a cruder regional fish sauce known as **plaa ráa** (literally, 'rotten fish'; see the boxed text Rotten Fish, Anyone? in the Staples & Specialities chapter). Most sômtam addicts prefer the more flavourful plaa ráa over náam plaa in this dish. Cooks may also add a little sugar – either **náam má-phráo** (coconut sugar) or **náamtaan pìip** (palm sugar) – as well as some shredded carrot for extra colour and texture. Another ingredient sometimes added to Lao-style sômtam is **má-kàwk**, a small, orange-coloured fruit with a very tart flavour. Sômtam is always made fresh to order, and in Isaan it's standard practice to 'customise' your order by offering guidelines, such as 'sômtam for three people; six chillies; not too sweet; no peanuts'. This dish may also be referred to as **tamsôm** and is sometimes made using sliced cucumber or green beans in place of papaya.

The third essential of Isaan cuisine is **khâo nǐaw** (sticky rice). The khon isǎan eat khâo nǐaw with nearly all their meals, rolling the almost translucent grains into balls, then dipping them into the various dishes on the table.

Another major culinary genre for the North-Eastern Thailand is **lâap**, a salad-like dish made by tossing minced meat, poultry or freshwater fish with lime juice, fish sauce, chillies, fresh mint leaves, chopped spring onion and **khâo khûa pòn** (uncooked rice that has been dry-roasted in a pan until it begins to brown, then pulverised with mortar and pestle). Other ingredients occasionally make their way into the mix, particularly kaffir lime and galangal for fish lâap, and garlic for chicken, duck and turkey lâap.

Generally, cooked meat is used to make lâap, but beef and water buffalo lâap are occasionally prepared raw. If you prefer to avoid this type of dish, ask for **lâap sùk** (cooked lâap), rather than **lâap dìp** (raw lâap). In Isaan, raw lâap is often referred to as **kâwy**, as in **kâwy wua** (raw beef lâap). Other than the raw meat, there is no difference in kâwy and lâap recipes. **Kâwy plaa** (raw fish lâap) is somewhat comparable to Latin American ceviche in the way the lime juice 'cooks' the fish, turning it white.

When beef is charcoal-grilled first, then mixed with the basic lâap ingredients, it's called **néua náam**

*Pork lâap, Northern Thai style*

tòk (literally, 'waterfall beef'). **Lâap pèt** (duck lâap), for which the city of Ubon Ratchathani is very famous, is available in two versions, **lâap pèt khão** (white duck lâap) and **lâap pèt daeng** (red duck lâap); the red one uses duck blood as part of the sauce, imparting a deep red colour to the entire dish.

Along with lime juice and chilli, khâo khûa pòn must be included or it's not true lâap. This ingredient imparts a roasted, savoury flavour to several Isaan dishes. Mix khâo khûa pòn with boiled or pickled bamboo shoots and you have **súp nàw mái** (literally, 'bamboo shoot soup'), another Isaan dish that is popular all over Thailand. Eggplant or jackfruit may also be treated similarly to produce **súp má-khẽua** and **súp kha-nũn** (or **súp màak mìi**, since the Isaan word for jackfruit is **màak mìi**).

Another tasty category of Isaan cuisine is **tôm** (soup made with lemongrass, galangal, spring onions, kaffir lime leaves and chilli), which is roughly equivalent to Central Thailand's **tôm yam** (chilli & lemongrass soup). A traditional Isaan meal isn't complete without a bowl of tôm on the table. Variations on the soup include **tôm wua** (tôm with beef tripe and liver) and **tôm kài sài bai má-khãam àwn** (tôm made with chicken and the flavourful young leaves of the tamarind tree). A speciality of the town of Ubon is **tôm fák** (tôm with green squash), which is often eaten with duck lâap.

Another popular soup available in Isaan is **jaew hâwn**. Basically a spicier version of **sùkîi** (see Central earlier in this chapter), this soup uses a spicy broth that's very similar in seasonings and preparation to tôm. As with sùkîi, it's always served in a hotpot or 'steamboat', an aluminium bowl with a strong, continuous heat source in the base to keep the broth boiling. Raw ingredients – mung bean starch noodles, thin-sliced beef, beef entrails, egg, water spinach, cabbage and cherry tomatoes – are cooked in the broth by the diners.

Commonly seen in Central and Southern Thai cuisine, **khanõm jiin** (rice noodles) get a slightly different treatment in Isaan. Instead of saucing

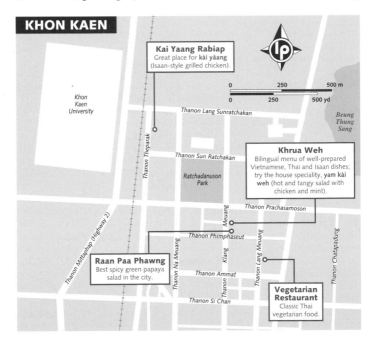

**KHON KAEN**

**Kai Yaang Rabiap**
Great place for **kài yãang** (Isaan-style grilled chicken).

Khon Kaen University

Thanon Lang Sunratchakan

Beung Thung Sang

0    250    500 m
0    250    500 yd

Thanon Sun Ratchakan

Ratchadanuson Park

**Khrua Weh**
Bilingual menu of well-prepared Vietnamese, Thai and Isaan dishes; try the house speciality, **yam kài weh** (hot and tangy salad with chicken and mint).

Thanon Prachasamoson

Thanon Theparak

Thanon Mittaphap (Highway 2)

Thanon Na Meuang

Meuang

Thanon Phimphaseut

Klang

Thanon Lang Meuang

Thanon Chatapadung

**Raan Paa Phawng**
Best spicy green papaya salad in the city.

Thanon Ammat

Thanon Si Chan

**Vegetarian Restaurant**
Classic Thai vegetarian food.

REGIONAL VARIATIONS

the noodles with a ground fish curry, cooks here mix ground pork with coconut milk, lemongrass and a milder dose of chillies. Sometimes this dish will be called by its Lao name, **khâo pûn**.

**Nêung plaa** is a very simple and healthy dish in which a whole freshwater fish is steamed with Thai lemon basil, lemongrass and any vegetables available. The fish is served with some of the water it is steamed in, which picks up all the flavours to produce a sort of broth.

One freshwater fish that won't be steamed is the near-mythical **plaa bèuk** (giant Mekong catfish). Although most are caught in the Mekong in Northern Thailand, a few are taken further downriver, passing through Isaan towns such as Nakhon Phanom. This town has several restaurants specialising in the giant catfish, usually only available fresh in May, then frozen for a few months afterwards. Because plaa bèuk is much too large to be served whole, it's usually cooked in slices or chunks, such as in **phàt phèt** (hot stirfry), **tôm yam** (chilli & lemongrass soup), **phàt krà-tiam phrík thai** (garlic- and black pepper-fried) or **òp mâw din** (baked in a clay pot). All of these are Central Thai cooking styles, implying that only visiting Bangkokians can afford the high prices (see the boxed text The Giant Mekong Catfish on the next page).

Largely a factor of poverty, the khon isāan are known to eat just about anything that moves, including many insects and reptiles such as **khài mót daeng** (red ant larvae; in soups), **maeng daa naa** (rice field water beetles; chilli dip), **kîng-kàa** (an iguana-type lizard; grilled), **túk-kae** (gecko; grilled) and **kòp** (frog; grilled or stuffed with ground pork and deep-fried). We've tried the ant larvae, water beetle and frog and found them all to be quite palatable. Conservationists note: villagers now raise all three, so you're not necessarily eating wildlife. The lizards, however, are another story. We suspect the reason you see fewer geckos in Thailand now, compared with 20 years ago, is that the khon isāan have eaten so many of them.

**REGIONAL VARIATIONS**

## DON'T MISS

- The famed Isaan chicken dish, **kài yâang**
- The spiciest salad, **sômtam**
- Eating sticky rice with your hands
- A freshly minced **lâap** salad
- Fishing for the giant Mekong catfish
- Daring to dine on red ant larvae, rice field water beetles and gecko

One Isaan oddity with more global appeal is **khài phǎm**, a very small, green plant that grows on the surface of ponds and bogs, rather similar to algae or spirulina. Being so high in protein, vitamin and mineral content some botanists believe khài phǎm to be the most nutritious vegetable food in the world. The khon isǎan add it to salads or simply stirfry it with a little oil and garlic.

## THE GIANT MEKONG CATFISH

A long stretch of the Mekong River between Northern and North-Eastern Thailand is an important fishing ground for the **plaa bèuk** (giant Mekong catfish, *Pangasianodon gigas* to ichthyologists). Probably the largest freshwater fish in the world, plaa bèuk takes between six and 12 years (no-one's really sure) to reach full size, when it will measure 2-3m in length and weigh up to 300kg. Locals say these fish swim all the way from Qinghai Province (where the Mekong originates) in northern China. In Thailand and Laos, its flesh is considered a major delicacy; the texture is very meaty but has a delicate flavour, similar to tuna or swordfish, only whiter in colour.

These fish are only taken between mid-April and May when the river depth is just 3-4m and the fish are swimming upriver to spawn in China's Erhai Lake. Before netting them, Thai and Lao fishermen hold a special annual ceremony to propitiate Chao Mae plaa bèuk, a female deity thought to preside over the giant catfish. Among the rituals comprising the ceremony are chicken sacrifices performed aboard the fishing boats. After the ceremony is completed, fishing teams draw lots to see who casts the first net, and then take turns casting.

Anywhere from 15 to 60 catfish are captured in a typical season, and the catfish hunters guild is limited to 40 men, all natives of Ban Hat Khrai (near Chiang Khong) in Northern Thailand. Fishermen sell the meat on the spot for up to 500B per kg (a single fish can bring up to 100,000B in Bangkok); most of it ends up in Bangkok or Chiang Mai restaurants, since local restaurants can't afford such prices. Sometimes you can sample the catfish during harvest season in a makeshift restaurant near the fishermen's landing in Ban Hat Khrai.

Because of the danger of extinction, Thailand's Inland Fisheries Department has introduced a breed-and-release programme for the plaa bèuk. Every time a female is caught, it is kept alive until a male is netted, then the eggs are removed (by massaging the female's ovaries) and put into a pan. The male is then milked for sperm and the eggs are fertilised in the pan. In this fashion well over a million plaa bèuk have been released into the Mekong since 1983.

# South
## Background

South of the Isthmus of Kra, the narrowest point in Thailand, the lengthy Thai-Malay Peninsula widens to encompass the 14 provinces of Southern Thailand. This region consists of flat, narrow plains along both coasts, which give way to inland mountains. Karst topography – limestone outcrops that jut up from the plains – add a distinctive profile to the region. Southern Thailand receives the country's highest annual rainfall, and some areas are still thick with rainforest, the last natural refuge of the Bengal tiger in Thailand.

Although under Thai political domination for several centuries, Southern Thailand has always remained culturally distinct from the other regions. Historically, this region is linked to cultures in ancient Indonesia, particularly the Sriwijaya empire, which ruled a string of principalities in what is today Southern Thailand, Malaysia and Indonesia. The 500-year Sriwijaya dynasty was based in Sumatra, and the influence of Malay-Indonesian culture is still apparent in the ethnicity, religion, art and language of the **thai pàk tâi** (Southern Thais).

*Southern Thai fisherman*

REGIONAL VARIATIONS

**DON'T MISS**

- The pungent and spicy kaeng tai plaa
- Turmeric smothered plaa khlúk kha-mîn
- Chinese-Thai buns and dumplings, washed down with kopíi, the famed Hokkien caffeine fix
- Flaky, tasty roti
- Thailand's own chicken biryani, khâo mòk kài

The thai pàk tâi dress differently, build their houses differently and eat differently from other Thais. Many thai pàk tâi are Muslim, particularly in the four southern provinces bordering Malaysia. In Satun Province, for example, 80% of the people profess Islam. In fact throughout the entire province, there are only 11 or 12 Buddhist temples, but 117 mosques. Thai Muslims often cover their heads and, among men, the long sarong is favoured over the **phâakhamāa** (short sarong) worn in other rural areas of the country.

A large minority of Chinese live in Southern Thailand, mostly in the cities where they tend to dominate the economy. Although Chinese can be found throughout Thailand, they are perhaps more apparent here, where their culture contrasts greatly with that of the Muslims. Other minority groups include the Sakai, who still hunt with blowpipes in the interior, and Moken (sea gypsies) along the coast and on nearby islands. Many of the Moken practise animism, which revolves around the placation of spirits who inhabit the sea, island forests and even their boats. The Moken often leave offerings of food, liquor and coloured strips of cloth at local shrines, and hold important yearly festivals to assure continuing fish harvests.

Three of the country's most important exports – rubber, tin and coconut – are produced in Southern Thailand, so the standard of living is a bit higher than in other provincial regions. The thai pàk tâi speak a dialect that confounds even visitors from other Thai regions. Diction is short and fast, and some of the vocabulary differs completely from that of other regions. In the provinces nearest Malaysia – Yala, Pattani, Narathiwat and Satun – many Thai Muslims speak Yawi, an old Malay dialect with similarities to modern Malay and Indonesian.

Architecture is also different in Southern Thailand and follows three basic threads. In rural areas, simple bungalows constructed from thatched palm leaves and bamboo strips affixed to wood or bamboo frames are common. A Malay style of construction can be seen in sturdy wooden houses with square tile roofs. In the older cities you'll come across splendid examples of Sino-Portuguese architecture, featuring arched windows, porticoes and tiled roofs.

Nakhon Si Thammarat and Phattalung are home to the unique **năng yài** (life-size shadow puppets carved from buffalo hide). Nakhon Si Thammarat is also known for its dance masks and for **khrêuang thōm** (nielloware, a Chinese silver and black alloy/enamel jewellery technique). Ko Yo, in Songkhla Province, is famous for its cotton weaving, and every other house on this little island has a loom or two. The provinces of Pattani and Narathiwat are renowned for their colourful batik textiles, which share many design characteristics with the batiks of Malaysia and Indonesia.

### Flavours & Influences

Bounded by water on two sides, it's not surprising that the thai pak tâi prepare an abundance of delectable seafood. **Aahǎan pàk tâi** (Southern Thai cuisine) combines Chinese, Malay and Thai elements to create brightly coloured and heavily spiced dishes.

Salty flavours predominate, with occasional overtones of sour and very little of the sweetness favoured in Central Thai cuisine. Shrimp paste features as much or more than fish sauce in typical Southern Thai dishes, and chillies are generously present as well.

### Foods

Ask someone from Central Thailand what dish they think of first when they think of the South, and chances are they'll say **kaeng tai plaa**, a very pungent and spicy curry made with fish stomach, green beans, pickled bamboo shoots and potatoes. Fresh **kha-mîn** (turmeric) turns this curry and many other Southern Thai dishes yellow. Another classic Southern Thai example, **kaeng lěuang** (literally, 'yellow curry') is a spicy dish of fish cooked with green squash, pineapple, green beans and green papaya. A delicious curry popular in Phuket and Ranong is **kaeng kaa-yuu**, which is made with fresh cashews. These are only three of more than a dozen common Southern Thai curries; virtually any vegetable, seafood or meat available in the south can be enjoyed in curry form. Cooks here are so adept at improvisation that on a city street in Phuket, you can walk by several rice & curry shops and almost never see the same curry twice.

Southern Thailand offers its own version of the **hàw mòk** (see Central earlier in this chapter) called **khài plaa mòk**, which consists of egg, fish and red curry paste steamed in a banana-leaf cup and topped with strips of kaffir lime leaves. Although quite similar to the Central Thai version,

## Kaeng Matsaman (Muslim Curry)

The recipe below leans toward the mild side, by Thai standards.

### Khrêuang kaeng mátsàman (Muslim curry paste)

| | | | |
|---|---|---|---|
| 5 | peeled shallots | 4 | green peppercorns |
| 2 | whole heads of garlic, peeled | 2 | cloves |
| 1 | teaspoon minced fresh galangal | 1 | teaspoon salt |
| 1 | tablespoon coriander seeds | | |
| 1 | teaspoon cumin seeds | | |
| 1 | teaspoon shrimp paste | | |
| 1 | tablespoon sliced fresh lemongrass | | |
| 4 | dried red phrík chíi fáa (sky pointing chillies) | | |

Slice open the dried chillies, shake out and discard the seeds and soak the chillies in warm water until they are soft and flexible.

Roast all other ingredients, one at a time, in a dry skillet or wok until aromatic and only slightly browned. Grind and mash all ingredients together in a mortar until a thick red-brown paste is formed.

1 cup (250ml) coconut cream
3 tablespoons Muslim curry paste
2 cups (500ml) coconut milk
500g beef cut into 5cm chunks (or chicken, usually with bone)
100g potatoes, peeled, quartered and boiled
5 small white onions, peeled
2 tablespoons roasted peanut halves
3 curry leaves
5 cardamom seeds
1 stick of cinnamon (3cm)
3 tablespoons palm sugar
3 tablespoons tamarind juice
3 tablespoons lime juice
3 tablespoons fish sauce

In an ample-sized pot, bring the coconut cream to a boil at medium heat. Add the curry paste and stir until the paste and cream are well blended and aromatic.

Add the coconut milk, meat, potatoes, onions, peanuts and curry leaves. Lower the heat, stir all the ingredients and let simmer. While the curry is cooking, briefly roast the cardamom and cinnamon in a dry pan or skillet until fragrant, then add to the pot. Let the curry simmer for a further 20-30 minutes or until the meat is tender.

Stir in the palm sugar, tamarind juice and fish sauce and cook for another 5-10 minutes. Serve with rice.

REGIONAL VARIATIONS

the curry paste used here is richer and spicier. The same description applies to the southern version of **kaeng mátsàman**, an Indian-influenced curry adopted by Central Thais as one of their own but which is far more common in Southern Thailand.

In **plaa khlúk kha-mîn**, fresh fish is rubbed with a paste of turmeric, garlic and salt before grilling or frying, rendering a golden hue and countering any 'fishy' smells. Central Thais find this use of turmeric rather strange, but quickly become converts once they've tasted it.

One dish that appears to have both equal Chinese and Malay influence is **khanŏm jiin náam yaa** (thin Chinese rice noodles doused in a Malay-style fish curry sauce). Although also seen in Central Thailand, the original southern version tends to be spicier and comes served with a large tray of fresh cucumbers, steamed long green beans, parboiled mung bean

---

### MATSAMAN DREAMS

Mátsàman kaeng kâew taa
hăwm yîiràa rót ráwn raeng
chaai dai dâi kleun kaeng
raeng yàak hâi fài făn hăa

Mátsàman, curried by the jewel of my eye,
fragrant with cumin, hot strong taste
Any man who has tasted her curry,
cannot help but dream of her.

Virtually every Thai child memorises this poem in grammar school, which it is said to reinforce the traditional Thai claim that a woman who prepares a good curry is **sanèh plaai ja-wàk** (the charm at the end of the ladle). King Rama II composed the verse during his 1809-24 reign, and it clearly shows us that Indian-style curries had established themselves in Siam by at least that era. The fact that a Buddhist king wrote an ode associated with a dish that translates as 'Muslim curry' furthermore suggests that the recipe had long been accepted in Thai food culture.

Kaeng mátsàman remains very much a standard in rice & curry shops, especially in Central and Southern Thailand. It can be very mild, or very hot, depending on the number of chillies added. This is unusual in that most other Thai curries stay at the higher end of the heat range. Yet one of the hottest Thai curries we ever ate was a small plate of **kaeng mátsàman kài** (Muslim curry with chicken) in a rice & curry shop in the mostly Chinese Thai town of Chainat in Central Thailand.

sprouts, grated papaya, pickled cabbage and fresh pineapple chunks. Every evening in the city of Trang, khanōm jiin vendors set up near the central clock tower and serve arguably the tastiest khanōm jiin dishes you'll find in the country.

Trang is even more famous for its traditional coffee shops, which are easily identified by their charcoal-fired aluminium boilers with stubby smokestacks. These shops are usually run by Hokkien Chinese, but patronised by all local ethnicities. They serve real filtered coffee along with a variety of Chinese-Thai snacks, typically **paa-thông-kŏh** (a light fried dough similar to an unsweetened doughnut), **salabao** (steamed buns filled with stewed pork or sweet bean paste), **khanōm jìip** (shrimp, or pork, filled Chinese dumplings), **mǔu yâang** (barbecued pork) and **jóhk** (thick rice soup or congee).

When ordering coffee in these places, use the Hokkien word **kopíi** rather than the Thai **kaafae**. To do otherwise would be to risk ending up with Nescafé or Khao Chong (a brand of coffee produced in Trang). As in the rest of Thailand, coffee is typically served with milk and sugar – ask for **kopíi dam** for sweetened black coffee or **kopíi dam, mâi sài náamtaan** for black coffee without sugar.

A very traditional Southern Thai breakfast is **khâo yam**, often prepared and sold from market stalls or from simple home-front stands. It's a delicious mixture of cooked dry rice, grated toasted coconut, bean sprouts, kaffir lime leaves, lemongrass and dried shrimp, with powdered chilli and lime on the side. A sauce called **náam khoei**, consisting of palm sugar, raw cane sugar, shrimp paste, fish sauce, salt, black pepper, shallots, galangal, kaffir lime leaves and lemongrass, is poured over the other ingredients, which are then tossed like a salad. Coupled with a cup of strong kopíi, there's no better way to greet the day.

The thai pàk tâi, especially rural Muslims, are also fond of **sà-tàw**, a large flat bean with a bitter taste. It is often boiled and eaten as a side dish, or can become the centre of attention in **kûng phàt sà-tàw** (stirfried with chillies, shrimp and shrimp paste). People from other regions often protest that cooked sà-tàw smells foul and causes flatulence, but – like durian – the taste can be very addictive.

**Roti**, a round, flat wheat bread descended from the Indian paratha, but now very much nativised to South-East Asia, has become a true favourite in Southern Thailand. Watching a cook pound round balls of pre-made dough, fling them into a gossamer thinness, then fry them on a hot, well-oiled griddle is all part of the roti dining experience. The best roti is light and fluffy, like a good French croissant, and only the roti cooks here seem to be able to make them this way.

*khâo yam, a traditional Southern Thai breakfast*

For breakfast, roti is often eaten as **roti kaeng** (dipped in the sauce from a chicken, beef or crab curry). Although found throughout the region, the best roti kaeng we've eaten has been in Satun, a province on the Malaysian border facing the Andaman Sea. Other roti dishes available are **roti khài** (cooked with egg), **mátàbà** (stuffed with chopped chicken or beef with onions and spices) and, for a snack eaten after the sun goes down, **roti klûay** (stuffed with fresh banana chunks or banana paste and sprinkled with sugar and condensed milk). No place makes roti klûay as well as the city of Nakhon Si Thammarat, where street vendors offer fresh coffee and tea and provide tables and chairs for you to linger at. Elsewhere, roti is strictly a takeaway proposition.

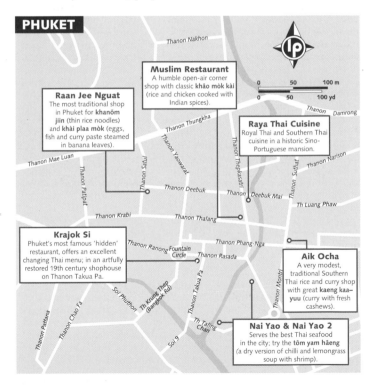

**PHUKET**

**Muslim Restaurant**
A humble open-air corner shop with classic **khảo mòk kài** (rice and chicken cooked with Indian spices).

**Raan Jee Nguat**
The most traditional shop in Phuket for **khanŏm jiin** (thin rice noodles) and **khài plaa mòk** (eggs, fish and curry paste steamed in banana leaves).

**Raya Thai Cuisine**
Royal Thai and Southern Thai cuisine in a historic Sino-Portuguese mansion.

**Krajok Si**
Phuket's most famous 'hidden' restaurant, offers an excellent changing Thai menu; in an artfully restored 19th century shophouse on Thanon Takua Pa.

**Aik Ocha**
A very modest, traditional Southern Thai rice and curry shop with great **kaeng kaa-yuu** (curry with fresh cashews).

**Nai Yao & Nai Yao 2**
Serves the best Thai seafood in the city; try the **tôm yam hâeng** (a dry version of chilli and lemongrass soup with shrimp).

Thanon Nakhon
Thanon Damrong
Thanon Thungkha
Thanon Yaowarat
Thanon Thepkasatri
Thanon Satul
Thanon Narison
Thanon Suthat
Thanon Mae Luan
Thanon Patipat
Thanon Deebuk
Thanon Deebuk Mai
Th Luang Phaw
Thanon Krabi
Thanon Thalang
Thanon Ranong
Thanon Phang-Nga
Fountain Circle
Thanon Rasada
Thanon Montri
Thanon Chao Fa
Soi Phuthon
Th Krung Thep (Bangkok Rd)
Thanon Takua Pa
Thanon Pattana
Th Taling Chan
Soi 9

0    50    100 m
0    50    100 yd

Hokkien Thais and Thai Muslims living in Phang-Nga, Krabi and Phuket savour a breakfast speciality known as **khanōm pao lâng**, a mix of black sticky rice, shrimp, coconut, black pepper and chilli steamed in a banana leaf packet.

A favourite among faràng as well as Thai Muslims is **khâo mòk kài**, rice and chicken cooked together along with rich Indian spices like clove, cinnamon and turmeric – the Southern Thai version of chicken biryani. This dish usually comes with a bowl of plain chicken broth, a roasted chilli sauce and a saucer of sliced cucumbers mixed with vinegar, sugar and a few sliced red chillies.

Chicken features in a more localised speciality found in the province of Yala. Named for Betong, a small town on the Thai-Malaysian border, **kài betong** consists of steamed chicken, chopped and seasoned with locally made soy sauce, stirfried together with **phàk náam** (a green vegetable grown in local creeks). It's no surprise that this dish seems to be of Chinese origin, as the population of Betong is predominately Chinese.

REGIONAL VARIATIONS

*Kids & Coconuts in Ko Samui*

REGIONAL VARIATIONS

# BANGLAMPHU – CENTRAL BANGKOK

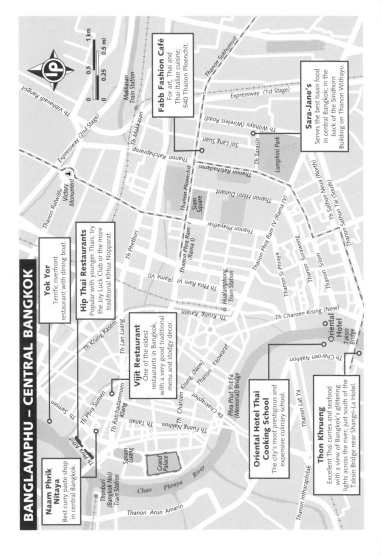

**Fabb Fashion Café**
For art, Thai and
Thai-Italian cuisine;
540 Thanon Ploenchit.

**Sara-Jane's**
Serves the best Issan food
in central Bangkok; in the
back of the Sindhorn
Building on Thanon Withayu.

**Yok Yor**
Terrific riverfront
restaurant with dining boat.

**Naam Phrik Nitaya**
Best curry paste shop
in central Bangkok

**Hip Thai Restaurants**
Popular with younger Thais; try
the Joy Luck Club or the more
traditional Khtua Nopparat.

**Vijit Restaurant**
One of the oldest
restaurants in Bangkok,
with a very good traditional
menu and stodgy decor.

**Oriental Hotel Thai Cooking School**
The city's most prestigious and
expensive culinary school.

**Thon Khrueng**
Excellent Thai curries and seafood
with a view of Bangkok's glittering
lights across the river, just south of the
Taksin Bridge near Shangri-La Hotel.

# Bangkok
## Background

Before it became the capital of Thailand, the settlement known as Bang Makok (literally, 'Makok Place', named for a grove of native **má-kàwk** trees) was only a very small part of what foreigners today call Bangkok. Back then, it was merely an outlying district of the capital, Thonburi Si Mahasamut on the east bank of the Chao Phraya River.

In 1782 Rama I moved the capital to the Bangkok district, believing the area to be more easily defended against naval attack. Artisans from Ayuthaya contributed several new temples to the city. Upon completion of the new capital in 1785, at a three-day consecration ceremony, the city was given a new name:

Krungthep mahanakhon bowon rattanakosin mahintara ayuthaya mahadilok popnopparat ratchathani burirom-udomratchaniwet mahasathan-amonpiman-avatansathir-sakkathatitya-visnukamprasit.

Roughly translated, this tongue-twister means:

Great city of angels, the repository of divine gems, the great land unconquerable, the grand and prominent realm, the royal and delightful capital city full of nine noble gems, the highest royal dwelling and grand palace, the divine shelter and living place of reincarnated spirits.

Fortunately it is shortened to Krung Thep in everyday usage. The name Bangkok persisted among foreign traders, and today the capital of Thailand is still known by its old name to most outside the kingdom.

Bangkok remains the most exciting and dynamic city in South-East Asia, with, for example, the region's largest foreign media correspondent base. Although today it's a city groaning under the weight of an overtaxed infrastructure, Bangkok continues to lure rural and working-class Thais, Asian and western investors, and curious visitors from around the world with its a phantasmagoric blend of the carnal, spiritual and entrepreneurial.

**REGIONAL VARIATIONS**

**DON'T MISS**

- Royal Thai cuisine, such as kaeng phèt pèt yâang
- The finest of international cuisine
- Endless, round-the clock variety of street foods

## Flavours & Influences

Thailand's sprawling capital, home to 10% of the country's population, brings together culinary styles from all corners of the kingdom and beyond. Virtually every regional speciality can be found somewhere in the city. Isaan cooking is particularly prevalent, partially because so many North-Eastern Thais have migrated to Bangkok looking for work, but also because Bangkokians love Isaan food. Although less common in the capital, you don't have to search very long to find Southern and Northern Thai dishes.

## Foods

Central Thai cooking, of course, dominates, as most Bangkokians have a preference for this style (see Central at the beginning of this chapter). One Bangkok-oriented twist on Central Thai cuisine, royal Thai cuisine, features menu items that were restricted to palace consumption until the late 1960s when King Bhumibol opened the palace cookbooks to commoners. The learned food observer may notice strong Chinese and Mon influences in royal Thai cuisine. For example, **kaeng phèt pèt yâang** (roast duck curry), takes duck roasted Chinese-style in five-spice seasoning and mixes it into Thai red curry. In many cases royal Thai cuisine is simply dressed-up Central Thai fare, as in **hàw mòk hāwy malaeng phuu** (hàw mòk cooked inside green mussel shells). Nowadays royal Thai cuisine has escaped not only the Bangkok palaces but the capital itself, so that it can no longer be considered the exclusive culinary domain of Bangkok chefs.

Bangkok does claim certain kinds of cooking that can't easily be found elsewhere in the country. Indian cuisine, for example, is virtually non-existent in the provinces (save for tourist-oriented Phuket and Chiang Mai), but relatively abundant in Bangkok, particularly in the partially Indian neighbourhoods of Bang Rak and Pahurat. If you're looking for Middle Eastern, French, Italian, Mexican, Burmese, Lao, Chinese, Korean, Japanese or German cuisines, you'll easily find them, particularly in the lanes off Thanon Sukhumvit and Thanon Silom. Shopping malls contain all the major American-style fast-food franchises, from Burger King to Starbucks, along with plenty of cafes specialising in different kinds of regional Thai cuisine.

No matter where you go in Bangkok, you're almost never more than 50m away from a restaurant or street food vendor. The variety of places to eat is simply astounding and defeats all but the most tireless food samplers in their quest to say they've tried everything. Eating out isn't restricted by the clock either; you'll find places to eat at any time here, in the city that never sleeps.

# shopping
## & markets

Despite the advent of supermarkets and 7-eleven stores, markets
are still the heart of Thailand. They are places where people from
all walks of life converge in search of the freshest coriander,
plumpest ducks and spiciest chillies. Armed with a shopping list
and well-honed bargaining skills, shopping in any of Thailand's
markets is an unforgettable experience. And with unique and
portable cooking utensils available, the memory of smells and
tastes needn't be the only thing you bring home.

## PRICES, BARGAINING & PRECAUTIONS

Prices in department stores and most non-tourist shops are fixed, but if you're shopping in a local market, and prices aren't marked, then bargaining is the norm. To find out start by asking **'lót raakhaa dâi mãi?'** (Can the price be reduced?)

Thais admire someone who can **tàw kèng** (bargain well), and good bargaining takes practice. First off you should have a general idea of what something should cost – try asking Thai acquaintances first – or at the very least have a firm idea of what you're willing to pay. If possible, have the vendor state a price first. We usually counter by offering half the asked price, and then going back and forth with the vendor until a mutually agreeable price is reached (often about 30% below the asking price). You may need to bargain harder in heavily touristed areas since the one week, all air-con type often pays whatever's asked, creating an artificial price zone between the local and tourist market. In such cases, a discount of 50% or more may be possible once the vendor knows you're aware of the 'real' price.

Thais aren't always trying to rip you off, so use some discretion when going for the bone on a price. There's a fine line between bargaining and niggling – getting hot under the collar over 5B makes both seller and buyer lose face. Likewise a frown is a poor bargaining tool. A cheerful demeanour will often net more savings than a hard stance, and acting like you don't absolutely have to have the item is always a good ploy.

**General Precautions:**
- Don't shop with touts, tour guides, tuk-tuk drivers or friendly strangers as they will inevitably – no matter what they say – take a commission on anything you buy, thus driving prices up.
- Watch out for pick-pockets in Bangkok's large municipal markets.
- Don't let vendors take your credit card out of your sight to run it through the machine. Unscrupulous merchants have been known to rub off three or four or more receipts.
- Before bargaining, be sure you want the item. It is considered bad form to start bargaining but not go through with a purchase.

## At the Market

Despite the arrival of shopping malls, supermarkets and department stores, **tàlàat** (traditional open-air markets) are still the most popular place to shop for foodstuffs. Such markets continue to flourish because Thai cooks value freshness above all, and transported produce wrapped in plastic, they reason, won't be as fresh as that found in the local grassroots tàlàat. It's also assumed – sometimes correctly, sometimes not – that everything found in the tàlàat will be less expensive than comparable goods stocked at a well-lit, air-conditioned supermarket.

Discerning Thais also like to see, feel and smell the food they're buying, impossible to do when the food is covered in plastic. Pre-packaging also breaks up the marvellous displays of a traditional market – pyramids of golden mangoes, silver mackerel side by side in their bamboo steamers. It also abandons the velvety touch of traditional banana and pandan leaf food wrappers, which keep dirt at bay but allow fragrances to escape.

Traditional markets come in all shapes and sizes. In Northern Thailand, for example, you might come across a small roadside tàlàat thrown together by a few shy Hmong tribeswomen with surplus **man kâew** (yam root or jicama), **nàw mái** (bamboo shoots) and **taeng moh** (watermelon) for sale. In this case, the market will consist of a palm-leaf canopy held up by bamboo poles.

Switch to a cavernous shelter with huge concrete pillars and acres of corrugated iron roofing. Running the length of the market are cement benches piled with every Thai foodstuff imaginable, from whole fresh sea bass to neat green piles of pomelo, perhaps even a stack of shining red New Zealand apples. Less picturesque are the blood-red carcasses of slaughtered beef and pork, and the floppy-headed, plucked chickens and ducks, hanging from iron hooks among buzzing flies in the market's butchery section. Another section is devoted to foodstuffs in cans and jars, and another to pots, pans, strainers, storage baskets and other cooking utensils. Virtually all municipalities build and maintain such **tàlàat thêhtsabaan** (municipal markets), funded by the renting out of stalls and spaces within. Vendors here aren't shy at all when it comes to finding a buyer, and spirited bargaining is the rule.

Somewhere between the impromptu roadside market and the heavily trafficked tàlàat thêhtsabaan is the **tàlàat nát** (appointment market). Common in small towns throughout the country, but especially in the heavily agricultural North and North-East, this type of market limits opening times to a few hours in the morning, known as **tàlàat cháo** (morning market) or in the early evening, known as **tàlàat láeng** (early

evening market). Such a diurnal set-up leaves the vendor time to work the fields and collect produce outside of market hours. The opening times also efficiently coincide with the times when people are most likely to be needing supplies for the day's meals.

One of the most intriguing of Thailand's many tàlàat nát are the **tàlàat náam** (water markets), more commonly known in English as floating markets. These take place on the canals of Central Thailand, usually in the early morning hours, wherever a group of boats loaded with merchandise convene in one spot for the purpose of buying and selling their wares. Local customers either paddle their own small craft alongside the market boats to make their purchases or, less commonly, squat at the canal's edge and conduct boat-to-shore transactions. In addition to boats filled with fresh produce, the typical tàlàat náam also features a few boats selling ready-to-eat meals such as **kūaytīaw** (rice noodles) and **khâo kacng** (curry & rice).

Bangkok once had several traditional tàlàat náam but the last of them disappeared about a decade ago, leaving behind the tourist-oriented floating market at Bang Sai. Authentic tàlàat náam can still be found in the canals of Ratchaburi, Samut Sakhon and Samut Songkhram provinces southwest of Bangkok, as well as at other points along the hundreds of kilometres of canals surrounding Bangkok on three sides.

The easiest floating market to get to from the capital is at Damnoen Saduak, on Khlong Damnoen Saduak in Ratchaburi Province (104km southwest of Bangkok, between Nakhon Pathom and Samut Songkhram). You can get buses to Damnoen Saduak from the southern bus terminal in Thonburi starting at 6am. Get there as early in the morning as possible to escape the tourist hordes or, better yet, spend the night in Damnoen Saduak and get up early before the tour buses arrive.

On a much smaller scale than the tàlàat, whether on water or on land, the small, family-run **ráan cham** sells **khǎwng cham** (sundries) such as vegetable oil, fish sauce, sugar, soy sauce, salt, coffee, dried noodles, canned food, rice, curry paste, eggs, liquor and cigarettes. If conducted from a boat, these suppliers are called **reua cham**. In urban areas the growth of supermarkets and 7-eleven stores has cut into the ráan cham business only slightly.

Markets where live animals such as cattle, pigs and water buffalo are traded will usually be found on the outskirts of town. In more remote areas of Thailand you may also come across markets unfortunately specialising in **aahǎan pàa** (forest food), that is, wildlife bought and sold for food. Although Thailand is a signatory to the UN Convention on International Trade in Endangered Species (CITES), this only covers the

SHOPPING

*Fruit market in rural Northern Thailand*

import and export of wildlife. Poaching and a domestic trade persists, although wildlife experts agree that the greatest danger faced by Thai fauna is neither hunting nor the illegal wildlife trade but rather habitat loss – a claim which holds true for most countries.

In both tàlàat thêhtsabaan and tàlàat nát, several vendors often proffer similar items side by side. Shopping around is expected, even considered part of the fun as the vendors banter amongst themselves, cheerfully denigrating a neighbour's product by saying things like 'you won't find any fresher water beetles than these – I plucked them from the rice paddy myself this morning', or 'sure mine cost more, but look how puny her tomatoes are!'

Fruit & vegetables are sold either by **kii-lôh** (kilogram) or by **lûuk** (piece). Spices are sold by **kram** (gram) or already packaged in a **thŭng** (bag). Meat, poultry and fish are almost always priced by the kilo, or on rare occasions, by the **tua** (body or unit, such as by chicken or by fish).

Of course if you don't speak Thai, much of this will pass right over your head. In many markets, vendors are usually adept at improvised sign language, but you'll do well to memorise a small repertoire of market vocabulary, beginning with Thai numbers (see the inside front cover).

*Soi Itsaranuphap, one of the busiest alleys in Bangkok's Chinatown*

## Specialist Shops

The evolution of traditional Thai merchandising all began with the village tàlàat nát. Once it reached the municipal market stage, vendors had begun to group themselves by the product they sold. In the next stage, represented by Bangkok's Chatuchak Weekend Market, walls were added to separate the sections and create individual booths. The

*Pre-packaged offerings to monks, Bangkok*

ongoing success of this famous market testifies to its appeal.

Immigrating Chinese merchants brought with them the **hâwng thǎew** (literally, 'row house'), a two storey affair in which the ground floor is reserved for stocking and selling, while the upper floor serves as a residence for the merchant's family. Some hâwng thǎew stand alone, though a more typical arrangement places them in a tight row with one unit sharing a common wall with the next. The architecture for such hâwng thǎew varies widely, from the classic early Sino-Portuguese buildings of urban Southern Thailand, to the garish modern units that combine a hotchpotch of incongruous architectural features.

Family members usually work as staff, so the hâwng thǎew offers the perfect self-contained selling unit, and many a hâwng thǎew has provided a comfortable – in some cases extravagant – living for its owners.

In smaller towns, residents will rely on local markets for many of their foodstuffs and cooking wares, but in the larger towns there's usually a central district where a group of hâwng thǎew specialise in one type of item. Bangkok's Chinatown, in the Sampeng neighbourhood near the Chao Phraya River, provides perhaps the best example anywhere in the country. Wander down one lane and you'll pass hâwng thǎew purveying stacks of fresh egg noodles, or pick another route and come face to face with baskets full of all different kinds of rice. Another block along the same street may carry nothing but pots and pans, or knives and cutting boards.

On a smaller scale, virtually every provincial capital in the kingdom has a neighbourhood with such specialist shops. Often this neighbourhood will have established itself next to or near the oldest market. In Chiang Mai, for example, specialist shops related to food and cooking are clustered around Warorot Market (known locally as Kaat Luang), which has been popular since the reign of Prince Inthawarorot (1870-97). Of course towns of this size will have several market districts, each with numerous hâwng thǎew riding the market's coat-tails.

## A Thai Picnic

Thais love to eat outdoors, whether in the back yard, at the beach, or next to a waterfall in a national park. Families, school groups, couples, co-workers – almost any group – will picnic on weekends or during Thai holidays such as **songkran** (Water Festival) or Chinese New Year. Such outdoor dining is so institutionalised here that only in remote places will picnickers have to bring their own food. In more accessible places, a row of rustic vendor stalls hammered together from bamboo, wood and palm leaf will have all the Thai favourites on hand.

Whether bought from vendors or carried in the car or day pack, the most popular picnic fare is Isaan cuisine, particularly the trio of grilled chicken, green papaya salad and sticky rice. Sticky rice works very well for picnics since it can be brought along in individual cane or wicker containers. Also, to the Thai palate, sticky rice tastes better than regular white rice when not fresh and hot. The ingredients for the necessary dipping sauces – lime, garlic, chillies and fish sauce – should be brought along in their raw, whole and/or bottled states. They'll be easier to carry, and in any case such sauces should be prepared just before eating for the sake of freshness.

The same prepare-on-site philosophy can be applied to **yam** (hot & tangy salad), another picnic favourite, especially if washed down with beer or Mekong whisky. Stock a Thai shoulder bag with whole shallots, limes, chillies, garlic, mint leaves and a pre-roasted eggplant, for example, and you have the makings of **yam má-khēua** (eggplant yam). The traditional Thai **khīang** (cutting board) is small enough to carry, or save weight by using a small plastic cutting board, available at any plasticware store.

Thais on car picnics may bring along a small bag of charcoal and a **tao fai** (firepot) for cooking. A tao fai can also be improvised on the spot with a few well placed flat rocks and an easily portable cooking grid.

One indispensable part of a Thai picnic is the light and easily rolled **sèua** (rice mat), Thailand's answer to the picnic blanket. Any large market will sell these mats in various sizes. Large groups wouldn't dream of heading out to picnic without a couple of guitars and hand-drums so that the group can sing the popular songs of the moment or, depending on their taste, more traditional tunes.

*Floating market at Damnoen Saduak, Ratchaburi Province, Central Thailand*

SHOPPING

## URBAN TRANSFORMATIONS

Thai cookery is now being promoted as a holiday activity, with classes moving out of the five-star hotels and becoming the focus of experiential homestays. At cooking classes at Baan Thai in Nonthaburi, or Center Place Guest House in Chiang Mai, the first task is to visit a market to learn about the ingredients used in classics like kaeng kĩaw-wãan (green curry).

So when will the first Thais take such a course? That's not as absurd as it sounds in a country where the streets literally smell of food. Even traffic fumes are masked by the visceral sting of stirfried chillies, the piscatory pique of seafood displayed outside restaurants, or the malty wafts of deep-fried ták-taen (grasshoppers).

Thais may eat whenever they're hungry, and regard food and socialising as inseparable twin concepts. However, the way that food is prepared and consumed is changing. It's an accelerating phenomenon, too, since a generation is growing up away from the tradition of passing on kitchen skills within extended families.

The Thai word for family, khrâwp khrua, literally means those who gather in the kitchen, but contemporary urban families are slowly dissolving. Television and malls are displacing the charcoal hearth, rice steamer and wok as the instinctive magnet. Urban birth rates are falling, grown children are moving downtown from their parents' mùu bâan (suburban estate), mothers are working, children are out of the house more and millions of workers migrate to the cities from ancestral farms.

As living units become smaller and domestic staff rarer, buying fresh from the morning market becomes less practical and affordable than eating out. Stalls occupy nearly every street, but half the customers aren't dining there. These are the mâe thũng phálaesàtìk (plastic bag mothers) with careers no time to cook. The continuous act of pouring phàt thai, sômtam or thâwt man plaa into bowls for their latch-key kids is severing a chain of knowledge passed from generation to generation. No wonder there are so many Thai cookbooks. We can't be far from the Thai equivalent of British chef Delia Smith teaching her television audience how to boil an egg.

With refrigerators proliferating and fresh markets disappearing from central Bangkok (Asoke Market and half of Pratunam Market are the latest victims), middle class Bangkokians are buying their sustenance from supermarkets such as Foodland, Tops or the British chain, Tesco. Beside the tubs of fresh produce are cool cabinets stacked with polystyrene trays of pre-measured ingredients neatly arranged under cellophane: meat, vegetables, herbs, curry paste and sachets of oily sauces. Just add water.

Habitually, part-finished dishes are never wasted; rice might be fried up for breakfast, meat merged with a curry, vegetables tipped into a soup or remainders passed on to domestic staff or even the dog. Recycling, even of discarded food, is a valuable resource in the Thai slums. Yet when Bangkok *METRO* magazine surveyed the rubbish bags of various city districts, chopping board waste was scarcer in affluent neighbourhoods. Incomprehensibly, there was even a shrink-wrapped individual portion of steamed rice – tossed out unopened.

Convenience is likewise the excuse for another trend – mass produced foodstuffs for instant hydration and consumption. Since it takes two or three days to cook, khǎa mǔu (pig leg stew) is now rarely made at home, while pre-mixed curry paste is more popular than ever.

Occupying entire aisles of supermarkets and 7-eleven stores are Thai-style instant noodles, all too often bought as an entire meal. Suitcases full of the popular MaMa brand instant noodles are also a common comfort food for Thais while abroad. Even noodle stalls – the lunchtime standby for Thais and Thai-Chinese alike – now often stock packet noodles in their glazed cabinets in place of freshly mixed, rolled and cut kǔaytǐaw or bà-mìi – not so much for speed's sake, but because customers are actually asking for MaMa noodles! We're talking heresy here.

It could be that food is going the way of so many other Thai traditions – notably architecture, silk, and basketry – whereby external impetus might be required for its preservation. Tourist expectations, foreign residents' anguish and the cultivated tastes of young Thai graduates are nudging a nascent trend towards wholesome Thai food. Ancient Ayuthaya-era recipes fill the menu at art bars like Banglamphu's Hemlock, royal Thai cuisine is no longer confined to the palace, and crop-replacement projects of His Majesty King Bhumibol are kindling interest in organic farming.

Reaction against western ways has characterised the economic recession since 1997. While often hypocritical, this has prompted quixotic protests against foreign fast-food chains and genetically modified goods, plus high duties on luxury imports. Rediscovery of local values has been a focus of Bangkok's 'Walking Street' festivals, which often emphasise indigenous food. There you'll find northern náam kaeng (curry stews) bubbling in ceramic pots, Chinese men pounding thùa tàt (peanut brittle) with huge mallets, and ladlefuls of **náam krà-jìap** (a red-tinted beverage made from roselle fruit) served as an alternative to canned soft drinks. The rarity of such treats makes many yearn for their greater availability – not just locally, but internationally.

*– Philip Cornwel-Smith*
*Philip is managing editor of Bangkok METRO magazine.*

## Things to Take Home
### Utensils

Most Thai dishes can be duplicated in modern kitchens, but there are a few utensils that will help make the job easier, and others which will make it more fun, if only for nostalgia's sake. Everything you need can be found in a city market district.

One of the most important Thai cooking tools, the **krà-thá** (wok), is now available in many parts of the world, as are **phai** (spatulas with curved edges). Likewise the **mâw din** (claypot used to bake certain rice and mung bean starch noodle dishes) is sometimes available in shops that carry Chinese cookware.

Much less common outside Thailand is the crescent-shaped **hùat** (bamboo steamer) used for cooking sticky rice. If you decide to buy a hùat, then you should also buy a **mâw khàek** (rounded narrow-necked pot) to go with it. Don't forget to pick up a few **krà-tìp khâo** (lidded baskets of woven reed or bamboo) for the table. They're cheap and light.

For making Thai curry pastes you'll need a mortar (**khrók**) and pestle (**sàak**) set. Mortars and pestles of various kinds are of course available elsewhere in the world, but for making curry pastes, make sure your mortar has very smooth sides. A larger **khrók din** (earthen mortar) and **sàak mái**

*Food vendor's goods, Bangkok*

(wooden pestle), dedicated to the making of sômtam, are heavy and bulky. For the purist they're indispensable, but you can pound out a reasonable sômtam with a sturdy mixing bowl and a large, heavy wooden spoon.

Likewise, the traditional **khĭang** (cutting board) is completely redundant if you already have a good cutting board. Chinese-style cleavers, such as the **mĭit mŭu** (pig knife) or the **bang taw** (cleaver) can usually be found just about anywhere, but it's good to get one here, where they are inexpensive and sturdy.

If you plan to grate your own coconut to make the freshest coconut milk, buy yourself a traditional **maew khùut má-phráo** (coconut grater). To strain the milk, any large metal sieve lined with cheesecloth will do (see the boxed text Ka-Thi in the Staples & Specialities chapter).

For traditional **kaafae thŭng** (bag coffee), pick up an easy-to-carry, inexpensive **thŭng kaafae**, a cone-shaped cloth bag fastened to a steel handle, which looks like a miniature butterfly net. To make Thai-style coffee load a few spoonfuls of ground coffee into the thŭng kaafae and pour hot water through the grounds over a pot. You can also use a thŭng kaafae to make traditional Thai tea, although to get the flavour and colour of real tamarind-seasoned **chaa thai**, you'd best buy the tea in Thailand. It's available both in 500g bags or in larger tins.

Anyone aiming to cook Thai food will need plenty of lime juice, and most western juicers – even the electric ones – are too big and clumsy for the job. You're better off picking up a **krà-chawn má-nao**, the double-handled sieve dedicated to squeezing juice from halved limes.

Any heat source back home will of course suffice for cooking a Thai meal, but remember that gas burners work best with round-bottomed pans. Although hardly necessary, and perhaps illegal in some countries, if you really want to recreate a rustic backyard Thai kitchen – or just want to amaze your friends by squatting down in the garden and whipping up a five-dish meal – you could buy yourself a traditional **tao fai** (firepot).

## Ingredients

Depending on where you live, Thai ingredients may not be readily available. Dried herbs and roots are pale substitutes for the real thing and not worth bothering with. If you have a green thumb and the space for cultivation, Thai herbs such as lemongrass and holy basil can easily be grown in a hothouse. Nevertheless, with the growing popularity of Thai cuisine, it is worth checking Asian grocery stores in large western cities.

Some packaged **khrêuang kaeng** (curry paste) from speciality shops travels fairly well and will keep a few weeks, or longer if you freeze it. Two Bangkok markets where you can find pre-packaged curry pastes are

Chatuchak Weekend Market and Banglamphu Market. **Kà-pì** (shrimp paste) is sold in similar, albeit smaller, plastic jars, and keeps for a similar length of time. Another common market item, **má-khāam pìak** (pressed tamarind seed) also travels well.

If you want a real Thai flavour in your cooking, buy a couple of bottles of **náam plaa** (fish sauce) to take home with you. Unless you plan to cook Thai very frequently, a bottle or two should last a year, and it's available at any market or grocery store in Thailand.

You can stock up on **phrík hâeng** (dried chillies) at any Thai market, and these will keep a very long time if sealed and kept in a cool, dry spot. Garlic, shallots and spring onions should be available just about anywhere in the world, as should cumin, cinnamon and cardamom, the three Cs common to the more Indian-influenced Thai curries.

Most recipes calling for palm or coconut sugar won't suffer if brown or granulated cane sugar is used instead.

Coconut milk sold in cans is widely available these days. You also may be able to purchase dried, unsweetened coconut from Indian shops or markets, and this seems to work fine for making your own coconut milk.

If your home town doesn't have a place that sells sticky rice, you may want to bring back a kilo or two. A short-grained Japanese rice – sometimes referred to as 'sticky rice' – is not a reasonable substitute, so it's better just to use regular white rice. Thai jasmine rice has become readily available in supermarkets and Asian markets.

A few packs of **kǔaytǐaw chanthabun** (dried rice noodles) are worth adding to your kit if they aren't available back home. Some of the world's Chinatowns will carry dried – sometimes even fresh – rice noodles.

# where to
# eat & drink

The choices for where to eat out in Thailand are as varied as the dishes available. And thankfully expense doesn't bear relation to quality or taste, as some of the finest Thai cuisine can be found on trestle tables in the kingdom's many night markets. For a more tailored meal there are plenty of vegetarian restaurants as well as ones specialising in regional cuisine. At the other end of the spectrum, upscale restaurants with starch-white tablecloths can be found in major towns and tourist centres, if that's what you're really after.

No doubt the early markets of Siam sold a few ready-to-eat dishes along with the raw ingredients for cooking meals at home. We can easily imagine that market-goers would occasionally seat themselves on mats beside the vendor, dipping balls of rice into curries and chilli dips to assuage the appetite before lugging the day's groceries away on foot or by bullock cart. If the historical reality matches our imagination, this would have been the beginnings of the **ráan khâo kaeng** (rice & curry shop).

The first ráan khâo kaeng was a lean-to affair situated just outside the palace walls in 17th century Ayuthaya. It was said to have served rice and curry to palace courtiers too busy to prepare meals for themselves.

The lack of other historical accounts implies that, in traditional Thai society, cooking and eating at home was overwhelmingly the custom. We might even assume that eating outside the home couldn't have been a more distasteful prospect. After motorised transport and railways came to Thailand in the early 20th century, linking Bangkok ever more closely with the countryside, a migration trend began. People from the provinces voluntarily left their homes in large numbers, seeking new opportunities. This probably provided a major boost to the concept of the ráan khâo kaeng.

After constitutional government was established in 1932, and the last of the semi-independent vassal states such as Chiang Mai came into the national fold, Bangkok became the nerve centre of a vast civil service. Coinciding with its growing success as a world port, Bangkok became a city full of people too busy to cook. The restaurant culture that subsequently evolved slowly spread to provincial capitals and smaller towns.

Other than simple ráan khâo kaeng in markets, Thai food wasn't available at most pre-WWII restaurants, which tended to be either Chinese or, more rarely, European. Real Thai restaurants – with full menus of kaeng, yam, tôm yam and phàt dishes – didn't appear until the beginning of the Cold War, when Indochinese conflict brought an influx of foreigners with diplomatic, military or commercial interests. It could be said that Thais discovered the enjoyment of a Thai meal outside their homes only after the experience received outside attention.

This self discovery coincided with tremendous economic development between 1963 and 1997, when per capita income levels in Thailand increased 19-fold. Save for Malaysia and South Korea, no other country in the world at that time produced more rapid economic growth or saw such a dramatic reduction in poverty. As a result of the new affluence, Thai restaurant cuisine boomed along with Thai art, music and other cultural forms. Nowadays Thailand boasts many more Thai restaurants than any other type of eatery, and it's hard to believe that barely 50 years ago finding a full-menu Thai restaurant was not an easy task.

# Where to Eat

Today urban Thais eat out almost as often as they eat at home, whether it means grabbing a chair at a street vendor table for a quick bowl of kŭaytĭaw, or driving in convoy with 15 family members to a pier-top restaurant for a weekend seafood feast. Watching where Thais congregate to eat is the best way of all to determine the potential quality of a **ráan aahăan** (food shop) or **rót khěn** (vendor cart). This axiom holds no matter what the budget level is.

The most common type of ráan aahăan throughout the kingdom consists of a garage-like space in a **hâwng thǎew** (row house), often rented rather than owned by the proprietors. What they do with the space ranges widely according to their tastes and budgets. Most aren't anything fancy, simply a collection of utilitarian tables and chairs lined up along the walls. As any Thai will be quick to point out, decor has nothing to do with food quality. Profit margins at typical restaurants are thin, and to keep the meals affordable

*Heuan Phen in Chiang Mai specialises in Northern Thai cuisine*

for the average Thai, the restaurateurs must economise wherever they can. Decoration may be limited to a few Singha Beer or Sang Thip Whisky posters, or something more incongruous like a faded picture of the Swiss Alps. Fluorescent lighting – cheap and cool – is the norm.

At a ráan khâo kaeng, pots of curry are placed on a table at the front of the shop, along with a large rice cooker. Typically the pots are not on a stove or heating element of any kind. Instead the curries are cooked early in the morning and, once lidded, they will stay warm for at least a few hours. Re-heating is not usually done, as it risks drying out or over-thickening the curry (a good curry should not be thinned with water, and to add more coconut milk would risk throwing the flavour balance off). The variety of beverages available are slim, often just water, **náam chaa** (weak Chinese tea) and a few soft drinks or fresh fruit juices. Most ráan khâo kaeng open around 7am and close around 1pm. Those that stay open longer usually cook the curries in two shifts, one batch in the morning before opening and a second around 11am, just before the lunch crowd arrives. It's rare for a ráan khâo kaeng to stay open past mid afternoon, as most Thais enjoy curry more as a daytime meal.

The more generic **ráan aahǎan taam sàng** (food-to-order shop) can usually be recognised by one or more tall refrigerated cabinets with clear glass windows at the front of the shop. These will be filled with many of the raw ingredients – Chinese kale, tomatoes, chopped pork, fresh or dried fish, noodles, eggplant, spring onions – for a standard repertoire of Thai and Chinese dishes. The ingredients are often there as a simple means of promotion, as the actual kitchen stocks much more. As the name of the eatery implies, the cook attempts to prepare any dish you can name, including any kind of rice or noodle dish as well as more complex multi-dish meals. You won't usually find curries at a ráan aahǎan taam sàng, but if they have them, the curries will usually be pre-prepared as at a ráan khâo kaeng. Most of the standard Thai dishes are available, including those in the tôm yam, yam and phàt categories. Almost any kind of beverage is available, from water and soft drinks to rice whisky and beer. Typical opening hours for a ráan aahǎan taam sàng are 10am-9pm, but they can be open at any time.

In larger cities you may find a few 24-hour ráan aahǎan taam sàng, especially if they serve **khâo tôm** (boiled rice soup), a popular late night meal. In fact **ráan khâo tôm** (boiled rice soup shops) and ráan aahǎan taam sàng frequently overlap in menu and function. A true ráan khâo tôm, however, carries a greater variety of khâo tôm accoutrements and will have more of a Chinese orientation. Both kinds of eateries often use the word **phochánaa** – a Thai-Sanskrit term meaning 'meals' – in their names, as in Sayam Phochanaa or Si Chaiya Phochanaa.

At the front of a **ráan kǔaytǐaw** (noodle shop) you'll see cabinets filled with piles of snowy white noodles, hanging next to pre-cooked meats, such as **mǔu daeng** (strips of bright red barbecued pork) or **pèt yâang** (roast duck). On a lower shelf sit little piles of chopped raw meats or poultry for custom cooking and on another shelf are any accompanying vegetables. Two steel boilers near the cabinet contain plain water (for dunking the fresh noodles) and soup broth. On the dining tables you'll find the traditional rack of condiments (see the boxed text Perk Up Your Noodle in the Staples & Specialities chapter). Noodle shops don't have standard opening hours. Some cater to the breakfast and lunch crowd, others are open from 11pm until dawn.

For **khâo man kài**, a Hainanese dish of sliced steamed chicken served over broth-cooked rice, look for cabinets similar to those at a noodle shop, but containing whole steamed chickens. A broth is always served in a bowl on the side, and a nearby rice cooker contains the aromatic **khâo man** (rice cooked in chicken broth and garlic). The typical khâo man kài shop is open for breakfast and lunch, though a few keep longer hours.

## Night Markets

One of the simplest and most pleasurable venues for dining out in Thailand is the night market, which can vary from a small cluster of metal tables and chairs alongside the road to more elaborate affairs that take up whole city blocks. What they all have in common are a conglomeration of **rót khĕn** (vendor carts) and their owners, who have decided that a particular intersection or unused urban lot makes an ideal location to set up their mobile kitchens.

You can distinguish a night market from a distance by the telltale string of fluorescent lighting tubes, often in white, pink and green, dangling at chaotic angles from a network of improvised electrical wiring. Steam from the vendor boilers and fryers diffuse the harsh light, as an orchestra of aromas waft on the evening air.

Night markets are among the most popular and economical venues for an evening meal. While breakfast or lunch may be quick and functional, a meal at a night market can be an evening in itself, starting with a drink and **kàp klâem** (drinking food) at one vendor, followed by a slow perusal of the other vendors to put together a feast.

There are two types of night market, firstly the **tàlàat laeng** (late afternoon market) or **tàlàat yen** (evening market), which sets up just before sunset and stays open till around 9 or 10pm – possibly later in large cities. The second is the **tàlàat tôh rûng** (open until dawn market), which begins doing business around 11pm and keeps going until sunrise. Most Thai towns have at least one of these markets. Typical places to look for them include in front of day markets, next to bus or train stations and at busy intersections.

## Upmarket Restaurants

More upmarket restaurants – the type that would offer printed menus – are usually only found in provincial capitals or tourist resorts. Average Thais prefer to order their favourite dishes without referring to a menu at all, so these more expensive restaurants only cater to an upper-class clientele with more international tastes. It is in such restaurants that you will find air-conditioning, tablecloths, and individual soup bowls.

There's no special name for this kind of restaurant, although the owners often bestow them with Thai names that have royal or historic connotations – Wang (palace), Tamnan (epic), Than Ying (a titled lady) – or that are intentionally humble – Baan (house or village), Rai (field) or Kratip (sticky rice basket). In Bangkok the current trend is to use English names for small, fashionable Thai restaurants, such as Joy Luck Club, Hemlock and Anna's Café.

Of course there are numerous restaurants catering specifically to foreign tourists, particularly in beach resort areas like Phuket, Ko Samui and Ko Pha-Ngan. The names of these establishments usually include words such as Palace, Princess, Royal, Orchid, Pearl, Siam or Siamese. The food at such restaurants tends to be toned down versions of authentic Thai cuisine – fine if Thai food isn't a passion, but best avoided if you're on a culinary journey.

Other kinds of Thai eateries fall into smaller, specialist categories. In Bangkok, for example, there are a number of **reua aahǎan** (food boat restaurants), which leave the restaurant's pier once or twice nightly for a one- or two-hour cruise on the Chao Phraya River. Such restaurants offer a regular Thai menu from the restaurant's riverside eatery, and a modest charge of around US$1 or US$2 per person for the cruise. It's a fine way to dine outdoors when the weather is hot, away from city traffic and cooled by river breezes. Several of the boats cruise under the illuminated Rama IX Bridge, the world's longest single-span cable-suspension bridge.

---

### THE GREEN BOWL

Look for restaurants with a sign bearing the familiar Shell logo next to the outline of a green rice bowl. This means that noted Thai food critic Thanad Sri, sponsored by the Shell oil company, has awarded at least one dish at that restaurant with his **Shell chuan chim** (Shell Invitation to Taste) designation. It's not a foolproof guarantee of quality however, as some restaurants hang onto their signs long after the kitchen has lowered its standards.

---

In provincial towns with rivers or lakes, you'll see the **phae aahǎan** (food raft), a floating platform moored to the bank. Although the rafts never move from their moorings, the cooling breezes off the water makes for pleasant dining. Be especially discerning when choosing a phae aahǎan, as the cooking sometimes comes a distant second to the location. Follow the usual rule of thumb – look for a crowd – and you should be fine.

Restaurants specialising in regional cuisines often include the name of a dish in the name of the restaurant. Thus the Nong Khai restaurant, Rim Khong Neua Nam Tok, specialises in **néua náam tòk** (waterfall beef) and other Isaan dishes, while Khao Sawy Haw in Chiang Mai serves **khâo sawy** (curry noodles). Restaurants specialising in seafood often use the English word 'seafood' in their names, such as Seafood Sombun. (For a description of street vendor food and food centres, see the Street Food chapter.)

*Night market, Chiang Mai*

## Vegetarians & Vegans

You can avoid eating meat and seafood with a little effort. The number of vegetarian restaurants is increasing, thanks largely to Bangkok's ex-Governor, Chamlong Srimuang, whose strict vegetarianism inspired a non-profit chain of **ráan aahǎan mangsàwírát** (vegetarian restaurants) in Bangkok and several provincial capitals. Many of these are sponsored by the Asoke Foundation, an ascetic (and somewhat heretic, in the eyes of the Thai orthodoxy) Theravada Buddhist sect that finds justification for vegetarianism in the Buddhist **suttas** (discourses of the Buddha). Look for restaurants with a green sign bearing large Thai numerals – each restaurant is numbered according to the order in which it was established. The food at these restaurants is usually served buffet-style and is very inexpensive. Most are open only from 7 or 8am until noon.

Other non-Asoke ráan aahǎan mangsàwírát usually serve either Thai or Chinese vegetarian food. Asoke-sponsored or not, the dishes at such eateries are always 100% vegan, that is they do not include any meat, poultry, fish, dairy or egg products whatsoever. Other easy, though less widespread, venues for vegetarian meals include Indian restaurants, which usually feature a vegetarian section on the menu. These are most prevalent in Bangkok, Chiang Mai, Pattaya and Phuket's Hat Patong. Indian vegetarian meals often include dairy products such as cheese and yoghurt. Chinese restaurants are also a good bet since many Chinese Buddhists eat vegetarian food during Buddhist festivals, especially in Southern Thailand.

Because so many people here follow vegetarian regimens, whether short- or long-term, for religious reasons, Thais in general are completely accustomed to the concept. Hence mentioning that you're vegetarian isn't likely to raise eyebrows. What does surprise them, however, is that you might choose to dine in a non-vegetarian restaurant, and then expect the cooks to alter their recipes to suit your regimen. Thai vegetarians generally stick to vegetarian restaurants or simply eat at home. Asking to alter a recipe automatically courts loss of face for diner and kitchen staff alike.

Therefore if you want to eat vegetarian at a non-vegetarian restaurant, you must be prepared. If you're game, the phrase: I'm vegetarian, in Thai is '**phǒm kin jeh**' (for men) or '**dì-chǎn kin jeh**' (for women). Like other Thai phrases, it's important to get the tones right – the key word, **jeh**, should rhyme with the English 'jay' without the 'y'. Loosely translated this phrase means 'I eat only vegetarian food', which includes no eggs and no dairy products – in other words, total vegan.

It might also be necessary to follow with the explanation '**phǒm/dì-chǎn kin tàe phàk**' (I eat only vegetables). Don't worry – this won't be interpreted to mean no rice, herbs or fruit. On the other hand, don't expect the average Thai restaurant to be 100% scrupulous in following your request. Cooks, especially busy cooks, will sometimes forget and allow a stray piece of meat into the pan, or season the dish with fish sauce. If this is absolutely unacceptable, you would do well to watch the cook prepare your dishes to make sure they end up completely free of meat and fish products.

Those interested in tapping into the Thai vegetarian movement can phone the Vegetarian Society of Bangkok (tel 02-254 5444/3502) for information on the group's activities. The society usually meets monthly to share a vegetarian feast, swap recipes and discuss the whys and where-fores of vegetarianism.

## Eating Alone

At ráan khâo kaeng, ráan khâo tôm and ráan aahǎan taam sàng – places where the **jaan diaw** (one plate) meal is the norm – you'll fit right in dining alone. Eating at places like these not only saves you from buying a dish and a plate of rice separately, but the portion will be ample for one.

At reua aahǎan, phae aahǎan and the more up-market restaurants, it's fairly unusual to dine solo. It's difficult for one person to eat a multi-dish meal alone, since most dishes are meant to feed at least two. Even if you order only one dish and some rice, it's not a balanced meal in Thai eyes. The most socially acceptable solution is to stick to jaan diaw places.

*Dining solo is not the norm*

## Tipping

Tipping is not normal practice in Thailand, although they are getting used to it in tourist hotels and restaurants. When dining in such establishments, check to see if there's a 'service charge' included in the bill; if there is, don't leave a tip. If there isn't, tip whatever you'd like, as there is no standard amount to leave.

In everyday ráan aahǎan elsewhere, a tip isn't expected. However if a meal costs 288B and you pay with three 100B notes, it's good form to leave the 12B coin change on the change tray. It's not so much a tip as a way of saying 'I'm not so money-grubbing as to grab every last baht'.

## Children

We have yet to encounter a restaurant anywhere in the kingdom that denied entry to children of any age, and most Thai restaurants of any type or size are happy to have children accompany adult diners. Don't expect high-chairs or child-size portions, however, as these are non-existent in all but a handful of the more expensive restaurants in Bangkok and resort areas. Children usually sit on the lap of their parents or other family members, and eat from the same plate.

Fast-food chains can be found in Bangkok, Chiang Mai, Phuket and Hat Yai, if that's the kind of food your child enjoys. Many of these establishments serve child-size portions or even have children's menus, two concepts completely alien to most Thai restaurants.

Bring along bibs if you're concerned about messy eating, and child-size eating utensils and drinking glasses if you need them. These also can be purchased here at the larger department stores.

Supermarkets and even some **ráan cham** (sundries shops) carry baby food in jars as well as snacks older kids might like. western-style breakfast cereals such as Quaker Oats and Kellogg's Corn Flakes are widely available in the cities, but less so in small towns.

# street food

At times, the streets in Thailand look more like food fairs than thoroughfares. Pots of steaming curry, carts of fresh fruit and lattices of dried squid can turn an evening stroll into a culinary exploration. And if you don't want to go to the food, let the food come to you on one of the many roaming vendor carts. It's Thailand's answer to meals-on-wheels.

Perhaps no more than a hundred years ago, the **tàlàat** (market) was the only place where Thais could acquire food they didn't grow themselves. Vendors brought their wares by bullock cart, hand cart, or on their backs. As market culture expanded with Siam's political and economic development, a few enterprising vendors began cooking simple dishes for shoppers. We can imagine these entrepreneurs carting all their cooking utensils and ingredients back and forth between home and market, and, faced with requests to serve customers along the way, devising ways of setting up and cooking anywhere.

Eventually an entire culinary subculture developed around the **rót khēn** (vendor cart). Instead of going to the tàlàat, customers waited for a piece of the tàlàat to come to them, carrying steaming noodles, fresh fruits or sweetmeats. This portable food culture lives on in Thailand, and you now find street vendors serving practically every single item from the Thai kitchen. Big cities, small towns, even villages feature these meals on wheels, an institution which perfectly suits the Thai penchant for enjoying a snack anytime, anywhere.

---

### ROAD RULES

In Bangkok a city law stipulates that all street vendors be off the street on Wednesdays, purportedly to clear the sidewalks for cleaning. A side benefit – unless you happen to be hungry – is being able to walk down the city's narrow lanes and main boulevards without bumping into a rót khēn.

---

A street vendor can choose virtually any venue, from a gridlocked intersection to backwater **soi** (lane), from the edge of a town to the edge of a beach, in which to temporarily set up shop – usually rent-free. At the end of the day or night, the rót khēn is packed up and pushed home, or simply shuttered and left on the spot. A vendor who finds a successful location may remove the wheels from the cart and build a more permanent roadside stall, complete with electric lights.

Prices at vendor stalls tend to be very low and are kept that way because of minimal overheads. The carts may be humble, but the clientele come from all walks of life. At a renowned fishball noodle vendor we frequent in Chiang Mai, push-bikes vie for parking spaces with Mercedes saloons. All-night street vendors with the right product and the right location have been known to take in an impressive nightly revenue of US$1000. Many successful vendors have been able to parlay their cart business into a restaurant or even a chain of restaurants. A Bangkok woman's **thâwt man plaa** (fried fishcake) stand so flourished that she was able to establish one of the city's best middle-class Thai restaurant chains, D'Jit Pochana.

Almost anything edible, whether Thai, Chinese or faràng, from bird's nest soup to Italian espresso to hamburgers, is available from a street vendor somewhere in Thailand. Even so, there are certain dishes to look for – dishes which tend to exceed the restaurant version in quality. Most in this category, in our opinion, happen to be Chinese or Sino-Thai foods.

Number one is **jóhk** (thick rice soup), sometimes served with thin slivers of fresh ginger and rough meatballs made of ground pork to make **jóhk mūu**, or less frequently with chicken to make **jóhk kài**. If you'd like, the cook will toss in a raw egg just before serving. Stir the steaming jóhk well, and the egg will cook itself in a minute or so. If you want the egg, say '**sài khài**', and if you don't, say '**mâi sài khài**'.

Noodles are another delicious and satisfying type of vendor dish, and as usual, the variety is astounding (see Kuaytiaw & Ba-Mii in the Staples & Specialities chapter). One noodle dish, **kūaytīaw phàt thai** (thin rice noodles stirfried with egg, tofu and dried shrimp), can be irresistible if bought from the right vendor. It's not uncommon to see Thais standing in line at a tried and true phàt thai vendor in the early evening.

It's a well-known fact that the best **sômtam** comes not from a restaurant but from a roadside rót khēn. This axiom holds if for no other reason than you can watch the vendor's every move, specifying exactly how much lime juice goes in, how many chillies get pounded and whether to add green beans or not.

We haven't found that this necessarily holds true for the other great Isaan dish, **kài yâang** (grilled chicken), and in fact we're not very big fans of anything barbecued or otherwise cooked in advance at roadside. One exception we make is for Malay-Indonesian style **sà-té** (satay), short skewers of barbecued beef, pork or chicken that are served with a spicy peanut sauce. The most popular sà-té is **sà-té mūu** (pork satay), followed by **sà-té néua** (beef satay), very popular among Southern Thai Muslims.

A favourite vendor dish with many visiting faràng is **khanōm khrók**, made by pouring a slightly salted and slightly sweetened mixture of coconut milk and rice flour into half-round dimples in a large, round iron grill which is heated over a charcoal firepot or portable gas burner. The little pastries cook in a matter of minutes and, when removed, each half is mated with another half to form an oval ball, then placed in a paper box to be sold. Some vendors add chopped chives to the pastry to create a flavour combination that certainly needs an acquired taste.

Other sweets found on the street include the ubiquitous **klûay thâwt** (batter-fried banana), which can be very good at one cart and rather rank at another. It's a good idea to have a look at the oil the bananas are fried in before investing in a bag of klûay thâwt. If the oil is very dark, or if it smells fishy, then you're better off looking elsewhere. The same vendors who make klûay thâwt often make **phèuak thâwt** (fried taro) as well.

After the sun goes down, one of the most popular vendor foods available is **roti** (round, flat wheat bread), a Southern Thai speciality found throughout the kingdom. In its simplest form, roti is quickly fried on a griddle, drizzled with sweetened condensed milk and granulated sugar and then rolled into a piece of paper in an attempt to keep the customer's hands clean (it never works). Bananas, chocolate, egg and many other

## NOODLES ON WHEELS

Although eating off the streets may not be advisable in many countries, sitting down for a bowl of noodles at one of Thailand's ubiquitous noodle stalls is safe and a culinary delight. In Thailand, the place of noodles and the vendors who transform them into culinary works of art, is profound.

For Thais, the mere mention of noodles has been known to turn heads, perk up ears and evoke emotional conversations. The quest for the perfect bowl of noodles has driven many to ferret out a recommended noodle vendor in a remote corner of town. It has been said that Thais have abandoned lavish parties and buffets of smoked salmon and caviar to travel absurd distances for the seductive creations of some new noodle vendor.

Many noodle vendors are celebrated for their broths, the recipes for which are shared only with the vendor's family. A vendor possessing a new angle to the perfect bowl of noodles can expect word to travel fast. Several years ago, a rumour circulated around Bangkok that a particular noodle vendor was dosing his soup with aphrodisiacs, whose miraculous effects were being celebrated by all who consumed it. The chef was an overnight sensation, amassing a quick fortune, but was soon driven into bankruptcy when he, and his noodles, were declared fraudulent.

Whether it's noodle soup prepared in a flavourful broth, or stirfried noodles served with curry, a trip to Thailand would not be complete without several samplings of noodle-based dishes.

The Thai noodle stall is typically a pushcart, equipped with a gas or charcoal stove, a large pot of steaming broth, and several ingredients, spread across an adjoining counter. With this simple set of supplies, the vendor works with a variety of noodles and preparations.

As with all street vendors, who don't have to pay rent or the list of other overheads endured by established eateries, noodle dishes can be quite cheap. For as little as US$0.65, you can buy a filling and delicious

fillings may also be added, depending on the vendor's repertoire (see South in the Regional Variations chapter).

You'll recognise the **plaa mèuk bîng** (dried, roasted squid) cart from the rows of dried squid dangling from a rack. The vendor takes down a dried squid, runs it through a hand-cranked press to flatten it further, then, holding it in a pair of tongs, roasts it briefly over hot coals. The smell may be off-putting, but the squid goes well with a bottle of cold beer.

In Isaan, food you won't find at any restaurant is **khài pîng**, eggs in their shells skewered on a sharp piece of bamboo and grilled over hot coals, and served with a simple **phrík náam plaa** (chillies in fish sauce).

**STREET FOOD**

---

meal while enjoying a convivial street stall atmosphere that is a natural and essential part of the Thai lifestyle.

### How To Order

At most noodle stalls, menus are non-existent, and vendors speak little, if any, English. This means attaining 'made to order' noodle creations can involve some experimentation. Because you must indicate the type of noodle desired, additional ingredients and style of preparation, the noodle experience can be a challenging and fun way to order a meal.

Sometimes the name of the dish will indicate its contents; other times it will refer to a famous style from a particular location in Thailand. Some typical Thai noodle dishes are **kŭaytĭaw phàt thai** (usually called **phàt thai** for short, thin rice noodles with dried or fresh shrimp, bean sprouts, fried tofu, peanuts, egg and seasonings), **kŭaytĭaw râat nâa** (or just **râat nâa**, braised noodles combined with pork or chicken, Chinese broccoli or Chinese kale and oyster sauce) and **kŭaytĭaw phàt khîi mao** (wide rice noodles, fresh basil leaves, chicken or pork, seasonings and a healthy dose of fresh sliced chillies).

Language failing, you can always point to the desired choices, or point to the tables of other diners. After a few noodle experiences, the observant traveller will begin to pick up a noodle vocabulary and should get better at ordering the types and styles of dishes desired.

Noodle vendors can be found on street corners, in alleys, along rivers, at markets and in canoes along canals. A good rule of thumb for choosing a noodle outlet is to find one that's crowded. Thai diners usually have good taste and their presence at a particular stall is often an indication that it is worth a try. But whatever you do, try noodles – a national dish that has been called 'the fuel that drives the engines of a kingdom'.

*by Steven Van Yoder*
*When he's not on the road sampling world cuisines,*
*Steven writes from his home in San Francisco.*

## CURBSIDE GOURMET

**Jerry Hopkins** worked as a correspondent and contributing editor for *Rolling Stone* for many years in Los Angeles, London and Africa. While living in the USA, he wrote several rock-star biographies, including the bestselling *No One Here Gets Out Alive*, a book about Jim Morrison that was later turned into the Oliver Stone film *The Doors*. Elvis Presley and Jimi Hendrix were also Hopkins' book subjects. Now a freelance writer living in Bangkok, Hopkins recently finished writing a book about exotic cuisines entitled *Strange Foods* (Tuttle/Periplus Editions). He continues to write for the Australian, German and American editions of *Rolling Stone* as well as *Condé Nast Traveler*, *Sawasdee* and other magazines.

**On street food:** If you're interested in Thai food, you *must* eat on the street. There's far greater variety, more dishes available than you'd find if you put all the restaurants together, and it's *cheap*. People ask 'aren't you afraid of getting sick?' If you're afraid of getting sick, stay home! Of the four or five times I've got sick from something I've eaten in Thailand, only once has it happened from street food. Every other time, it happened at a 'nice' restaurant or hotel. Street dining is one of the things I like best about Thai food; you sit on little stools like in kindergarten, and get toilet paper for napkins, and trucks and buses keep roaring past – talk about ambience!

**On eating bugs:** I liked all this stuff, or at least was interested in it, before I started researching *Strange Foods*. All my life it's been 'Oh, what's that?! Let me try it!' Except for those big water bugs which look like huge cockroaches, I kept walking around them! I was avoiding them like a snake. Finally one day, a very good Thai friend bought a giant bag of those things from a street vendor on Soi Nana Tai, and taught me how to peel off the carapace and strip off the legs. Once you get all that outside stuff off, the inside is kind of like soft cashews.

It's a matter of what you grew up with. There's a quote attributed to King James "it was a brave man who ate the first oyster". In Isaan, the eating of insects is so normal it's not even discussed. People say 'Oh those poor people have to eat that because they're poor'. No, they *like* it!

**Would Jim Morrison have liked Thai food?** Probably not. Let's face it, when he was hungry, he'd order a Singapore Sling! Jim didn't eat much.

**Elvis Presley?** If it was deep fried he probably would have eaten it.

*Streetside barbecued fish*

Another dish you won't find in any restaurant – except perhaps in a few Chinese-style coffee shops – is **paa-thâwng kōh** (deep-fried chunks of wheat dough), similar to an unsweetened doughnut. Typically you'll find these only in the early morning between 6 and 8am, or in the evening after 8pm. Sometimes the same vendor sells warm **náam tâo-hûu** (soy milk) for dunking. Sometimes paa-thâwng kōh is served with **jóhk** (thick rice soup), in which case the custom is to cut the pastries into pieces, using a pair of large sewing scissors usually left on the table for this purpose. Stirred into the jóhk, the pastry pieces give the dish more texture and flavour.

Carts stocked with fresh **phōn-lá-mái** (fruit) are common, and like the plaa mèuk pîng carts, they're always on the move. Typically, pineapple, papaya, guava and watermelon are available year-round, while other fruits are seasonal. Most fruit is sliced fresh in front of the customer, although they may already be peeled. The fruit is then slipped into a small plastic bag along with a bamboo skewer to spear the fruit with, and a smaller plastic bag containing a mixture of salt, sugar and powdered chilli. Most Thais like to dip pieces of fruit into this mixture before eating.

The best place to buy traditional **khǎwng wǎan** (sweet stuff) is from vendor carts (see Khawng Waan in the Staples & Specialities chapter).

## Hygiene

We've eaten hundreds of meals cooked by street vendors in Thailand, and have yet to encounter ill effect, and we consider Thailand to have one the highest standards of vendor hygiene in South-East Asia.

Nonetheless precautions are worth taking. Firstly, avoid eating cooked vendor foods that aren't either refrigerator cold or stove hot. If you don't see it cooked in front of you, don't eat it. Sausages or barbecued meats that have been sitting out all afternoon could be particularly hazardous.

Secondly, avoid vendor stands where health standards are clearly below average. In Bangkok and other large cities, the competition usually drives substandard vendors out of business, but in small and medium-sized towns that's not necessarily the case. If the cook looks unclean, or if the food cabinets have more than a few flies, keep on walking.

One very big grey area is the fruit vendor. Garden variety travel health advice says 'if you can't peel it yourself, don't eat it'. If you obeyed this maxim, you would never get to sample the delights of the Thai fruit stand. Experience seems to support our belief that the risks inherent in eating peeled fruits in Thailand are no higher than the risks of eating any other vendor food. But as with all vendor food, use your discretion.

# a thai
# banquet

These days Thai cuisine can be found internationally. Many of the world's major cities have at least one Thai restaurant, and the sales of Thai cookbooks continue to boom. But buyer beware, as many dishes and recipes on offer will be compromised to suit the palette of the uninitiated. It's good to know that all the fire of an authentic spicy **tôm yam** (chilli & lemongrass soup) can be recreated for unsuspecting friends, in the comfort of your own kitchen.

Back home with your suitcase or backpack full of traditional Thai cooking utensils and a few hard-to-find ingredients, it won't take long before you're feeling nostalgic for Thai food. When that happens, it's time to take a crack at impressing your friends by throwing a Thai dinner party. Thai is the perfect party food, as it doesn't require a lot of preparation or cooking time compared to many other cuisines. It's a breeze for your friends too, as Thai dinner hosts never expect guests to bring anything, not even a bottle of wine. The host provides everything.

Remember that Thai meals aren't normally served in courses, so you'll need to plan your dishes so that they're more or less ready at the same time. The exception is **kàp klâem** (drinking food). Whether or not alcohol is served, you might as well take advantage of the nearest thing Thai cuisine has to an appetiser, for party guests to nibble on before the main meal.

## Yam Met Ma-Muang Himaphaan
### (Hot & Tangy Salad with Cashew Nuts)

Yam mét má-mûang himáphaan makes a tasty kàp klâem (drinking food) dish. The most simple recipes consist of fried cashew nuts on a plate with little piles of chopped spring onions or shallots, sliced fresh chillies, wedges of lime, salt and sometimes dried shrimp on the side. The customers then squeeze the lime over the nuts and mix everything together.

Here's a more sophisticated cashew nut yam we dreamt up after several visits to a little Mekong view restaurant in Khong Jiam.

| | |
|---|---|
| ½ | kilo cashews, fresh or dry roasted |
| 8 | fresh red and green chillies (any kind will do, depending on how hot you'd like this dish to be), sliced into small rounds |
| 6 | fresh cherry tomatoes |
| 4 | shallots, sliced into small wedges |
| ¼ | cup dried shrimp |
| 1 | teaspoon green peppercorns, fresh or bottled (but drained) |
| 3 | tablespoons lime juice |
| | salt, to taste |

Roast the cherry tomatoes in a hot oven or over an open flame until the skins blister and crack. Peel the tomatoes and set aside.

Fry the cashews in a small amount of cooking oil until fragrant and golden. Take care not to overcook or burn them.

Toss all the ingredients together. Serve with cold Singha Beer or iced Mekong whisky with lime and soda.

A **yam** (hot & tangy salad) such as **yam mét má-mûang hìmáphaan** (yam with cashew nuts) is easy to prepare, or go for the slightly more ambitious **yam wún sên** (yam with mung bean starch noodles) or **yam plaa mèuk** (yam with squid). A Northern Thai **náam phrík nùm** (chilli-eggplant dip) with steamed vegetables also makes a good **kàp klâem**, as does **mîang kham**, a do-it-yourself appetiser in which chunks of ginger, shallot, peanuts, coconut flakes, lime and dried shrimp are wrapped in wild tea leaves or lettuce. Concerning your guests' chilli tolerance, you may want to prepare two different plates, one with less chilli – in mîang kham, you can omit the chillies altogether. Another thing to remember before overworking yourself is that one Thai dish normally feeds two people.

For the drinkers in your party, consider providing Mekong whisky along with a traditional **chút** (a set of ice, halved limes and mixers). Also remember that a spicy yam goes much better with a light drink than a double shot of Mekong or the like. If you can get Singha Beer, all the better, but any strong lager will do nicely. Most wines won't complement Thai food. Reds are especially inappropriate as the tannin tends to clash with the chillies and lime. For guests who might prefer wine, consider providing a chilled crisp white.

Now to the most important planning task – creating a good balance of differently flavoured dishes. Pick a classic seafood **tôm yam** (chilli & lemongrass soup), such as **tôm yam kûng** (tôm yam with shrimp) or **tôm yam pó tàek** (tôm yam with mixed seafood). Up the chilli ante with either a **kaeng khîaw-wãan** (green curry) or a **phàt phèt** (literally, 'hot stirfry').

With the chilli quotient simmering a blander vegetable dish is called for, say either **phàt phàk ruam** (stirfried mixed vegetables) or **phàt phàk khá-náa** (stirfried Chinese kale). Almost any vegetable or selection of vegetables will do, lightly stirfried with the right seasonings – a little fish sauce, a little soy or oyster sauce, fresh ground black pepper and minced garlic.

---

## PUTTING ON A SPREAD

To add further ambience to the dinner party, consider draping the dining table with Thai textiles you've brought back from your trip – not the antique ones from Northern and North-Eastern Thailand, but the ordinary everyday **phâakhamãa**, the short simple cotton sarong woven in chequered patterns and traditionally worn by rural Thai men. You could also use **phâa sîn**, a longer sarong with small printed patterns, worn by women when lounging around their homes during hot weather.

# Miang Kham

If we had to pick one dish that most exemplifies Thai cuisine, it wouldn't be tôm yam kûng, phàt thai or even kaeng phèt. Rather we'd choose **mîang kham**; just bite into a wad of it and it fairly shouts 'Thailand'.

Here's how it's done. Prepare a plate of tiny chunks of lime, ginger and shallot, toasted grated coconut, roasted peanuts, fresh whole phrík khîi nûu (mouse-dropping chillies) and dried shrimp.

At the centre of the plate, place a stack of fresh, clean **bai chá-phluu** (wild tea leaf) or substitute red-leaf lettuce or butter lettuce, as well as a small bowl filled with **náam mîang** (see recipe below). Using your fingers, work your way around the plate, picking up one of each ingredient and placing it on a bai chá-phluu or lettuce leaf. Sprinkle the coconut on last, dribble a little náam mîang over the contents, and fold the corners of the leaf over the mixture to form a parcel.

Pop the whole thing in your mouth, bite down, chew and pay attention to what happens next. First the lime juice comes bursting out, and floods your mouth with a lime taste at the same time that the salty-sweet, honey-like sauce coats your tongue. Next you're likely to sense a spicy infusion of ginger, followed by the crunch of peanuts, the roasted taste of the coconut, the bitterness of the lime peel and then the salty-sea feel of the dried shrimp. The last thing to arrive is the chilli.

### náam mîang

| | | | |
|---|---|---|---|
| ½ | cup minced ginger | ½ | cup minced shallots |
| 1 | tablespoon shrimp paste | 1 | tablespoon fish sauce |
| ¼ | cup (60ml) water | | |
| | palm sugar or honey to taste | | |

Pound the ginger, shallots and shrimp paste into a paste. Add the water, fish sauce and palm sugar or honey and stir. Cook in a small saucepan until all ingredients are well blended, then set aside to cool. Don't let it get too thick – you should be able to pour it, albeit slowly.

### khrêuang mîang

½ cup of each of the following:
> unsalted, unseasoned roasted peanuts
> roasted unsweetened coconut flakes
> ginger, peeled and cut into 1cm cubes
> shallots cut into 1cm cubes
> lime cut into 1cm cubes
> whole phrík khîi nûu (mouse dropping chillies)
> dried shrimp

30 to 40 **bai chá-phluu** (wild tea leaves) or substitute red-leaf lettuce or butter lettuce

## Laap Pet (Spicy Duck Salad)

The key to this flavourful Isaan dish is the **khâo khûa pòn**, made by taking uncooked rice that has been dry-roasted in a pan until it begins to brown, and pulverising it with a mortar & pestle. The powder need not be too fine.

- 1 whole duck
- 4 shallots, chopped
- 2-3 spring onions, chopped
- 4 cloves garlic, minced
- 8 lemongrass leaves (not the root)
- 10 fresh mint leaves
- 4 teaspoons khâo khûa pòn
- 3 teaspoons dried phrík chíi fáa (sky pointing chillies) flakes or powder
- 4 tablespoons lime juice
- 2 tablespoons fish sauce or to taste

Remove all the meat from the duck, discard the skin and chop the meat into small pieces, almost minced. If there's a lot of duck fat, some of it can be removed and discarded, but leave some for the next step.

Stirfry the duck meat in a dry wok on medium heat. If there's not enough duck fat in the meat to keep it from sticking, add a few drops of cooking oil. Take care not to overcook the duck, drain all the excess moisture out of the wok. If you prefer a moister dish, skip this step.

Add all the remaining ingredients except the mint leaves to the wok and stirfry for another couple of minutes or until the shallots soften.

Mix in the mint leaves and toss everything together in the wok until the mint is warmed through but not wilted.

Serve with sticky rice.

A THAI BANQUET

A chicken-based dish with a slight spiciness will fill the space between chilli-blasted and bland. If you didn't serve a cashew yam – or just like cashews – make up a platter of **kài phàt mét má-mûang hìmáphaan** (chicken stirfried with dried chillies and cashews). Or else get out the barbecue grill and bring in an Isaan classic, **kài yâang** (grilled chicken).

So far you have enough to feed eight people according to the traditional formula. If you really want to fill them up, consider making something with a whole fish, either the Southern Thai **plaa tàet diaw** (half-day dried fish, fried and served with a spicy mango salad) or the Isaan dish with mild to medium chilli heat, **nêung plaa** (fish steamed with lemongrass). For another easy dish with very distinctive flavours, get out the cutting board and put together a **lâap** (spicy minced meat salad) of beef, duck or turkey.

Before cooking anything, prepare some rice using the traditional Thai method (see Khâo in the Staples & Specialities chapter) or cut corners with a rice cooker. The important thing is that the rice stops boiling about 15 minutes before serving, so it's cooked through but not burning hot. A decent rice cooker will keep rice warm and moist for at least an hour or two.

## Phat Phak Ruam (Stirfried Mixed Vegetables)

Thais have several ways of preparing this dish, often with oyster sauce in the Cantonese fashion. This one is very simple and very Thai.

| | |
|---|---|
| 1 | cup fresh mushrooms, sliced into thick pieces |
| 1 | head of cauliflower, cut into flowerets |
| 1 | carrot, sliced into flat ovals |
| 10 | Chinese cabbage leaves |
| 2 | cloves garlic, minced |
| 3 | tablespoons chicken or vegetable stock |
| 2 | teaspoons fish sauce |
| ½ | teaspoon sugar |
| 3 | tablespoons vegetable oil |

Heat the oil in a wok until a drop of water tossed in immediately sizzles. Stirfry the garlic until aromatic and golden, then add the cauliflower and stirfry on medium heat for about 20 seconds.

Add the stock and carrots and continue stirfrying for another minute or so, then add the cabbage and mushrooms and stirfry for 2 minutes.

Add the fish sauce and sugar and continue cooking until the sugar is well dissolved. Remove from the heat and serve hot with steamed rice and **phrík náam plaa** (a simple concoction of sliced fresh red and green mouse dropping chillies floating in fish sauce).

Most Thai meals end with a plate of assorted sliced fresh fruit. For a really special dessert, prepare **khâo nǐaw má-mûang** (sliced fresh ripe mangoes served with sticky rice sweetened with coconut milk) or **sǎngkhayǎa fák thawng** (pumpkin custard).

*Mangoes and sweetened sticky rice*

If you want a Thai soundtrack for your dinner party there's a lot to choose from. The best upcountry Thai party music just might be **lûuk thûng** (literally, 'children of the fields'), the syncopated music style from North-East Thailand. Among the many lûuk thûng recording artists, Phairot is a perennial Thai favourite and always a good bet. Take lûuk thûng a step further into electric instrumentation, mix it with international folk,

---

**BUYING MUSIC**

Cassette tapes and CDs of Thai music are readily available throughout the country, from department stores, music shops and street vendors. Cassettes of Thai music cost US$1.50 to US$2.25, much less expensive than the average US$12 for a CD.

## Plaa Taet Diaw (Once-Dried Fish)

Around the Gulf of Thailand, this dish is usually made with **plaa sãmlii** (cottonfish), but we've eaten versions made with several other kinds of fish, including the freshwater **plaa chãwn** (serpent-headed fish). The only requirement is that it be a firm-fleshed fish, one that can take frying. The Thais will often make the flesh drier and firmer by drying the fish in the sun for a half day or so, hence the name.

1    fresh whole fish weighing about 300g, cleaned and
        without the head
      enough cooking oil to fill the pan about 5cm deep
1    large green mango, pitted and julienned
4    phrik khĩi nũu (mouse-dropping chilli), sliced into small rounds
      juice of one lime
2    tablespoons fish sauce
1    tablespoon sugar
½    cup unseasoned, unsalted roasted peanuts (optional)

First, make the mango salad by tossing together the julienned green mango, sliced chillies, lime juice, fish sauce and sugar. Mix until the sugar dissolves.

Split the fish open lengthways and remove the bones. Pat the inside and outside dry with paper towels. Fry the fish in hot oil until well done – the inside flesh should begin to look as if it were breaded.

Drain the fried fish, place on a platter, and cover with the mango salad. Top with peanuts if desired.

vary the tempos and you've got **phleng phêua chiiwít** (literally, 'songs for life'). Created by a 1970s group called Caravan and considerably extended by Thailand's most famous rock group, Carabao, in the 1980s, phleng phêua chiiwít continues to be one of the most popular Thai musical genres and is very much at home at a party. Carabao and other bands like them have crafted an exciting fusion of Thai classical and lûuk thûng forms with hard rock and even metal.

For something more mellow, put on some 'Thai jazz', a misnomer for an experimental fusion of international jazz with Thai classical and folk motifs using a mix of Thai and western instruments. The leading exponents of this genre are Tewan Sapsanyakorn, Kangsadarn, Boy Thai (who adds Brazilian samba to the mix), Todd Lavelle, Nupap Savantrachas and Fong Nam.

# fit
### & healthy

Low in fat, high in nutrition, Thai cuisine is good for you. While enjoying Thailand's many dining opportunities, though, don't forget your common sense. Number one rule: if it's fresh cooked – or kept stove hot or refrigerator cold – you're probably OK.

Don't plan on hitting the ground running, especially if you're on a long trip. Allow yourself time to adjust physically and mentally to your new environment, especially in the first week. Factor in some time to take a breather, recover from jet lag and catch up on sleep. Don't overdo the booze or the chillies; work up to your usual party vigour slowly.

For a health guide, look no further than Lonely Planet's pocket-size *Healthy Travel Asia*.

## Hygiene

Thailand has one of the highest standards of hygiene in South-East Asia and most visitors suffer no ill effect whatsoever from the food. Thoroughly cooked food is safest but not if it has been left to cool or if it has been reheated. Uncooked or incompletely cooked shellfish such as mussels, oysters and clams should be avoided as well as undercooked meat.

How food is prepared is more important than where. Heating kills germs so a plate of noodles cooked in a steaming hot wok in front of you at a street stall is probably safer than food left on display in an upmarket hotel buffet.

## Water

Thais don't drink tap water, and you shouldn't either. Drink bottled water or beverages such as soft drinks or fruit juice. All water served in restaurants or in homes is purified (usually boiled or taken from a five-gallon dispenser in the kitchen) and is free. If you're paranoid, ask for **náam deum khùat** (bottled drinking water), which will cost a few baht.

Water used to make coffee or tea is of course boiled and safe to drink. Ice is produced from purified water under hygienic conditions and is therefore theoretically safe. During transit to the local restaurant, however, conditions may not be so hygienic (you may see blocks of ice being dragged along the street), but it's very difficult to resist in the hot season. The rule of thumb is that if it's chipped ice, it probably came from an ice block (which may not have been handled well) but if it's ice cubes or 'tubes', it was delivered from the ice factory in sealed plastic.

In rural areas, villagers mostly drink collected rainwater. Most people can drink this without problems, but some people can't tolerate it.

In Thailand, virtually no one bothers with filters, tablets or iodine since bottled water is so cheap and readily available. Try to purchase glass water bottles, however, as these are recyclable (unlike the plastic disposable ones). Even better for the environment, you can prepare your own drinking water by boiling it for a minute or two and then letting it cool.

*One man and his rooster, Central Thailand*

FIT & HEALTHY

## Fluid Balance

Plain water is the best antidote to dehydration. Always have a supply and remind yourself to sip from it regularly.

Use how much urine you're passing as a rough guide to whether you're getting dehydrated. Small amounts of dark urine suggest you need to increase your fluid intake. Passing reasonable quantities of light yellow urine indicates that you've got the balance about right. As a rough guide, drink enough so you produce a reasonable quantity of light-coloured urine every three to four hours while you're awake.

## Eating the Right Stuff

Eating well should be fun, but it's also about making sure you get enough of the right nutrients to enable you to function at your best, mentally and physically. When you're on the road, your diet will be different from normal; in addition, a different lifestyle, stress and new activities may mean your nutritional requirements are increased.

With the help of this book you'll be able to identify available foods for a diverse and nutritious diet. But when you eat can be as important as what you eat. If you're on the move, be careful not to miss meals as this will make you more easily fatigued and vulnerable to illness.

## Fading Away?

Losing weight when you're travelling is pretty common. There are lots of reasons for this, including getting sick, having a change in diet and perhaps being more active. You may have a bit of padding to spare, but keep an eye on how much weight you're losing and don't allow yourself to shed too much, as this may put you at risk of illness, as well as draining you of energy.

If you've just turned vegetarian – or aren't eating meat here – be aware that your body takes a bit of time to adjust, so it's worth taking a bit of care with your diet. Good plant sources of nutrients include:

**protein**   soya protein, pulses, bread, rice, noodles, seeds, potatoes

**calcium**   tofu, seeds, green leafy vegetables, nuts, bread, dried fruit

**iron**   pulses, green vegetables, dried fruits, nuts; absorption of iron is increased by consuming a source of vitamin C at the same time (fruit, fruit juice or vegetables). Tea, coffee, and phytate and oxalates from plants will reduce the absorption of iron

## Diarrhoea

Despite taking precautions you may still get a bout of mild travellers diarrhoea, but a few rushed toilet trips with no other symptoms is not indicative of a serious problem. Diarrhoea caused by contaminated food or water is more serious. Dehydration is the main danger with any diarrhoea, particularly for children where dehydration can occur quickly.

If diarrhoea strikes, you should rest – this gives your body the best chance to fight whatever is making you ill. Drink plenty of fluids and check you're not getting dehydrated – weak black tea with a little sugar, carbonated drinks allowed to go flat and diluted 50% with water, are all

---

### THE SIX BASICS

Everybody needs six basics for life: water, carbohydrates, protein, fat, vitamins and minerals. Obviously foods aren't a pure source of just of one type of nutrient, they contain various elements in different quantities, so the best way to make sure you get enough of the right things is to eat a varied diet. You shouldn't find this difficult here, where the diet consists of a carbohydrate staple (rice, noodles) which is eaten with a protein source (meat, fish, tofu, beans) and vegetables. Fresh fruit is widely available.

As a guide, you need to eat a variety of foods from each of five core groups:

- **bread** (roti), **other cereals** (rice, noodles) – eat lots of these, they provide carbohydrate, fibre, some calcium and iron, and B vitamins

- **fruit & vegetables** – eat lots of these, they give you vitamin C, carotenes (vitamin A), folic acid, fibre and some carbohydrate

- **milk and dairy products** – eat moderate amounts for calcium, zinc, protein, vitamin B12, vitamin B2, vitamin A and vitamin D

- **meat, fish, nuts, beans** – these provide iron, protein, B vitamins (especially B12; meat only), zinc and magnesium; eat in moderation

- **fat and sugary foods** (butter, oil, margarine, cakes, biscuits, sweets, etc) – eat sparingly from this group, which mainly provides fat, including essential fatty acids, some vitamins and salt.

Bear in mind that if you're already sick, your requirements change and you may need to increase the amounts of some food groups to increase your intake of protein, vitamins and minerals, for example.

good. Be aware of how often you're passing urine and what colour it is (see Fluid Balance earlier in this chapter).

Note any other symptoms – diarrhoea can occur in many other illnesses, including malaria and hepatitis. Remember, diarrhoea is contagious so be scrupulous about washing your hands after you use the toilet.

Lomotil or Imodium can be used to bring relief, although they do not actually cure the problem. In certain situations, the need for antibiotics may be indicated by: diarrhoea with blood and mucous (gut-paralysing drugs like Imodium or Lomotil should be avoided in this situation); watery diarrhoea with fever and lethargy; persistent diarrhoea for more than five days; severe diarrhoea, if it is logistically difficult to stay in one place. In cases like these, seek medical help. Bangkok, Phuket and Chiang Mai have the best clinics and hospitals in Thailand; many have English-speaking doctors on staff.

## What to Eat

It's easy to get hung up about what, if anything, to eat when you have diarrhoea. But relax, use your common sense and try to tune in to what your body is telling you – if you feel like eating, go ahead, especially starchy foods which are known to promote salt and water absorption (such as rice, noodles, non-oily roti and crackers). If you don't feel like eating, don't force yourself to. Unless you're really roughing it, you're going to be basically well nourished and able to withstand a couple of days with little or no food. It may make you feel a bit wobbly, so make sure you add a bit of sugar or honey to your drinks to keep your energy levels up.

Your overworked guts will appreciate small amounts of food at regular intervals rather than great big meals. This may help make you feel less nauseated too. You may find that eating brings on cramps and you have to dash to the toilet. We all have a natural reflex whereby eating

---

### Food on the Runs

When you have diarrhoea, it's good to eat:

- plain rice
- roti if it's not too oily
- plain noodles
- dry biscuits, salty or not too sweet
- bananas

If possible, it's best to avoid:

- fruit & vegetables, except bananas
- dairy products, including yoghurt
- spicy foods
- greasy foods

increases the activity of the gut, but this can get exaggerated in a diarrhoeal illness. It doesn't make you a great dinner companion, but you'll probably find that once you've answered the call of nature you can return to finish your meal.

Contrary to the spirit of this book, you should stick to a more limited diet while you have diarrhoea and as you recover. Go easy on fibre providers like fruit, vegetables and nuts. Bananas are good as they tend to stop you up, and are a source of potassium and glucose. As the diarrhoea clears up and you start to get your appetite back, gradually add in more foods until you're back to normal and can resume your culinary escapade.

## Indigestion

A change in diet, stress, anxiety and spicy foods can all make 'indigestion' (burning pains in your upper abdomen) and heartburn (burning in your gullet, often with an acid taste in your mouth) more likely when you're travelling. The discomfort is often worse when you're hungry or just after meals. Smoking and alcohol exacerbate it.

Simple measures you could try are to eat small, regular meals – don't eat a huge meal just before you go to bed. It can be difficult, but try to avoid spicy hot foods. Milk and yoghurt can be soothing, as can eating plain, starchy foods like noodles or roti.

You could consider trying antacids (there are many products available without prescription), although stomach acid has a protective effect against infective agents, so taking antacids may make you more vulnerable to gut infections.

## Children's Health

Like many places in South-East Asia, travelling with children in Thailand can be a lot of fun, as long as you come with the right attitudes, equipment and the usual parental patience. All the usual health tips regarding food, heat and diarrhoea mentioned earlier should be followed with extra care, as kids tend to jump into everything with both feet.

Finicky eaters may find noodles more to their liking than many spicy Thai dishes. Of course there's always McDonald's, Pizza Hut and other western fast-food chains in the larger cities.

For the most part, parents needn't worry too much about health concerns though it pays to lay down a few ground rules – such as regular hand-washing – to head off potential medical problems. Children should be warned not to play with animals since rabies is relatively common in Thailand.

## Heat

Thailand's full-on tropical climate can get to you, so take it slow until you've fully acclimatised. Drink plenty of liquids to replace all the water lost via perspiration. Use sunscreen, even when overcast.

Thais bathe at least twice a day; taking cool showers can be of great help. Use talcum powder to prevent 'prickly heat', an itchy rash caused by trapped perspiration.

Contrary to popular belief, salt tablets interfere with the absorption of water by the body. 'Dehydrating' or 'electrolyte' solutions can have a similar effect if consumed too often.

When the weather is hot, avoid the sun between 11am and 6pm – stick to the shade. Avoid overexerting yourself or eating a big meal at this time of the day – have a siesta or read that airport novel.

*Cooling off, Southern Thailand*

## Diabetes

If you are diabetic, bring plenty of supplies and everything you will need, then pack some more. If you're travelling with a companion it's a good idea to split your supplies between you in the event your luggage is lost. Also leave some with a hotel or a friend. Carry your prescription or other documentation so local police won't think you're dealing in drugs.

**MSG: FRIEND OR FOE**

Many noodle stands and restaurants season dishes – particularly soups – with monosodium glutamate (MSG), also known by its Japanese name, ajinomoto, or its Thai name **phǒng chuu rót**. Although it's use in Thailand doesn't match China, Vietnam or Japan, you'll see it now and then. Many visitors try to avoid this natural substance, believing they are allergic to it, or that it's dangerously high in sodium.

For the record, MSG is a simple compound of glutamate, water and sodium (about two-thirds less by weight than in table salt). Glutamate, an amino acid that occurs naturally in virtually every food, is a major component of most natural protein sources. Like salt and sugar, MSG has been used in Asia for centuries, originally as a distillate of seaweed. Today it's produced through a natural fermentation and evaporation process using molasses made from sugar cane or sugar beets. Despite its white, crystalline appearance, it is not a synthetic substance, nor does it necessarily compound one's intake of sodium. When a little MSG is used during food preparation, the flavour-enhancing properties mean far less salt needs to be used during and after cooking. Although often presumed to have no flavour of its own, MSG has an identifiable taste to those familiar with its culinary uses – the Japanese call this flavour umami, often translated as 'savoury'.

Contrary to popular myth, the human body metabolises glutamate added to food the same way it metabolises glutamate already found in food. Although some people report physical reactions to MSG (the so-called 'Chinese restaurant syndrome'), every placebo-controlled food research study on humans thus far published has concluded that such reactions can almost always be traced not to MSG but rather to psychological syndromes (a legacy of late 1960s food scares) or to food allergies triggered by ingredients other than MSG. The American College of Allergy and Immunology in 1991 concluded that MSG could not be considered an allergen. If you insist that you have a direct sensitivity to MSG (despite your own everyday ingestion of glutamates present naturally in foods), just say '**mâi sài phǒng chuu rót**' (don't add MSG).

## Allergies

Anyone with an allergy to shrimp should be aware that a lot of Thai dishes contain shrimp paste or dried shrimp. You may want to check first by asking '**aahǎan níi sài kûng hâeng rěu kà-pì mǎi?**' (Does this food contain dried shrimp or shrimp paste?).

**Recommended Reading**

If you're going to Thailand, have a look at Lonely Planet's *Thailand*, one of Lonely Planet's bestselling guidebooks, ever since it was first released in 1982. Other LP guides to Thailand include *Bangkok* and *Thailand's Islands & Beaches*.

LP's *Thai Phrasebook* will help you get up to speed with the language, a necessity if you hope to do any serious culinary exploring in Thailand.

Among our favourite Thai cookbooks is *Thailand The Beautiful Cookbook: Authentic Recipes from the Regions of Thailand*, by Panurat Poladitmontri and Judy Lew. It's big and looks more like a coffee-table tome than a real cookbook, but the recipes are authentic and easy to follow. *Real Thai: The Best of Thailand's Regional Cooking* by ex-US Peace Corps volunteer Nancie McDermott is a more manageable paperback size and contains lots of good tips on Thai food culture. McDermott's more recent *Real Vegetarian Thai* caters for the vegetarian crowd, also good.

*Keo's Thai Cuisine*, by the Lao chef-owner at Honolulu's well established Keo's Thai restaurant, presents westernised versions – with fantasised dish names such as 'Evil Jungle Prince' (no such dish name exists in Thai) – of many dishes popular among Hawaiian residents. *The Elegant Taste of Thailand: Cha Am Cuisine*, by Pinyo Srisawat et al, does the same for the Cha Am restaurant in Berkeley, California, only better.

The introductory cultural background material in *The Taste of Thailand* by London's Vatcharin Bhumichitr is very well written (ghost-written?) but contains many errors (examples: The book says 'the ideal Thai meal includes small bowls of clear soup for each diner', something we've never seen in a Thai home). The recipes tend to be more Chinese than Thai. *The Food of Thailand: Authentic Recipes from the Golden Kingdom* contains an introductory chapter written by William Warren and authentic recipes borrowed by the executive chef for the Beaufort Sukhothai in Bangkok from cookbooks available locally in Thailand. Put this book and *The Taste of Thailand* together for a relatively well-rounded view of Thai cuisine.

The best chilli book we've seen, though sadly lacking in Thai varieties, is *Peppers of the World* by Dave DeWitt and Paul Bosland.

**Multimedia**

*The Spice of Life*, a CD-ROM issued by Silkworm Books in Chiang Mai, contains a complete and well illustrated overview of ingredients in Thai cooking and a good introduction to Thai food culture. It's bundled with a 238-page book, *Thai Cooking Companion*, which repeats the ingredients section found on the CD-ROM, along with some of the cultural information and 183 pages of recipes.

FIT & HEALTHY

# eat your words

## language guide

## Pronunciation

The following is a guide to the transliteration system used in this book. It is based on the Royal Thai General System of Transcription (RTGS), the most widely used system in Thailand, with some minor changes to help you to pronounce Thai as accurately as possible. As transliterations give only an approximate guide to pronunciation, we've included this guide for those who want to try their hand at pronouncing Thai more like a native speaker.

### Vowels

The meanings of some words change depending on whether they have a long or short vowel, so take care to make this distinction. Long vowels are indicated in the transliterations by doubling the vowel or by adding the letter **h** to it.

| | |
|---|---|
| a | as the 'u' in 'nut' |
| aa | as the 'a' in 'father' (twice as long as a) |
| ae | as the 'a' in 'bat' |
| e | as the 'e' in 'hen' |
| eh | like the 'a' in 'hay' but flat (twice as long as e) |
| i | as the 'i' in 'it' |
| ii | as the 'ee' in 'feet' (twice as long as i) |
| o | as the 'o' in 'bone', but shorter |
| oh | as the 'oe' in 'toe' (twice as long as o) |
| oe | as the 'u' in 'hut' but with the mouth more closed |
| u | as the 'u' in 'flute', but shorter |
| uu | as the 'oo' in 'food' (longer than u) |

### Vowel Combinations

| | |
|---|---|
| ai | as the 'i' in 'pipe' |
| ao | as the 'ow' in 'now' |
| aw | as the 'aw' in 'jaw' |
| eu | as the 'i' in 'sir' |
| eua | eu + a |
| ia | as the 'ia' in 'Fiat' |
| iaw | as the 'io' in 'Rio' |
| iu | as the 'ew' in 'new' |
| oei | oe + i |
| ua | u + a |
| uay | u + ai |

### Consonants

In Thai, **k**, **p** and **t** can be pronounced with or without a puff of breath, with breath signified by the letter **h**. Don't be confused by **ph**, which means 'p' with breath, not the 'f' sound in 'photo'. Note, however, that the combination **ch** is pronounced as in English 'cheese'.

| k | as the 'k' in 'skunk' |
|---|---|
| kh | as the 'k' in 'kite' |
| p | as the 'p' in 'spit' |
| ph | as the 'p' in 'pet' |
| t | as the 't' in 'stamp' |
| th | as the 't' in 'time' |
| ng | as the 'ng' in 'sing' |
| j | similar to the 't' in 'rapture' or 'culture' |
| r | similar to the 'r' in 'run' but the tongue taps the roof of the mouth. In everyday speech it's often pronounced like 'l', and sometimes omitted altogether. |

## Tones

Thai has five tones, which can often determine a word's meaning.

| good | dii | mid (level, mid-range tone indicated by the absence of a tone mark) |
|---|---|---|
| new | mái | high (level tone produced at the top of the vocal range) |
| wood | mài | low (level tone produced at the bottom of the vocal range) |
| not/burn | mâi | falling (pronounced as though emphasising a word, such as 'No!') |
| not? | mǎi | rising (similar to the inflection given to the question 'Yes?') |

# Useful Phrases
## General

Have you eaten yet? (common greeting)
    **thaan khâo láew rĕu yang?**      ทานข้าวแล้วหรือยัง

I've eaten already.
    **thaan láew**      ทานแล้ว

## Family Meals

You're a great cook!
    **tham aahǎan kèng mâak**      ทำอาหารเก่งมาก

It's delicious.
    **aràwy**      อร่อย

Are the ingredients local?
    **khrêuang prung maa jàak tháew níi mái?**      เครื่องปรุงมาจากแถวนี้ไหม

I've never eaten food like this.
    **mâi khoei thaan aahǎan bàep níi**      ไม่เคยทานอาหารแบบนี้

Could you pass the (salt) please?
    **khǎaw ... nàwy**      ขอ...หน่อย

Thanks very much for the meal.
    **khàwp khun mâak tîi líang aahǎan**      ขอบคุณมากที่เลี้ยงอาหาร

I really liked it.
    **châwp mâak**      ชอบมาก

## Vegetarian Needs

I eat only vegetarian food. (for men)
**phŏm kin jeh**      ผมกินเจ

I eat only vegetarian food. (for women)
**dì-chăn kin jeh**      ดิฉันกินเจ

I don't eat meat or dairy products.
**phŏm/dì-chăn mâi kin néua**      ผม/ดิฉันไม่กินเนื้อสัตว์
**sàt rĕu aahăan thîi tàam jàak nom**      หรืออาหารที่ทำจากนม

Do you have any vegetarian dishes?
**mii aahăan jeh măi?**      มีอาหารเจไหม

Does this dish have meat?
**aahăan jaan níi sài**      อาหารจานนี้ใส่เ
**néua sàt măi?**      นื้อสัตว์ไหม

Can I get this without the meat?
**sàng mâi sài néua sàt dâi măi**      สั่งไม่ใส่เนื้อสัตว์ได้ไหม

I'm allergic to…
**phŏm/dì-chăn pháe …**      ผม/ดิฉันแพ้...

---

### DELICIOUS IS THE WORD

How to say 'very tasty' in four Thai dialects:

| | |
|---|---|
| **sâep ii-lĭi** | North-East |
| **ràwy jang hûu** | South |
| **àràwy mâak** | Central |
| **lam tâe** | North |

---

I don't eat …    **phŏm/dì-chăn kin … mâi dâi**    ผม/ดิฉันกิน...ไม่ได้
   meat      **néua sàt**      เนื้อสัตว์
   chicken      **kài**      ไก่
   fish      **plaa**      ปลา
   seafood      **aahăan thaleh**      อาหารทะเล
   pork      **mŭu**      หมู

I eat only vegetables.
**phŏm/dì-chăn kin tàe phàk**      ผม/ดิฉันกินแต่ผัก

I eat only vegetarian food.
**phŏm/dì-chăn kin jeh**      ผม/ดิฉันกินเจ

I don't want any meat at all.
**phŏm/dì-chăn mâi**      ผม/ดิฉันไม่เ
**ao néua sàt loei**      อาเนื้อสัตว์เลย

No fish or chicken.
**mâi sài plaa rĕu kài**      ไม่ใส่ปลาหรือไก่

(I/we) want vegetables only.
**sài tàe phàk**     ใส่แต่ผัก

Please don't use fish sauce.
**karúnaa mâi sài náam plaa**     กรุณาไม่ใส่น้ำปลา

**Special Needs**
Does it contain eggs/dairy products?
**níi sài khài rēu nom mái?**     นี่ใส่ไข่หรือนมไหม

I'm allergic to …
**phõm/dì-chãn pháe …**     ผม/ดิฉันแพ้...

| Does it contain …? | **níi sài … mái?** | นี่ใส่...ไหม |
|---|---|---|
| wheat | **khâo sãa-lii** | ข้าวสาลี |
| salt | **kleua** | เกลือ |
| sugar | **náam taan** | น้ำตาล |

Please don't use MSG.
**karúnaa mâi sài phõng chuu-rót**     กรุณาไม่ใส่ผงชูรส

Don't add egg.
**mâi sài khài**     ไม่ใส่ไข่

## Eating Out
restaurant
**ráan aahãan**     ร้านอาหาร

cheap restaurant
**ráan aahãan**     ร้านอาหารราคาถูก
**raa-khaa thùuk**

Do you speak English?
**phûut phaasãa angkrìt dâi mái?**     พูดภาษาอังกฤษได้ไหม

Table for …, please.
**khãw tò sãmràp … khon**     ขอโต๊ะสำหรับ...คน

**Choosing from the Menu**
Can I see the menu please?
**khãw duu raaikaan**     ขอดูรายการอาหาร
**aahãan dâi mái?**     ได้ไหม

Do you have a menu in English?
**mii raaikaan aahãan**     มีรายการอาหารเ
**pen phaasãa angkrìt mái?**     ป็นภาษาอังกฤษไหม

What does it include?
**maa dûay kàp a-rai bâang?**     เสริฟกับอะไรบ้าง

What do you recommend?
**mii a-rai náe nam?**     มีอะไรแนะนำ

I'd like ...
   khãw ...                                                      ขอ...

Is service included in the bill?
   ruam khâa bawrikaan                                           รวมค่าบริการแ
   láew châi mái?                                                ล้วใช่ไหม

## Taking a Punt
What's the speciality of this region?
   khãwng thîi nîi mii a-rai phí-sèht?                            ของที่นี่มีอะไรพิเศษ

What do you have that's special?
   mii a-rai phí-sèht?                                           มีอะไรพิเศษ

What is that?
   nán a-rai?                                                    นั่นอะไร

What are they eating?
   khon nán thaan a-rai?                                         คนนั้นทานอะไร

I'll try what they're having.
   yàak dâi kàp khâo bàep nán                                    อยากได้กับข้าวแบบนั้น

## Useful Questions
What's in this dish?
   jaan níi sài a-rai?                                           จานนี้ใส่อะไร

Not too spicy please.
   khãw mâi phèt mâak                                            ขอไม่เผ็ดมาก

Is that dish spicy?
   nán phèt mái?                                                 นั่นเผ็ดไหม

(I) don't like it hot and spicy.
   mâi châwp phèt                                                ไม่ชอบเผ็ด

(I) like it hot and spicy.
   châwp phèt                                                    ชอบเผ็ด

It's not hot.
   mâi phèt                                                      ไม่เผ็ด

I didn't order this.
   níi phõm/dì-chãn mâi dâi sàng                                 นี่ผม/ดิฉันไม่ได้สั่ง

Can I have a (beer) please?
   kháw (bia)?                                                   ขอ...(เบียร์)

Do you have a highchair for the baby?
   mii kâo îi dèk mái?                                           มีเก้าอี้เด็กไหม

Anything else?
   a-rai ìik mái?                                                อะไรอีกไหม

| Can you please bring me ...? | khǎw ... dâi mǎi? | ขอ...ได้ไหม |
|---|---|---|
| fish sauce | náam plaa | น้ำปลา |
| fish sauce with chillies | phrík náam plaa | พริกน้ำปลา |
| more beer | bia ìik | เบียร์อีก |
| powdered chilli | phrík pon | พริกป่น |
| sliced lime | má-nao hàn | มะนาวหั่น |
| some salt | kleua nàwy | เกลือหน่อย |
| some water | náam nàwy | น้ำหน่อย |
| some rice | khâo nàwy | ข้าวหน่อย |
| some wine | wain nàwy | ไวน์หน่อย |
| an ashtray | thîi khìi bùrii | ที่เขี่ยบุหรี่ |
| a cup | thûay | ถ้วย |
| a fork | sâwm | ส้อม |
| a glass | kâew | แก้ว |
| a knife | mîit | มีด |
| a napkin | kràdàat chét pàak | กระดาษเช็ดปาก |
| a plate | jaan plào | จานเปล่า |
| a spoon | cháwn | ช้อน |

Thank you, that was delicious.
**khàwp khun mâak, aràwy mâak** ขอบคุณมาก,อร่อยมาก

| This food is ... | aahǎan níi ... | อาหารนี้... |
|---|---|---|
| burnt | mâi koen pai | ไหม้มั้เกินไป |
| cold | yen | เย็น |
| delicious | aràwy | อร่อย |
| flavourful | rót jàt | รสจัด |
| spoiled | bùut/ pen ráa | บูด/เป็นรา |
| stale | mâi sòt | ไม่สด |
| undercooked | mâi sùk | ไม่สุก |
| very oily | man mâak | มันมาก |

Please bring the bill.
**khǎw bin** ขอบิล

## Self-Catering
Where is the nearest (market)?
**(tàlàat) thîi klâi thîi** (ตลาด) ที่ใกล้ที่
**sùt yùu thîi nǎi?** สุดอยู่ที่ไหน

How much?
**thâo rai** เท่าไร

| How much (for) ...? | ... thâo rai? | ...เท่าไร |
|---|---|---|
| both | tháng sǎwng | ทั้งสอง |
| per fruit | lûuk-lá | ลูกละ |
| per piece | chín-lá | ชิ้นละ |
| this | níi | นี้ |

| How much altogether? | | |
|---|---|---|
| **tháng mòt thâo rai?** | | ทั้งหมดเท่าไร |
| Can I have... | **khǎw ...** | ขอ... |
| a bottle | **khùat** | ขวด |
| a box | **klawng** | กล่อง |
| a can | **krà-bāwng** | กระป๋อง |
| a packet | **sawng** | ซอง |
| a bag | **thǔng** | ถุง |

Can I taste it?
   **chim dâi mai?**                                ชิมได้ไหม
What is the local speciality?
   **aahǎan phéun**                              อาหารพื้น
   **meuang kheu a-rai?**                      เมืองคืออะไร
Give me (half) a kilo, please.
   **khǎw (khrêung) kiiloh**                  ขอ(ครึ่ง)กิโล
I'd like (six pieces).
   **khǎw (hòk chín)**                        ขอ(6ชิ้น)
Where can I buy (sugar)?
   **séu (náam taan) dâi thîi nǎi**          ซื้อ(น้ำตาล)ได้ที่ไหน
I'd like to buy ...
   **yàak jà séu ...**                       อยากจะซื้อ...

| Where can I find ...? | **jà séu ... dâi tîi nǎi?** | จะซื้อได้ที่ไหน |
|---|---|---|
| bread | **khanǒm pang** | ขนมปัง |
| butter | **noei** | เนย |
| chillies | **phrík** | พริก |
| coconut milk | **kàthí** | กะทิ |
| curry paste | **khrêuang kaeng** | เครื่องแกง |
| eggs | **khài** | ไข่ |
| fish sauce | **náam plaa** | น้ำปลา |
| fresh vegetables | **phàk sòt** | ผักสด |
| fruit | **phǒn-lá-mái** | ผลไม้ |
| honey | **náam phêung** | น้ำผึ้ง |
| jam | **yaem** | แยม |
| lemongrass | **tàkhrái** | ตะใคร้ |
| milk | **nom jèut** | นมจืด |
| palm sugar | **náam taan pìip** | น้ำตาลปีบ |
| pepper | **phrík thai** | พริกไทย |
| rice | **khâo** | ข้าว |
| salt | **kleua** | เกลือ |
| spices | **khrêuang prung aahǎan** | เครื่องปรุงอาหาร |
| sticky rice | **khâo nǐaw** | ข้าวเหนียว |
| sugar | **náam-taan** | น้ำตาล |
| sweet basil | **bai hǒhráphaa** | ใบโหระพา |
| vegetable oil | **náam man phêut** | น้ำมันพืช |
| yoghurt | **nom prîaw** | นมเปรี้ยว |

Will this keep in the fridge?
**kèp nai tûu yen dâi mái?**                    เก็บในตู้เย็นได้ไหม

How much per (kilo)?
**(kiiloh) lá thâo rai?**                        กิโลละเท่าไร

Do you have anything cheaper?
**mii a-rai thîi thùuk-kwàa mái?**              มีอะไร ที่ถูกกว่าไหม

Is this the best you have?
**níi dii thîi-sùt mái?**                        นี่ดีที่สุดไหม

## At the Bar

What would you like?
**deum a-rai?**                                  ดื่มอะไร

I'll have …
**ao …**                                         เอา

Shall we go for a drink?
**pai kin lâo mái?**                             ไปกินเหล้าไหม

No ice.
**mâi sài náam khãeng**                          ไม่ใส่น้ำแข็ง

Can I have ice, please?
**khãw náam khãeng dâi mái?**                    ขอน้ำแข็งได้ไหม

Same again, please.
**mẽuan doem**                                   เหมือนเดิม

Thanks, but I don't feel like it.
**mâi pen rai, mâi ao,**                         ไม่เป็นไร, ไม่เอา,
**khàwp khun khráp/khá**                          ขอบคุณครับ/ค่ะ

I don't drink (alcohol).
**mâi kin (lâo)**                                 ไม่กิน(เหล้า)

This is hitting the spot.
**dâi thîi láew**                                ได้ที่แล้ว

I'm a bit tired, I'd better get home.
**nèuay láew,**                                  เหนื่อยแล้ว,
**nâa jà klàp bâan**                              น่าจะกลับบ้าน

Where is the toilet?
**hâwng náam yùu thîi nãi?**                     ห้องน้ำอยู่ที่ไหน

Is food available here?
**thîi nîi sàng aahãan dâi mái?**               ที่นี่สั่งอาหารได้ไหม

I'm feeling drunk.
**rúusèuk mao láew**                             รู้สึกเมาแล้ว

I think I've drunk too much.
  khít wâa kin lâo
  mâak koen pai

คิดว่ากินเหล้า
มากเกินไป

I feel ill.
  rúusèuk mâi sabaai

รู้สึกไม่สบาย

I want to throw up.
  yàak jà ûak

อยากจะอ้วก

I'm hung over.
  yang mao

ยังเมา

Excuse me.
  khăw thôht

ขอโทษ

I was here first.
  phŏm/dì-chăn maa kàwn

ผม/ดิฉันมาก่อน

So, do you come here often?
  maa thîi nîi bawy mái?

มาที่นี่บ่อยไหม

I really, really love you.
  rák thoe mâak jang loei

รักเธอมากจังเลย

What did I do last night?
  mêua kheun chan tham a-rai?

เมื่อคืนฉันทำอะไร

| I'll have… | khăw | ขอ… |
|---|---|---|
| a big bottle of beer | bia khùat yài | เบียร์ขวดใหญ่ |
| a bottle of wine | wain khùat nèung | ไวน์ขวดหนึ่ง |
| a glass of beer | bia kâew nèung | เบียร์แก้วหนึ่ง |
| a glass of wine | wain kâew nèung | ไวน์แก้วหนึ่ง |
| a small bottle of beer | bia khùat lék | เบียร์ขวดเล็ก |
| (two) glasses | kâew (săwng) bai | แก้ว(สอง) ใบ |
| 750-ml bottle | klom | กลม |
| 350-ml bottle | baen | แบน |
| Chang beer | bia cháang | เบียร์ช้าง |
| draught beer | bia sòt | เบียร์สด |
| distilled spirits | lâo | เหล้า |
| herbal liquor | lâo yaa dawng | เหล้ายาดอง |
| jungle liquor | lâo theuan | เหล้าเถื่อน |
| (moonshine) | | |
| Mekong & Coke | mâe-khăwng khóhk | แม่โขงโค้ก |
| Mekong whisky | mâe-khăwng | แม่โขง |
| Singha beer | bia sĭng | เบียร์สิงห์ |
| white liquor | lâo khăo | เหล้าขาว |
| (clear, brandless liquors) | | |

## A

| | | |
|---|---|---|
| ambience | banyaakàat | บรรยากาศ |
| angle bean | thùa phuu | ถั่วพู |
| aubergine | mákhĕua | มะเขือ |

## B

| | | |
|---|---|---|
| baby corn | khâo phôht àwn | ข้าวโพดอ่อน |
| baby food (tinned) | aahăan dèk kràpăwng | อาหารเด็กกระป๋อง |
| bake(d) | òp | อบ |
| bag | thŭng | ถุง |
| bamboo shoots | nàw mái | หน่อไม้ |
| banana | klûay | กล้วย |
| banana flower bud | hŭa plii | หัวปลี |
| to bargain well | tàw kèng | ต่อเก่ง |
| basil (sweet) | bai hŏhráphaa | ใบโหระพา |
| bean (angle) | thùa phuu | ถั่วพู |
| bean (long) | thùa fák yao | ถั่วฝักยาว |
| bean pod (twisted cluster) | sà-tàw | สะตอ |
| beef | néua | เนื้อ |
| beer | bia | เบียร์ |
| draught beer | bia sòt | เบียร์สด |
| hill | bin | บิล |
| bitter | khŏm | ขม |
| black bean sauce | tâo jîaw dam | เต้าเจี้ยวดำ |
| black pepper | phrík thai | พริกไทย |
| boiled | tôm | ต้ม |
| boiled water | náam tôm | น้ำต้ม |
| bottle | khùat | ขวด |
| bottle for baby | khùat nom | ขวดนม |
| bottled drinking water | náam dèum khùat | น้ำดื่มขวด |
| bottle gourd | náam tâo | น้ำเต้า |
| bottle opener | thîi pòet khùat | ที่เปิดขวด |
| bowl | chaam | ชาม |
| bread | khanŏm bang | ขนมปัง |
| breakfast | aahăan cháo | อาหารเช้า |
| brown rice | khâo klâwng | ข้าวกล้อง |
| butter | noei | เนย |

## C

| | | |
|---|---|---|
| cabbage (long, white) | phàk kàat khăo plii | ผักกาดขาวปลี |
| cabbage (mustard) | phàk kàat khĭaw | ผักกาดเขียว |
| can opener | thîi pòet kràpăwng | ที่เปิดกระป๋อง |
| capsicum (pepper) | phrík | พริก |
| cardamom | lûuk krà-waan | ลูกกระวาน |
| cashew | mét má-mûang hìmáphaan | เม็ดมะม่วงหิมพานต์ |

| English | Thai (romanized) | Thai |
|---|---|---|
| catfish | plaa dùk | ปลาดุก |
| celery (Chinese) | khêun chàai | ขึ้นฉ่าย |
| cheese | noei khǎeng/chiis | เนยแข็ง/ชีส |
| chicken | kài | ไก่ |
| –fried with chillies | phàt phrík | ผัดพริก |
| –fried with holy basil and chillies | phàt bai kà-phrao | ผัดใบกระเพรา |
| –stew | tǔn | ไก่ตุ๋น |
| –with cashews | phàt mít má-mûang | ไก่ผัดเม็ดมะม่วง |
| –with ginger | phàt khǐng | ไก่ผัดขิง |
| –with mushrooms | phàt hèt | ไก่ผัดเห็ด |
| chilli | phrík | พริก |
| chilli ('mouse-dropping') | phrík khîi nǔu | พริกขี้หนู |
| Chilli Festival (celebrated in Nan Province) | thêhtsakaan phrík | เทศกาลพริก |
| Chinese celery | khêun chàai | ขึ้นฉ่าย |
| Chinese dumplings | khanom jìip | ขนมจีบ |
| Chinese kale | phàk kha-náa | ผักคะน้า |
| Chinese key | krà-chai | กระชาย |
| Chinese New Year | trùt jiin | ตรุษจีน |
| Chinese radish | hǔa chai tháo | หัวไชเท้า |
| chocolate | cháwk-koh-lêht | ช็อกโกเลต |
| chopsticks | tà-kìap | ตะเกียบ |
| cilantro (coriander) | phàk chii | ผักชี |
| cinnamon | òp choei | อบเชย |
| clams & oysters (generic) | hǎwy | หอย |
| cleaver | bang taw | บั้งต |
| to close, closed | pìt | ปิด |
| cockle | hǎwy khraeng | หอยแครง |
| coconut | máphráo | มะพร้าว |
| coconut extract | kà-tí | กะทิ |
| coconut grater | krà-tàai khùut má-phráo | กระต่ายขูดมะพร้าว |
| coffee | kaafae | กาแฟ |
| hot coffee with milk & sugar | kaafae ráwn | กาแฟร้อน |
| iced coffee with sugar, no milk | oh-líang | โอเลี้ยง |
| traditional filtered coffee | kaafae thǔng (ko-píi in Southern Thailand) | กาแฟถุง (โกปี๊) |
| convolvulus (water variety; a herbaceous plant with funnel-shaped flowers) | phàk bûng | ผักบุ้ง |
| cooked/ripe | sùk | สุก |
| cooking pot | mâw | หม้อ |
| coriander leaf | phàk chii | ผักชี |

| | | |
|---|---|---|
| coriander root | râak phàk chii | รากผักชี |
| coriander seed | mét phàk chii | เม็ดผักชี |
| corn | khâo phôht | ข้าวโพด |
| baby corn | khâo phôht àwn | ข้าวโพดอ่อน |
| (to) cost | raakhaa | ราคา |
| cow pea | thùa fàk yao | ถั่วฝักยาว |
| crab | puu | ปู |
| steamed crab | puu nêung | ปูนึ่ง |
| steamed crab claws | kâam puu nêung | ก้ามปูนึ่ง |
| cumin | yîiràa | ยี่หร่า |
| cup | thûay | ถ้วย |
| curry, curried | kaeng | แกง |
| curry paste | khrêuang kaeng | เครื่องแกง |
| curry powder | phŏng kàrìi | ผงกะหรี่ |
| custard (coconut) | sangkha-yaa ma-phráo | สังขยามะพร้าว |
| custard (egg) | mâw kaeng | หม้อแกง |
| custard (Thai) | sangkha-yaa | สังขยา |
| custard-apple | náwy nàa | น้อยหน่า |
| cutting board | khĭang | เขียง |

## D

| | | |
|---|---|---|
| deep-fried dishes | mûat thâwt | หมวดทอด |
| deep-fry | thâwt | ทอด |
| dinner | aahăan yen | อาหารเย็น |
| dipping sauces | náam jîm | น้ำจิ้ม |
| dried, dry | hâeng | แห้ง |
| dried shrimp | kûng hâeng | กุ้งแห้ง |
| to drink | khrêuang dèum; dèum | เครื่องดื่มวดื่ม |
| drunk (inebriated) | mao | เมา |
| duck | pèt | เป็ด |
| duck stew | pèt tŭn | เป็ดตุ๋น |
| dumplings (Chinese) | khanŏm jìip | ขนมจีบ |
| durian | thúrian | ทุเรียน |

## E

| | | |
|---|---|---|
| to eat | thaan khâo (polite) | ทานข้าว |
| | kin khâo (informal) | กินข้าว |
| eel (freshwater) | plaa lăi | ปลาไหล |
| eel (saltwater) | plaa lòt | ปลาหลด |
| egg | khài | ไข่ |
| hard-boiled egg | khài tôm | ไข่ต้ม |
| coddled egg | khài lûak | ไข่ลวก |
| fried egg | khài dao | ไข่ดาว |
| omelette stuffed with vegetables & pork | khài yát sài | ไข่ยัดไส้ |
| plain omelette | khài jiaw | ไข่เจียว |
| scrambled egg | khài kuan | ไข่คน |

| | | |
|---|---|---|
| egg custard | khanŏm mâw kaeng; sāngkhayǎa | ขนมหม้อแกง,สังขยา |
| eggplant | mákhĕua | มะเขือ |
| egg yolk (sweet shredded) | fǎwy thawng | ฝอยทอง |

## F

| | | |
|---|---|---|
| farmer | chao naa | ชาวนา |
| fat (oil) | man | มัน |
| to feel full | ìm | อิ่ม |
| fire | fai | ไฟ |
| fish | plaa | ปลา |
| fish ball soup | kaeng jèut lûuk chín | แกงจืดลูกชิ้น |
| fish cakes | thâwt man plaa | ทอดมันปลา |
| fish sauce | náam plaa | น้ำปลา |
| grilled fish | plaa phao | ปลาเผา |
| ground fish curry | hàw mòk | ห่อหมก |
| steamed fish | plaa nêung | ปลานึ่ง |
| sweet & sour fish | plaa prîaw waan | ปลาเปรี้ยวหวาน |
| whole fish cooked in ginger & chillies | plaa jǐan | ปลาเจี๋ยน |
| flat fried wheat bread | roti | โรตี |
| floating markets | tàlàat náam | ตลาดน้ำ |
| flour | pâeng | แป้ง |
| food | aahǎan | อาหาร |
| food shop or restaurant | ráan aahǎan | ร้านอาหาร |
| fork | sâwm | ส้อม |
| French fries | man faràng thâwt | มันฝรั่งทอด |
| fresh (not stale) | sòt | สุด |
| fresh-squeezed juice | náam khán | น้ำคั้น |
| freshwater eel | plaa lǎi | ปลาไหล |
| fried in large pieces | thâwt | ทอด |
| fried in small pieces/stirfried | phàt | ผัด |
| fried with chilli paste & sweet basil | phàt phèt | ผัดเผ็ด |
| | phàt kràthiam phrík thai | ผัดกระเทียมพริกไทย |
| fried with ginger | phàt khǐng | ผัดขิง |
| frog | kòp | กบ |
| fruit juice | náam phŏn-lá-mái | น้ำผลไม้ |
| full (to feel) | ìm | อิ่ม |

## G

| | | |
|---|---|---|
| galangal, Thai ginger | khàa | ข่า |
| garden | sǔan | สวน |

| garlic | krà-tiam | กระเทียม |
| gas burner | tao káet | เตาแก๊ส |
| giant white radish | hūa phàk kàat | หัวผักกาด |
| ginger | khǐng | ขิง |
| ginger (Thai, galangal) | khàa | ข่า |
| glass | kâew | แก้ว |
| Golden Orange Festival (Nan Province) | thêthsakaan sôm sǐo thawng | เทศกาลส้มสีทอง |
| good | dii | ดี |
| gourd | fák; bùap | ฟัก, บวบ |
| green bean | thùa fàk yao | ถั่วฝักยาว |
| green tea | chaa jiin | ชาจีน |
| grilled (chillies, fish & shrimp) | phǎo | เผา |
| grilled (everything else) | yâang | ย่าง |
| ground peanuts | thùa pòn | ถั่วป่น |
| grouper/reef cod | plaa kāo | ปลาเก๋า |
| guava | faràng | ฝรั่ง |

## H

| ham | haem | แฮม |
| holy basil | bai kà-phrao | ใบกะเพรา |
| honey | náam phêung | น้ำผึ้ง |

## I

| ice | náam khǎeng | น้ำแข็ง |
| ice bucket | thōh | โถ |

## J

| jackfruit | kha-nǔn | ขนุน |
| Japanese eggplant | mákhēua yao | มะเขือยาว |
| … juice | náam … | น้ำ... |
| fresh-squeezed juice | náam khán | น้ำคั้น |
| fruit juice | náam phǒn-lá-mái | น้ำผลไม้ |

## K

| kaffir lime leaf | bai má-krùt | ใบมะกรูด |
| kitchen | hâwng khrua | ห้องครัว |
| knife | mîit | มีด |

## L

| ladies fingers/okra | kràjíap mawn | กระเจี๊ยบมอญ |
| lemongrass | tà-khrái | ตะไคร้ |

| | | |
|---|---|---|
| lettuce | phàk kàat hāwm | ผักกาดหอม |
| lighter | fai chék | ไฟแช็ค |
| lime | má-nao | มะนาว |
| lime juice | náam mánao | น้ำมะนาว |
| lobster | kûng mangkawn | กุ้งมังกร |
| longan fruit | lam yài | ลำใย |
| long bean | thùa fák yao | ถั่วฝักยาว |
| long white cabbage | phàk kàat khāo plii | ผักกาดขาวปลี |
| lunch | aahāan klaang wan | อาหารกลางวัน |

## M

| | | |
|---|---|---|
| mackerel | plaa thuu | ปลาทู |
| mandarin orange | sôm khīaw-wāan | ส้มเขียวหวาน |
| mango | má-mûang | มะม่วง |
| Mango Fair (celebrated in Chiang Mai) | thêhtsakaan má-mûang | เทศกาลมะม่วง |
| mangosteen | mang-khút | มังคุด |
| margarine | noei thiam | เนยเทียม/มาการีน |
| marijuana | kanchaa | กัญชา |
| market | tàlàat | ตลาด |
| appointment market | tàlàat nát | ตลาดนัด |
| early evening market *or* late afternoon market | tàlàat láeng | ตลาดแลง |
| evening market | tàlàat yen | ตลาดเย็น |
| morning market | tàlàat cháo | ตลาดเช้า |
| municipal market | tàlàat thêhtsabaan | ตลาดเทศบาล |
| open until dawn market (from around 11pm or midnight till sunrise) | tàlàat tôh rûng | ตลาดโต้รุ่ง |
| water markets *or* floating markets | tàlàat náam | ตลาดน้ำ |
| matches | mái khìit fai | ไม้ขีดไฟ |
| melon (winter or snake) | fák nguu | ฟักงู |
| menu | raai kaan aahāan | รายการอาหาร |
| milk | nom jèut | นมจืด |
| powdered milk (for baby) | nom phōng | นมผง |
| mint leaf (spearmint) | bai sàránàe | ใบสะระแหน่ |
| more | ìik | อีก |
| mortar | khrók | ครก |
| 'mouse-dropping' chilli | phrík khîi nūu | พริกขี้หนู |
| mung bean sprouts | thùa ngâwk | ถั่วงอก |
| mussel (green) | hāwy malaeng phùu | หอยแมลงภู่ |
| mustard cabbage | phàk kàat khīaw | ผักกาดเขียว |

## N

| | | |
|---|---|---|
| noodles (rice) | kūaytīaw | ก๋วยเตี๋ยว |

## O

| English | Thai (romanized) | Thai |
|---|---|---|
| ocean perch/seabass | plaa kà-phong | ปลากะพง |
| oil | náam man | น้ำมัน |
| okra/ladies fingers | kràjíap mawn | กระเจี๊ยบมอญ |
| omelette | khài jiaw | ไข่เจียว |
| to open, open (adj) | pòet | เปิด |
| orange juice | náam sôm | น้ำส้ม |
| to order | sàng | สั่ง |
| oyster | hāwy naang rom | หอยนางรม |

## P

| English | Thai (romanized) | Thai |
|---|---|---|
| pandan leaf | bai toey | ใบเตย |
| papaya | málákaw | มะละกอ |
| papaya smoothie | náam málákaw pàn | น้ำมะละกอปั่น |
| to pay | jàai | จ่าย |
| pea (cow) | thùa fák yao | ถั่วฝักยาว |
| peanut | thùa lísōng | ถั่วลิสง |
|   fried peanuts | thùa thâwt | ถั่วทอด |
|   ground peanuts | thùa pòn | ถั่วป่น |
| pepper (black) | phrík thai | พริกไทย |
| pepper (capsicum) | phrík | พริก |
| pestle | sàak | สาก |
| piece | chín | ชิ้น |
| pineapple | sàppàrót | สับปะรด |
| pineapple juice (fresh) | náam sàppàrót khán | น้ำสับปะรดคั้น |
| plate | jaan | จาน |
| pomelo | sôm oh | ส้มโอ |
| polygonum (Vietnamese mint) | phàk phai | ผักไผ่ |
| pork | mūu | หมู |
| cooking pot | mâw | หม้อ |
|   claypot used to bake rice & mung bean noodle dishes | mâw din | หม้อดิน |
| pot for preparing sticky rice | mâw khàek | หม้อแขก |
| potatoes | man faràng | มันฝรั่ง |
| prawns | kûng | กุ้ง |
|   batter-fried prawns | kûng chúp | กุ้งชุบแป้งทอด |
|   fried prawns | kûng thâwt | กุ้งทอด |
|   grilled prawns | kûng phao | กุ้งเผา |
|   prawn & lemongrass soup with mushrooms | tôm yam kûng | ต้มยำกุ้ง |
|   prawns stirfried with roasted chillies | kûng phàt phrík phão | กุ้งผัดพริกเผา |
| price | raakhāa | ราคา |

ENGLISH – THAI GLOSSARY

# R

| | | |
|---|---|---|
| radish (Chinese) | hūa chai tháo | หัวไชเท้า |
| radish (giant white) | hūa phàk kàat | หัวผักกาด |
| rambeh fruit; small, reddish-brown, sweet, apricot-like | máfai | มะไฟ |
| rambutan fruit; red, hairy-skinned fruit with grape-like interior | ngáw | เงาะ |
| raw | dìp | ดิบ |
| reef cod or grouper | plaa kāo | ปลาเก๋า |
| restaurant or food shop | ráan aahāan | ร้านอาหาร |
| rice | khâo | ข้าว |
| fried rice with ... | khâo phàt ... | ข้าวผัด... |
| rice noodles | kūaytīaw | ก๋วยเตี๋ยว |
| steamed white rice | khâo sūay | ข้าวสวย |
| sticky rice | khâo nīaw | ข้าวเหนียว |
| white rice | khâo jâo | ข้าวเจ้า |
| roast | yâang | ย่าง |
| rose-apple; fruit; small, apple-like texture, very fragrant | chom-phûu | ชมพู่ |
| roti (flat bread) | roti | โรตี |

# S

| | | |
|---|---|---|
| salad (hot & tangy) | yam | ยำ |
| salt | kleua | เกลือ |
| saltwater eel | plaa lòt | ปลาหลด |
| salty | khēm | เค็ม |
| sapodilla fruit | lámút | ละมุด |
| sardine | plaa saa-diin | ปลาซาร์ดีน |
| satay | sà-té | สะเต๊ะ |
| beef | néua | สะเต๊ะเนื้อ |
| chicken | kài | สะเต๊ะหมู |
| pork | mūu | สะเต๊ะหมู |
| sauce | náam râat aahāan | น้ำราดอาหาร |
| sausage | sâi kràwk | ไส้กรอก |
| scallions | tôn hāwm | ต้นหอม |
| seabass | plaa kà-phong | ปลากะพง |
| seafood | aahāan tháleh | อาหารทะเล |
| to sell | khāai | ขาย |
| sesame | ngaa | งา |
| shallot | hāwm daeng | หอมแดง |
| shark fin soup | hūu chalaam | หูฉลาม |
| shiitake | hèt hāwm | เห็ดหอม |

| shop | ráan | ร้าน |
|---|---|---|
| food shop | ráan aahǎan | ร้านอาหาร |
| food-to-order shop | ráan aahǎan taam sàng | ร้านอาหารตามสั่ง |
| rice soup shop | ráan khâo tôm | ร้านข้าวต้ม |
| noodle shop | ráan kǔaytǐaw | ร้านก่วยเตี๋ยว |
| rice & curry shop | ráan khâo kaeng | ร้านข้าวแกง |
| sundries shop | ráan khǎwng cham | ร้านของชำ |
| sundries shop on water | reua khǎwng cham | เรือของชำ |
| vegetarian restaurant | ráan aahǎan mangsàwírát | ร้านอาหารมังสวิรัติ |
| shrimp | kûng | กุ้ง |
| sieve | krà-chawn | กระชอน |
| smoothie (papaya) | náam málákaw pàn | น้ำมะละกอปั่น |
| snake gourd | bùap nguu | บวบงู |
| snow peas | thùa lan-tao | ถั่วลันเตา |
| soda water | náam sohdaa | น้ำโซดา |
| soup | kaeng jèut | แกงจืด |
| soup stock | náam súp | น้ำซุป |
| chicken stew | kài tǔn | ไก่ตุ๋น |
| duck stew | pèt tǔn | เป็ดตุ๋น |
| fish ball soup | kaeng jèut lûuk chín | แกงจืดลูกชิ้น |
| mild soup with vegetables & pork | kaeng jèut | แกงจืด |
| mild soup with vegetables, pork & bean curd | kaeng jèut tâo-hûu | แกงจืดเต้าหู้ |
| prawn & lemongrass soup with mushrooms | tôm yam kûng | ต้มยำกุ้ง |
| rice soup with ... | khâo tôm ... | ข้าวต้ม... |
| chicken | kài | ไก่ |
| fish | plaa | ปลา |
| shrimp | kûng | กุ้ง |
| soup with chicken, galanga root & coconut | tôm khàa kài | ต้มข่าไก่ |
| soybean | thùa lěuang | ถั่วเหลือง |
| soy sauce | náam sii-yú | น้ำซีอิ๊ว |
| spatula | phai | พาย |
| spearmint (mint leaf) | bai sàránàe | ใบสะระแหน่ |
| special | phí-sèht | พิเศษ |
| spicy | phèt | เผ็ด |
| spinach (water variety) | phàk bûng | ผักบุ้ง |
| spiny lobster | kûng mangkawn | กุ้งมังกร |
| spoon | cháwn | ช้อน |
| spring onions | tôn hǎwm | ต้นหอม |
| spring rolls (fresh) | paw pía sòt | ปอเปยะสด |
| spring rolls (fried) | paw pía thâwt | ปอเปยะทอด |

| | | |
|---|---|---|
| squash | fák; bùap | ฟัก, บวบ |
| squid | plaa mèuk | ปลาหมึก |
| squid stirfried with chillies & basil | plaa mèuk phàt phèt | ปลาหมึกผัดเผ็ด |
| staple | aahāan làk | อาหารหลัก |
| steamed (fish & rice only) | nêung | นึ่ง |
| sticky rice | khâo nīaw | ข้าวเหนียว |
| stirfried dishes | mùat phàt | หมวดผัด |
| stirfry | phàt | ผัด |
| stock | náam súp | น้ำซุป |
| straw mushrooms | hèt faang | เห็ดฟาง |
| sugar | náamtaan | น้ำตาล |
| sugar pea | thùa lan-tao | ถั่วลันเตา |
| sweet | wāan | หวาน |
| sweet basil | bai hōhráphaa | ใบโหระพา |
| sweet shredded egg yolk | fāwy thawng | ฝอยทอง |
| sweet stuff | khāwng wāan | ของหวาน |

## T

| | | |
|---|---|---|
| tamarind | ma-khāam | มะขาม |
| tasty (very) | aràwy mâak | อร่อยมาก |
| tea | chaa | ชา |
| Chinese green tea | chaa jiin | ชาจีน |
| hot Thai tea with milk & sugar | chaa ráwn | ชาร้อน |
| hot Thai tea with sugar | chaa dam ráwn | ชาดำร้อน |
| iced Thai tea with milk & sugar | chaa yen | ชาเย็น |
| iced Thai tea with sugar only | chaa dam yen | ชาดำเย็น |
| weak Chinese tea | náam chaa | น้ำชา |
| to be thirsty | hīw náam | หิวน้ำ |
| tilapia (fish) | plaa nin | ปลานิล |
| tinned (canned) baby food | aahāan dèk kràpāwng | อาหารเด็กกระป๋อง |
| tin opener | thîi pòet kràpāwng | ที่เปิดกระป๋อง |
| tip (gratuity) | khâa bawríkaan (khâa thíp) | ค่าบริการ |
| tobacco | yaa sùup | ยาสูบ |
| tofu | tâo-hûu | เต้าหู้ |
| toilet | sûam | ส้วม |
| toilet paper | kràdàat cham-rá | กระดาษชำระ |
| tomatoes | mákhēua-thêht | มะเขือเทศ |
| toothpaste | yaa sī fan | ยาสีฟัน |
| torch ginger | kà-laa | กาหลา |
| turmeric | kha-mîn | ขมิ้น |
| twisted cluster bean pod | sà-tàw | สะตอ |

## V

| | | |
|---|---|---|
| vegetable oil | náam man phêut | น้ำมันพืช |
| vegetables | phàk | ผัก |
| Vegetarian Festival | thêhtsakaan kin jeh | เทศกาลกินเจ |
| vegetarian food | aahǎan mangsàwírát | อาหารมังสวิรัติ |
| very tasty | aràwy mâak | อร่อยมาก |
| Vietnamese mint | phàk phai | ผักไผ่ |
| vinegar | náam sôm sǎai chuu | น้ำส้มสายชู |
|   vinegar with chillies | phrík náam sôm | พริกน้ำส้ม |

## W

| | | |
|---|---|---|
| to want (something) | yàak dâi | อยากได้ |
| water | náam | น้ำ |
|   boiled water | náam tôm | น้ำต้ม |
|   bottle | khùat | ขวด |
|   bottled drinking water | náam dèum khùat | น้ำ |
|   Chinese tea | chaa jiin | ชาจีน |
|   cold water | náam yen | น้ำเย็น |
|   plain water | náam plào | น้ำเปล่า |
|   soda water | náam soh-daa | น้ำโซดา |
| water convolvulus | phàk bûng | ผักบุ้ง |
| watercress | phàk kàat náam | ผักกาดน้ำ |
| watermelon | taeng moh | แตงโม |
| water spinach | phàk bûng | ผักบุ้ง |
| wheat bread, flat | roti | โรตี |
| where? | thîi nǎi? | ที่ไหน |
| wheat noodles | bà-mìi | บะหมี่ |
| white cabbage | phàk kàat khǎo plii | ผักกาดขาวปลี |
| white rice | khâo jâo | ข้าวเจ้า |
| whole, all | tháng mòt | ทั้งหมด |
| wine | wain | ไวน์ |
|   red wine | wain daeng | ไวน์แดง |
|   white wine | wain khǎo | ไวน์ขาว |
| winter or snake melon | fák nguu | ฟักงู |
| wok | krà-thá | กระทะ |
| wonton | kíaw | เกหยว |
|   fried wonton | kíaw kràwp | เกหยวกรอบ |
|   wonton soup | kíaw náam | เกหยวน้ำ |
|   wonton soup with | bà-mìi kíaw | บะหมี่เกหยว |
|     egg noodles | | |

## Y

| | | |
|---|---|---|
| yard-long bean | thùa fák yao | ถั่วฝักยาว |
| yoghurt | nom prîaw | นมเปรี้ยว |

## Thai Culinary Dictionary

The Thai alphabet consists of 44 consonants and 32 vowels. Thai words and sentences are written from left to right, though vowel signs may be written before, above, below, around *and/or* after consonants, depending on the letter. Lists of Thai words are alphabetised phonetically, in the order in which letters are pronounced, rather than in the order in which they are written.

# ก

กบ
  kòp frog, used as food in Northern and North-Eastern Thailand

กระเจี๊ยบมอญ
  kràjíap mawn okra

กระชอน
  krà-chawn sieve

กระชอนมะนาว
  krà-chawn má-nao a double-handled sieve used for squeezing juice from halved limes

กระชาย
  krà-chai Chinese key, a root in the ginger family used as a traditional remedy for a number of gastrointestinal ailments

กระดาษชำระ
  kràdàat cham-rá tissue

กระติ๊บข้าว
  krà-típ khâo lidded baskets of woven reed or bamboo for serving sticky rice

กระต่ายขูดมะพร้าว
  krà-tàai khùut má-phráo (*see* maew khùut má-phráo)

กระทะ
  krà-thá wok

กระเทียม
  krà-thiam garlic

กระยาสารท
  kràyaasàat a rice and peanut sweet, popular at certain Buddhist festivals

กรัม
  kram gram

กลม
  klom 750ml bottle (for whisky)

กล้วย
  klûay banana

กล้วยไข่
  klûay khài 'egg banana'; native to Kamphaeng Phet

กล้วยทอด
  klûay thâwt batter-fried banana

กล้วยน้ำว้า
  klûay náam wáa a thick-bodied, medium-length banana

กล้วยบวดชี
  klûay bùat chii 'bananas ordaining as nuns'; banana chunks floating in a

| ก | ข | ค | ง | จ | ฉ | ช | ซ | ฌ | ญ | ฎ | ฏ | ฐ | ฑ | ฒ | ณ | ด | ต | ถ | ท |
|---|---|---|---|---|---|---|---|---|---|---|---|---|---|---|---|---|---|---|---|
| k | k/h | kh | ng | j | ch | ch | s | ch | y | d | t | th | th | th | n | d | t | th | th |

white syrup of sweetened and slightly salted coconut milk

**กล้วยเล็บมือนาง**
klûay lép meu naang, 'princess fingernail banana'; native to Chumphon Province in Southern Thailand

**กล้วยหอม**
klûay hǎwm 'fragrant banana'

**กล่องข้าว**
kawng khâo Northern Thai for krà-típ khâo (baskets for serving sticky rice)

**กล้า**
klâa rice sprouts

**ก๋วยจั๊บ**
kǔay jáp a thick broth of sliced Chinese mushrooms and bits of chicken or pork

**ก๋วยเตี๋ยว**
kǔay tǐaw rice noodles, made from pure rice flour mixed with water to form a paste which is then steamed to form wide, flat sheets

**ก๋วยเตี๋ยวจันทบูรณ์**
kǔay tǐaw chanthabun dried rice noodles from Chantaburi province

**ก๋วยเตี๋ยวน้ำ**
kǔay tǐaw náam rice noodles served in a bowl of plain chicken or beef stock along with bits of meat and pickled cabbage, and a garnish of coriander leaf

**ก๋วยเตี๋ยวผัด**
kǔay tǐaw phàt fried rice noodles with sliced meat (usually pork or chicken, occasionally beef), Chinese **kale**, soy sauce and various seasonings, a favourite crowd-pleaser at

temple festivals all over the country.

**ก๋วยเตี๋ยวผัดขี้เมา**
kǔay tǐaw phàt khîi mao 'drunkard's fried noodles'; wide rice noodles, fresh basil leaves, chicken or pork, seasonings and a healthy dose of fresh sliced chillies

**ก๋วยเตี๋ยวผัดไทย**
kǔay tǐaw phàt thai a plate of thin rice noodles stirfried with dried or fresh shrimp, beansprouts, fried tofu, egg and seasonings (phàt thai for short)

**ก๋วยเตี๋ยวราดหน้า**
kǔay tǐaw râat nâa noodles braised in a light gravy made with cornstarch-thickened stock, then combined with either pork or chicken, as well as Chinese broccoli or Chinese kale and oyster sauce

**ก๋วยเตี๋ยวราดหน้าทะเล**
kǔaytǐaw râat nâa tháleh kǔaytǐaw râat nâa with seafood

**ก๋วยเตี๋ยวเรือ**
kǔaytǐaw reua 'boat noodles'; a concoction of dark beef broth and rice noodles originally sold only on boats that frequented the canals of Rangsit

**ก๋วยเตี๋ยวลูกชิ้นปลา**
kǔay tǐaw lûuk chín plaa rice noodles with fishballs

**ก๋วยเตี๋ยวเส้นจันทน์**
kǔay tǐaw sên jan local name for rice noodles in Chanthburi

**ก๋วยเตี๋ยวแห้ง**
kǔay tǐaw hâeng dry kǔay tǐaw

**ก๋วยเตี๋ยวแห้งสุโขทัย**
kǔay tǐaw hâeng sùkhōthai Sukothai

ธ น บ ป ผ ฝ พ ฟ ภ ม ย ร ล ว ศ ษ ส ห ฬ อ ฮ
th n b p ph f ph f ph m y r l w s s s h l aw h

dry rice noodles; thin rice noodles served in a bowl with peanuts, barbecued pork, ground dried chilli, green beans and bean sprouts

ก้อย
**kâwy** raw **lâap**

ก้อยวัว
**kâwy wua** beef **kâwy** or raw beef **lâap**

กะทิ
**kà-thí** coconut milk

กะปิ
**kà-pì** shrimp paste

กะหรี่
**kàrìi** Thai version of the Anglo-Indian term 'curry'

ก๊ก
**kák** 188ml bottle (for whisky, etc)

กัญชา
**kanchaa** marijuana

กับข้าว
**kàp khâo** any dish eaten with rice

กับแกล้ม
**kàp klâem** drinking food, dishes specifically meant to be eaten while drinking alcoholic beverages

กาแฟ
**kaafae** coffee

กาแฟดำ
**kaafae dam** black coffee with sugar

กาแฟดำไม่ใส่น้ำตาล
**kaafae dam mâi sài náamtaan** black coffee without sugar

กาแฟต้ม
**kaafae tôm** 'boiled coffee' usually made using a modern coffeemaker

กาแฟถุง
**kaafae thǔng** 'bag coffee'; traditional filtered coffee with condensed milk & sugar

กาแฟร้อน
**kaafae ráwn** hot coffee with condensed milk & sugar

กาแล
**kalae** carved wooden 'X' motif which adorns house gables in Northern Thailand

กาหลา
**kaa-lǎa** torch ginger; thin-sliced flower buds from a wild ginger, sometimes used in the Southern Thai rice salad **khâo yam**

กิ้งก่า
**kîng-kàa** an iguana-type lizard used as food in Isaan

กินข้าว
**kin khâo** 'consume rice'; eat

กินใจ
**kin jai** 'eat heart'; expression for being impressed by something or someone

กินบุญ
**kin bun** when one eats food prepared for any religious occasion, one is said to kin bun, 'eat merit'

กิโล
**kii-lôh** kilogram

กุ้ง
**kûng** refers to a variety of different shrimps, prawns and lobsters

กุ้งกุลาดำ
**kûng kùlaa dam** tiger prawn

| ก | ข | ค | ง | จ | ฉ | ช | ซ | ฌ | ญ | ฎ | ฏ | ฐ | ฑ | ฒ | ณ | ด | ต | ถ | ท |
|---|---|---|---|---|---|---|---|---|---|---|---|---|---|---|---|---|---|---|---|
| k | k/h | kh | ng | j | ch | ch | s | ch | y | d | t | th | th | th | n | d | t | th | th |

กุ้งชุบแป้งทอด
**kûng chúp pâeng thâwt** batter-fried shrimp

กุ้งผัดขิง
**kûng phàt khǐng** prawns stirfried in ginger

กุ้งผัดสะตอ
**kûng phàt sà-tàw** sà-tàw (beans) stirfried with chillies, shrimp and shrimp paste. A Southern Thai dish.

กุ้งมังกร
**kûng mangkawn** 'dragon prawn'; refers to lobster

เกลือ
**kleua** salt

เกี๊ยว
**kíaw** won-ton, a triangle of bà-mìi dough wrapped around ground pork or ground fish

เกี๊ยวทอด
**kíaw thâwt** fried kíaw

แกง
**kaeng** the classic chilli-based curries for which Thai cuisine is famous, as well as any dish with a lot of liquid (thus it can refer to soups). The word may also be used as a verb meaning 'to make a kaeng'.

แกงกะหรี่ไก่
**kaeng kàrìi kài** similar to an Indian curry, containing potatoes and chicken

แกงกาหยู
**kaeng kaa-yûu** curry made with fresh cashews, popular in Phuket and Ranong; also known as **kaeng mét má-mûang hìmáphaan** in Central Thai

แกงขนุน
**kaeng kha-nǔn** jackfruit curry, favoured in Northern Thailand but found elsewhere as well

แกงเขียวหวาน
**kaeng khǐaw-wǎan** green curry

แกงคั่วส้มสัปปะรด
**kaeng khûa sôm sàpàrót** pan-roasted pineapple curry with sea crab

แกงแค
**kaeng khae** famous Northern Thai soup made with 'sawtooth coriander' and bitter eggplant

แกงจืด
**kaeng jèut** 'bland soup'; plain Cantonese-influenced soup in which cubes of soft tofu, green squash, Chinese radish, bitter gourd, ground pork and mung bean noodles are common ingredients

แกงจืดวุ้นเส้น
**kaeng jèut wún sên** mung bean noodle soup, **kaeng jèut** with **wún sên**

แกงไตปลา
**kaeng tai plaa** Southern Thai curry made with fish stomach, green beans, pickled bamboo shoots and potatoes

แกงป่า
**kaeng pàa** 'forest curry'; a spicy curry which uses no coconut milk

แกงผักหวาน
**kaeng phàk waan** Northern soup with 'sweet greens'

แกงผักฮ้วน
**kaeng phàk hèuan** Northern Thai soup containing tamarind juice

| ธ | น | บ | ป | ผ | ฝ | พ | ฟ | ภ | ม | ย | ร | ล | ว | ศ | ษ | ส | ห | ฬ | อ | ฮ |
|---|---|---|---|---|---|---|---|---|---|---|---|---|---|---|---|---|---|---|---|---|
| th | n | b | p | ph | f | ph | f | ph | m | y | r | l | w | s | s | s | h | l | aw | h |

แกงเผ็ด
  **kaeng phèt** 'hot curry' or red curry

แกงเผ็ดเป็ดย่าง
  **kaeng phèt pèt yâang** duck roasted Chinese-style in five-spice seasoning and mixed into Thai red curry

แกงพะแนง
  **kaeng phánaeng** similar to regular red curry but thicker, milder and without vegetables

แกงมอญ
  **kaeng mawn** Mon curry

แกงเม็ดมะม่วงหิมพานต์
  **kaeng mét má-mûang hìmáphaan** curry made with fresh cashews; *(see* **kaeng kaa-yūu***)*

แกงมัสมั่น
  **kaeng mátsàman** Indian-influenced Muslim curry featuring cumin, cinnamon and cardamom

แกงราดข้าว
  **kaeng râat khâo** curry over rice

แกงเลียง
  **kaeng liang** spicy soup of green or black peppercorns rather than chillies, sponge gourd, baby corn, cauliflower and various greens, substantiated with pieces of chicken, shrimp or ground pork. Probably one of the oldest recipes in Thailand.

แกงส้ม
  **kaeng sôm** a soupy, salty, sweet & sour curry made with dried chillies, shallots, garlic and Chinese key pestled with salt, **kà-pì** and fish sauce

แกงหยวก
  **kaeng yùak** a Northern Thai curry featuring banana palm heart and jackfruit

แกงเหลือง
  **kaeng lēuang** literally, yellow curry; a spicy Southern Thai dish of fish cooked with green squash, pineapple, green beans and green papaya

แกงฮังเล
  **kaeng hangleh** a rich Burmese-style curry with no coconut milk; a Northern Thai speciality

แกงโฮ๊ะ
  **kaeng hó** spicy Northern Thai soup featuring pickled bamboo shoots

แก้ว
  **kâew** glass

แก้วเปล่า
  **kâew plào** plain glass

โกปี๊
  **kopíi** Hokkien dialect for coffee, used especially in Trang Province

โกปี๊ดำ
  **kopíi dam** sweetened black coffee, in Trang

โกปี๊ดำไม่ใส่น้ำตาล
  **kopíi dam, mâi sài náamtaan** black coffee, no sugar, in Trang

ไก่
  **kài** chicken

ไก่ตุ๋น
  **kài tūn** steamed chicken soup generally featuring a broth darkened by soy sauce and spices such as cinnamon, star anise or Chinese five-spice mixtures. Cabbage or beansprouts give the soup some crunch, while Chinese celery provides fragrance.

ไก่ทอด
  **kài thâwt** fried chicken

THAI CULINARY DICTIONARY

| ก | ข | ค | ง | จ | ฉ | ช | ซ | ฌ | ญ | ฎ | ฏ | ฐ | ฑ | ฒ | ณ | ด | ต | ถ | ท |
|---|---|---|---|---|---|---|---|---|---|---|---|---|---|---|---|---|---|---|---|
| k | k/h | kh | ng | j | ch | ch | s | ch | y | d | t | th | th | th | n | d | t | th | th |

250

ไก่เบตง
kài betong Betong dish of steamed chicken, chopped and seasoned with locally made soy sauce, stirfried with **phàk náam** (green vegetable)

ไก่ปิ้ง
kai pîng (*see* **kài yâang**)

ไก่ผัดขิง
kài phàt phrík khīng chicken stirfried with ginger, garlic and chillies, seasoned with fish sauce

ไก่ผัดเม็ดมะม่วงหิมพานต์
kài phàt mét má-mûang hìmáphaan sliced chicken stirfried in dried chillies and cashews

ไก่ย่าง
kài yâang Isaan-style grilled chicken; **pîng kai** or **kai pîng** in Isaan dialect, refers to the Isaan method of rubbing chickens in a marinade of garlic, coriander root, black pepper and salt or fish sauce before cooking them slowly over hot coals

ไก่สามอย่าง
kài sāam yàang 'three kinds of chicken'; chicken, chopped ginger, peanuts, chilli peppers and bits of lime to be mixed and eaten by hand

ไก่ห่อใบเตย
kài hàw bai toey chicken marinated in soy sauce and wrapped in pandan leaves along with sesame oil, garlic and coriander root, then fried or grilled and served with a dipping sauce similar to the marinade

## บ

ขนม
khanōm Thai sweets

ขนมครก
khanōm khrók a slightly salted and slightly sweetened mixture of coconut milk and rice flour poured into half-round dimples in a large, round iron grill

ขนมจีน
khanōm jiin 'Chinese Pastry', rice noodles produced by pushing rice flour paste through a sieve into boiling water, served on a plate and doused with various curries. In the North-East the noodles are sauced with a ground fish curry, and mixed with ground pork, coconut milk, lemongrass and a milder dose of chillies. Also known by its Lao name, **kháo pûn**.

ขนมจีนชาวน้ำ
khanōm jiin sao náam noodle dish featuring a mixture of pineapple, coconut, dried shrimp, ginger and garlic served with khanōm jiin

ขนมจีนทอดมัน
khanōm jiin thâwt man thin rice noodles with fried fish cake from Phetchaburi

ขนมจีนน้ำเงี้ยว
khanōm jiin náam ngíaw a sweet and spicy Yunnanese noodle dish with pork rib meat, tomatoes and black-bean sauce fried with a curry paste of chillies, coriander root, lemongrass, galangal, turmeric, shallots, garlic and shrimp paste

ขนมจีนน้ำยา
khanōm jiin náam yaa thin Chinese rice noodles doused in a Malay-style ground fish curry sauce served with fresh cucumbers, steamed long green beans, parboiled mung bean sprouts,

| ธ | น | บ | ป | ผ | ฝ | พ | ฟ | ภ | ม | ย | ร | ล | ว | ศ | ษ | ส | ห | อ | ฮ |
|---|---|---|---|---|---|---|---|---|---|---|---|---|---|---|---|---|---|---|---|
| th | n | b | p | ph | f | ph | f | ph | m | y | r | l | w | s | s | s | h | aw | h |

grated papaya, pickled cabbage and fresh pineapple chunks. A Southern Thai speciality.

ขนมจีบ
**khanǒm jìip** shrimp or pork filled Chinese dumplings

ขนมถ้วย
**khanǒm thûay** sweet made from tapioca flour and coconut milk steamed in tiny porcelain cups

ขนมเทียน
**khanǒm thian** 'candle pastry'; a mixture of rice or corn flour, sweetened coconut milk and sesame seeds, steamed in a tall slender banana leaf packet

ขนมเบื้อง
**khanǒm bêuang** Vietnamese vegetable crepe prepared in a wok

ขนมเปาลั้ง
**khanǒm pao láng** mix of black sticky rice, shrimp, coconut, black pepper and chilli steamed in a banana leaf packet, favoured by Thai Muslims in Ao Phang-Nga

ขนมหม้อแกง
**khanǒm mâw kaeng** a double-layered baked custard from Phetchaburi, made with pureed mung beans, eggs, coconut milk and sugar. There are many local variations on this popular dessert, including versions that insert fresh durian or lotus seeds.

ขนุน
**kha-nǔn** jackfruit; also known as **màak mìi** in Isaan dialect

ขม
**khǒm** bitter

ขมิ้น
**kha-mîn** turmeric, popular in Southern Thai cooking

ขวด
**khùat** bottle

ขวดเล็ก
**khùat lék** 330ml bottle (beer)

ขวดใหญ่
**khùat yài** 660ml bottle (beer)

ของ คาว
**kawng khâo** a cylindrical woven basket used to hold sticky rice

ของ ชำ
**khǎwng cham** refers to sundries like vegetable oil, fish sauce, sugar, soy sauce, salt, coffee, dried noodles, canned food, rice, curry paste, eggs, liquor and cigarettes

ของ หวาน
**khǎwng wǎan** 'sweet stuff'; refers to all foods whose primary flavour characteristic is sweetness

ขัน
**khǎn** small lidded serving bowls

ขัน โตก
**khan tòhk** low round dining table in Northern Thailand; also refers to ceremonial dinners in which attendees sit on the floor around a low, round cane (or lacquerware) table, eating Northern Thai dishes from small plates and bowls while watching musical and dance performances – a staple of the tourist industry in Chiang Mai.

ข่า
**khàa** galangal; also known as Thai ginger

ขาย
**khāai** sell

ข้าว

**khâo** rice

ข้าวแกง

**khâo kaeng** curry over rice

ข้าวกลาง

**khâo klaang** 'middle rice'; rice that matures mid-season

ข้าวกล่ำ

**khâo klam** a type of sticky rice with a deep purple, almost black hue, for use in desserts and, in Northern Thailand, to produce a mild home-made rice wine of the same name

ข้าวกล้อง
**khâo klâwng** brown rice

ข้าวเกรียบกุ้ง
**khâo krìap kûng** shrimp chips

ข้าวคั่วปน

**khâo khûa pòn** uncooked rice that has been dry-roasted in a pan till it begins to brown, then is pulverised with a mortar and pestle; one of the most important ingredients in **lâap**

ข้าวเจ้า
**khâo jâo** white rice

ข้าวแช่

**khâo châe** soupy rice eaten with small bowls of assorted foods

ข้าวแช่เพชรบุรี

**khâo châe phêtburii** moist chilled rice served with sweetmeats, a hot season Mon speciality

ข้าวซอย

**khâo sawy** a Shan or Yunnanese egg-noodle dish with chicken or beef curry, served with small saucers of shallot wedges, sweet-spicy pickled cabbage, lime and a thick red chilli sauce, popular in Northern Thailand

ข้าวต้ม

**khâo tôm** boiled rice soup, a popular late-night meal

ข้าวต้มกะทิ

**khâo tôm kà-thí** khanōm made of sticky rice, coconut milk and grated coconut wrapped in a banana leaf

ข้าวต้มมัด

**khâo tôm mát** khanōm made of sticky rice and coconut milk, black-beans or banana pieces wrapped in a banana leaf

ข้าวต้นฤดู
**khâo tôn rá-duu** early season rice

ข้าวนาปี
**khâo naa pii** one-field-per-year rice

ข้าวนาปรัง
**khâo naa prang** off-season rice

ข้าวเบา
**khâo bao** 'light rice'; early season rice

ข้าวเปล่า
**khâo plào** plain rice

ข้าวประดับดิน

**khâo pràdàp din** 'earth-adorning rice' small lumps of rice left as offerings at the base of temple stupas or beneath banyan trees during Buddhist festivals

ข้าวปุ้น

**khâo pûn** Lao/Isaan term for **khanōm jiin**

ข้าวผัด
**khâo phàt** fried rice

| ธ | น | บ | ป | ผ | ฝ | พ | ฟ | ภ | ม | ย | ร | ล | ว | ศ | ษ | ส | ห | อ | ฮ |
|---|---|---|---|---|---|---|---|---|---|---|---|---|---|---|---|---|---|---|---|
| th | n | b | p | ph | f | ph | f | ph | m | y | r | l | w | s | s | s | h | aw | h |

**THAI CULINARY DICTIONARY**

ข้าวผัดใบกะเพรา
**khâo phàt bai kà-phrao** chicken or pork stirfry served over rice

ข้าวโพด
**khâo phôht** corn

ข้าวโพดอ่อน
**khâo phôht àwn** baby corn measuring 8-10cm

ข้าวมันไก่
**khâo man kài** Hainanese dish of sliced steamed chicken over rice cooked in chicken broth and garlic

ข้าวยำ
**khâo yam** rice salad of cooked dry rice, grated toasted coconut, bean sprouts, kaffir lime leaves, lemongrass and dried shrimp, with powdered chilli and lime on the side. A traditional Southern Thai breakfast.

ข้าวราดแกง
**khâo râat kaeng** curry over rice

ข้าวไร่
**khâo râi** plantation rice or mountain rice

ข้าวสวย
**khâo sŭay** cooked rice, literally 'beautiful rice'

ข้าวสาร
**khâo sãan** unmilled rice

ข้าวหนัก
**khâo nàk** 'heavy rice'; late rice

ข้าวเหนียว
**khâo nĭaw** sticky rice that is popular in Northern and North-Eastern Thailand. Many Thai dishes from these regions are always served with khâo nĭaw, which is eaten with the fingers rather than with a fork and spoon.

ข้าวเหนียวมะม่วง
**khâo nĭaw má-mûang** sliced fresh ripe mangoes served with sticky rice sweetened with coconut milk.

ข้าวหมกไก่
**khâo mòk kài** Southern version of chicken biryani; rice and chicken cooked together with clove, cinnamon and turmeric, served with a bowl of plain chicken broth, a roasted chilli sauce and a saucer of sliced cucumbers mixed with vinegar, sugar and a few sliced red chillies

ข้าวหมูแดง
**khâo mŭu daeng** red pork over rice

ข้าวหลาม
**khâo lãam** sticky rice and coconut steamed in a bamboo joint, a Nakhon Pathom speciality

ข้าวหอมมะลิ
**khâo hãwm málí** fragrant jasmine rice

ขิง
**khĭng** ginger, as known in the west

ขึ้นฉ่าย
**khêun chàai** Chinese celery

เขียง
**khĭang** flat, circular cutting board made of dense tamarind wood about 5cm thick

ไข่
**khài** egg

ไข่เจียว
**khài jiaw** a Thai omelette, popular and offered as a side dish or filler for a multidish meal. The Central Thai method of cooking this dish is to mix the beaten eggs with a little water and

| ก | ข | ค | ง | จ | ฉ | ช | ซ | ฌ | ญ | ฎ | ฏ | ฐ | ฑ | ฒ | ณ | ด | ต | ถ | ท |
|---|---|---|---|---|---|---|---|---|---|---|---|---|---|---|---|---|---|---|---|
| k | k/h | kh | ng | j | ch | ch | s | ch | y | d | t | th | th | th | n | d | t | th | th |

lime juice, then drop the mixture into a very hot wok containing a couple centimetres of cooking oil.

**ไข่ปิ้ง**
khài pîng eggs in their shells skewered on a sharp piece of bamboo and grilled over hot coals

**ไข่ปลาหมก**
khài plaa mòk Southern dish of egg, fish and red curry paste steamed in a banana-leaf cup and topped with strips of kaffir lime leaves

**ไข่ผัดเห็ดหูหนู**
khài phàt hèt hǔu nǔu eggs stirfried with mouse-ear mushrooms

**ไข่ผัม**
khài phǎm a small, green plant that grows on the surface of ponds, bogs and other still waters, eaten in Isaan; similar to spirulina, extremely high in protein, vitamins and minerals

**ไข่มดแดง**
khài mót daeng red ant larvae; used in soups in the North-East

**ไข่ยัดไส้**
khài yát sài an omelette wrapped around a filling of fried ground pork, tomatoes, onions and chillies

# ค

**คนเมือง**
khon meuang 'city-state people', a euphemism for Chiang Mai natives

**คนอีสาน**
khon isǎan North-Eastern Thai people

**ครก**
khrók small stone mortar

**ครกดิน**
khrók din large earthen mortar

**ครกไม้**
khrók mái large wooden mortar

**ความเป็นไทย**
khwaam pen thai 'being Thai'; or Thai-ness

**เค็ม**
khēm salty

**เครื่องแกง**
khrêuang kaeng curry paste created by mashing, pounding and grinding an array of ingredients with a stone mortar and pestle to form an aromatic, extremely pungent-tasting and rather thick paste; also known as **náam phrík kaeng**

**เครื่องแกงเผ็ด**
khrêuang kaeng phèt red **khrêuang kaeng** made with dried red chillies

**เครื่องดื่ม**
khrêuang dèum beverage; drink (n)

**เครื่องถม**
khrêuang thǒm a silver and black alloy/enamel jewellery technique borrowed from China many centuries ago; nielloware

**แคน**
khaen a reed instrument with two long rows of bamboo pipes strung together; indigenous to Isaan and Laos

# ง

**งานบวช**
ngaan bùat Buddhist monastic ordination ceremony; also **banpaja**

ธ น บ ป ผ ฝ พ ฟ ภ ม ย ร ล ว ศ ษ ส ห อ ฮ

thn b p ph f ph f ph m y r l w s s s h l aw h

งานวัด
ngaan wát temple fair

เงาะ
ngáw rambutan

# จ

จังหวัด
jangwàat province

จัด
jàt rich or strong in flavour

จาน
jaan plate

จานเดียว
jaan diaw 'one plate' meal

จ่าย
jàai pay (v)

จืด
jèut plain, bland

เจ้าที่
jâo thîi 'place lord'; the presiding spirit of any house or building site

เจ้าเมือง
jâo meuang city-state chieftains

แจ่ว
jàew a thick and spicy Isaan chilli sauce; also known as náam jàew

แจ่วฮ้อน
jaew hâwn Isaan version of Central Thailand's popular Thai sukiyaki, but includes mung bean noodles, thin-sliced beef, beef entrails, egg, water spinach, cabbage and cherry tomatoes as ingredients

โจ๊ก
jóhk thick rice soup or congee

โจ๊กไก่
jóhk kài thick rice soup with chicken

โจ๊กหมู
jóhk mǔu thick rice soup with pork meatballs

# ช

ชนบท
chonábòt the most rural Thai countryside

ชมพู่
chom-phûu rose-apple

ช้อน
cháwn spoon

ช้อนโต๊ะ
cháwn tó tablespoon

ชะอม
cha-om a bitter acacia leaf

ชา
chaa tea

ชาขิง
chaa khǐng an infusion of ginger and hot water sweetened with sugar or honey, a popular herbal tea

ชาจีน
chaa jiin Chinese tea

ชาดำเย็น
chaa dam yen chilled chaa thai with sugar, and sometimes lime, also known as chaa dam yen sài má-nao

ชาดำร้อน
chaa dam ráwn hot chaa thai with sugar

ชามะนาว
chaa má-nao chilled black tea with sugar and lime

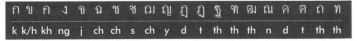

ชาเย็น
chaa yen a tall glass of iced **chaa thai** sweetened with sugar and condensed milk in which the milk is added last to create a thick, cloud-like layer on top of the tea

ชาร้อน
chaa ráwn hot **chaa thai** with sugar and condensed milk

ชาไทย
chaa thai tamarind-seasoned tea

ชาวนา
chao naa farmer

ชาวเล
chao leh sea gypsies

ชาวเหนือ
chao nēua Northern Thais

ชิ้น
chín piece

ชุด
chút 'set' of ice, halved limes, mixers and rice whisky

## ซ

ซอย
soi lane

ซาลาเปา
salabao steamed buns filled with stewed pork or sweet bean paste

ซาวน้ำ
sao náam a sauce of pineapple, dried shrimp, coconut, ginger and garlic used as a topping for **khanōm jiin** (rice noodles)

ซีอิ๊วขาว
sii-íw khāo 'white soy'; a light soy sauce

ซีอิ๊วดำ
sii-íw dam 'black soy'; a heavy dark soy sauce

ซุปขนุน
súp kha-nūn see **súp màak mìi**

ซุปขนุน
súp màak mìi jackfruit soup with **khâo khûa pòn**, lime juice and chilli, an Isaan speciality; also known as **súp kha-nūn**

ซุปมะเขือ
súp má-khēua eggplant soup with **khâo khûa pòn**, lime juice and chilli, an Isaan speciality

ซุปหน่อไม้
súp nàw mái literally, bamboo shoot soup; boiled or pickled bamboo shoots with khâo khûa pòn, lime juice and chilli, an Isaan speciality

แซบอีหลี
sâep ii-līi 'very tasty' in North-Eastern dialect

## ด

ดิบ
dìp raw

ดื่ม
dèum to drink

เด็ก
dèk child

เด็กครัว
dèk khrua child cook (for women)

## ต

ต้นกล้วย
tôn klûay cross-section of the heart of the banana stalk or tree

| ธ | น | บ | ป | ผ | ฝ | พ | ฟ | ภ | ม | ย | ร | ล | ว | ศ | ษ | ส | ห | อ | ฮ |
|---|---|---|---|---|---|---|---|---|---|---|---|---|---|---|---|---|---|---|---|
| th | n | b | p | ph | f | ph | f | ph | m | y | r | l | w | s | s | s | h | aw | h |

ต้นตาล
    tôn taan sugar palm, grown mostly in Phetburi Province

ต้นหอม
    tôn hāwm 'fragrant plant'; spring onion or scallions

ต้ม
    tôm Isaan soup similar to **tôm yam** made with lemongrass, galangal, spring onions, kaffir lime leaves and fresh whole **phrík khîi nũu**, seasoned before serving with lime juice and fish sauce; also known as **tôm sâep**

ต้มไก่ใส่ใบมะขามอ่อน
    tôm kài sài bai má-khāam àwn Isaan **tôm** made with chicken and tamarind leaves

ต้มข่าไก่
    tôm khàa kài literally 'boiled galangal chicken'; often translated as 'chicken coconut soup'; includes lime, chilli and coconut milk. A Central Thai dish.

ต้มแซ่บ
    tôm sâep see tôm

ต้มเปรี้ยว
    tôm prîaw 'boiled sour'; **tôm yam** soup with added tamarind

ต้มฟัก
    tôm fák Isaan tôm made with green squash, often eaten with duck **lâap** (salad)

ต้มยำ
    tôm yam soup made with chilli, lemongrass, lime and usually seafood

ต้มยำกุ้ง
    tôm yam kûng shrimp **tôm yam**

ต้มยำโป๊ะแตก
    **tôm yam** pó tàek
    **tôm yam** with mixed seafood

ต้มยำแห้ง
    tôm yam hâeng a dry version of **tôm yam kûng**

ต้มวัว
    tôm wua Isaan **tôm** made with beef tripe and liver

ตลาด
    tàlàat market

ตลาดเช้า
    tàlàat cháo 'morning market'

ตลาดโต้รุ่ง
    tàlàat tôh rûng 'open until dawn market' usually open from around 11pm or midnight till sunrise

ตลาดเทศบาล
    tàlàat thêhtsabaan municipal market

ตลาดนัด
    tàlàat nát 'appointment market'

ตลาดน้ำ
    tàlàat náam 'water markets' or floating markets

ตลาดเย็น
    tàlàat yen evening market

ตลาดแลง
    tàlàat láeng 'early evening market' or 'late afternoon market'

ต่อเก่ง
    tàw kèng to bargain well

ตะกรับ
    tà-kràp a clay grate used to hold the fuel inside a cooking pot, also known as a **rang phêung**

ตะเกียบ
    tà-kìap chopsticks

ก ข ค ง จ ฉ ช ซ ฌ ญ ฎ ฏ ฐ ฑ ฒ ณ ด ต ถ ท
k k/h kh ng j ch ch s ch y d t th th th n d t th th

ตะโก้
    **tà-kôh** popular steamed sweet made from tapioca flour and coconut milk over a layer of sweetened seaweed gelatine

ตะใคร้
    **tà-khrái** lemongrass, used in curry paste, **tôm yam**, **yam** and certain kinds of **lâap**

ตัว
    **tua** body or unit, eg per chicken or per fish

ตำรับกับข้าว
    **tamráp kàp khâo** literally 'formula with rice'; basic handed-down recipes

ตำส้ม
    **tamsôm** (*see* **sômtam**)

ตำหมากหุ่ง
    **tam màak hûng** (*see* **sômtam**)

ตืบข้าว
    **típ khâo** Isaan for **krà-típ khâo** (baskets for serving rice)

ตรุษจีน
    **trùt jiin** Chinese New Year

ตุ๊กแก
    **túk-kae** gecko, used as food in Isaan

เตาแก๊ส
    **tao káet** gas burner

เตาไฟ
    **tao fai** 'fire stove'; a thick-walled firepot made from clay mixed with sand, rice husk and ashes

เต้าเจี้ยว
    **tâo jîaw** paste of salted, fermented soybeans. There are two kinds of **tâo jîaw**, one yellow, one black.

เต้าเจี้ยวดำ
    **tâo jîaw dam** black-bean sauce

เต้าหู้
    **tâo-hûu** tofu

แตงโม
    **taeng moh** watermelon

โตก
    **tòhk** a low, round dining table made of lacquered wood or woven bamboo traditional to Northern Thailand

ไตรรัตน์
    **triratana** 'triple gems' of the Buddhist faith, the Buddha, the Dhamma and the Sangha

# ถ

ถ้วย
    **thûay** cup

ถั่วงอก
    **thùa ngâwk** mung bean sprouts

ถั่วทอด
    **thùa thâwt** fried peanuts

ถั่วป่น
    **thùa pon** ground peanuts

ถั่วฝักยาว
    **thùa fàk yao** long bean, yard bean, green bean, or cow pea

ถั่วพู
    **thùa phuu** angle bean; a long green, bean-like vegetable which when cut into cross sections produces a four-pointed star

ถั่วลันเตา
    **thùa lan-tao** snow peas

ถั่วลิสง
    **thùa lísŏng** peanut

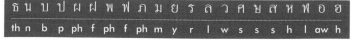

| ธ น | บ | ป | ผ | ฝ | พ | ฟ | ภ | ม | ย | ร | ล | ว | ศ | ษ | ส | ห | ฬ | อ | ฮ |
|------|---|---|---|---|---|---|---|---|---|---|---|---|---|---|---|---|---|---|---|
| th n | b | p | ph | f | ph | f | ph | m | y | r | l | w | s | s | s | h | l | aw | h |

ถั่วเหลือง
thùa lĕuang soybean

ถุง
thŭng bag

ถุงกาแฟ
thŭng kaafae a cone-shaped cloth bag fastened to a steel handle used for making filtered coffee

โถ
thŏh large lidded bowl/ice bucket

# ท

ทอด
thâwt deep fry

ทอดมันกุ้ง
thâwt man kûng fried shrimp cake

ทอดมันปลา
thâwt man plaa fried fishcake

ทับทิมกรอบ
tháp thim kràwp 'crisp rubies'; red-dyed chunks of fresh water chestnut in a white syrup of sweetened and slightly salted coconut milk

ทานข้าว
thaan khâo to eat (polite)

ทิพรส
Thiparot 'Divine Taste'; a famous brand of bottled fish sauce

ทุเรียน
thúrian durian

เทศกาลกินเจ
thêhtsakaan kin jeh Vegetarian Festival (celebrated by the Chinese community in certain parts of Thailand)

เทศกาลพริก
thêhtsakaan phrík Chilli Festival (celebrated in Nan Province)

เทศกาลมะม่วง
thêhtsakaan má-mûang Mango Fair (celebrated in Chiang Mai)

เทศกาลส้มสีทอง
thêhtsakaan sôm sĭi thawng Golden Orange Festival (celebrated in Nan Province during the orange harvest)

ไทยปักษ์ใต้
thai pàk tâi the Southern Thais

# น

นมจืด
nom jèut milk

น้อยหน่า
náwy nàa custard-apple

น้ำ
náam water or juice

น้ำกระเจี๊ยบ
náam krà-jíap a red-tinted beverage from the roselle fruit, which boasts a long list of health-enhancing properties. Can be rendered as a tea. (chaa) if brewed with hot water.

น้ำกลั่น
náam khán fresh-squeezed juice

น้ำแข็ง
náam khăeng ice

น้ำแข็งกด
náam khăeng kòt frozen sweets made with ice, sugar, and a little fruit juice

น้ำแข็งเปล่า
náam khăeng plào plain ice

น้ำแข็งใส
náam khăeng săi desserts with ice

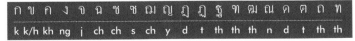

ก ข ค ง จ ฉ ช ซ ฌ ญ ฎ ฏ ฐ ฑ ฒ ณ ด ต ถ ท
k k/h kh ng j ch ch s ch y d t th th th n d t th th

น้ำเคย
**náam khoei** a sauce consisting of palm sugar, raw cane sugar, shrimp paste, fish sauce, salt, black pepper, shallots, galangal, karrir lime leaves and lemongrass, used with **khâo yam** (rice salad); a Southern Thai speciality

น้ำเงี้ยว
**náam ngíaw** a sweet and spicy topping for **khanŏm jiin**, common in far Northern Thailand

น้ำจิ้ม
**náam jîm** dipping sauces

น้ำจิ้มไก่
**náam jîm kài** chicken dipping sauce, a mixture of dried red chilli flakes, honey (or sugar) and rice vinegar

น้ำจิ้มอาหารทะเล
**náam jîm aahăan tháleh** seafood dipping sauce, **phrík náam plaa** (chilli in fish sauce) with the addition of minced garlic, lime juice & sugar

น้ำแจ่ว
**náam jàew** Isaan dipping sauce for chicken, made by pounding dried red chilli flakes with shallots, shrimp paste and a little tamarind juice to make a thick jam-like sauce; also known as **jàew**

น้ำชา
**náam chaa** weak Chinese tea, usually free in restaurants

น้ำซีอิ๊ว
**náam sii-yú** soy sauce

น้ำซุป
**náam súp** stock

น้ำโซดา
**náam sohdaa** soda water

น้ำดื่ม
**náam dèum** drinking water

น้ำดื่มขวด
**náam dèum khùat** bottled drinking water

น้ำต้ม
**náam tôm** boiled water

น้ำตาล
**náam taan** plain white sugar

น้ำตาลปี๊บ
**náamtaan pìip** soft, light palm sugar paste. The most raw form of palm sugar.

น้ำตาลสด
**náam taan sòt** sugar palm juice

น้ำเต้า
**náam tâo** bottle gourd

น้ำเต้าหู้
**náam tâo-hûu** soy milk

น้ำแตงโม
**náam taeng moh** watermelon juice

น้ำปู
**náam puu** Northern Thai condiment made by pounding small field crabs into a paste and then cooking the paste in water until it becomes a slightly sticky black liquid; **nâam pūu** in Northern Thai dialect

น้ำปู๋
**náam pūu** (see **náam puu**)

น้ำปั่น
**náam pon** fruit blended with ice; fruit smoothie

น้ำปลา
**náam plaa** fish sauce, a thin, clear, amber sauce made from fermented anchovies and used to salt Thai

| ธ | น | บ | ป | ผ | ฝ | พ | ฟ | ภ | ม | ย | ร | ล | ว | ศ | ษ | ส | ห | ฬ | อ | ฮ |
|---|---|---|---|---|---|---|---|---|---|---|---|---|---|---|---|---|---|---|---|---|
| th | n | b | p | ph | f | ph | f | ph | m | y | r | l | w | s | s | s | h | l | aw | h |

**THAI CULINARY DICTIONARY**

dishes (much as soy sauce is used in East Asia)

น้ำเปล่า
náam plào plain water

น้ำผลไม้
náam phǒn-lá-mái fruit juice

น้ำพริก
náam phrík a thick chilli and shrimp paste dip usually eaten with fresh raw or steamed vegetables/a spicy-sweet peanut sauce used as a topping for **khanǒm jiin** (rice noodles)

น้ำพริกกะปิ
náam phrík kà-pì náam phrík made with shrimp paste and fresh **phrík khîi nǔu** ('mouse dropping' chilli), usually eaten with **plaa thuu** (mackerel) that has been steamed and fried, or fried **plaa châwn** (serpent-headed fish, a freshwater variety). A Central Thai dish.

น้ำพริกแกง
náam phrík kaeng (see **khrêuang kaeng**)

น้ำพริกข่า
náam phrík khàa Northern Thai chilli dip made with galangal; often served with steamed or roasted fresh mushrooms

น้ำพริกชี้ฟ้า
náam phrík chíi fáa an Isaan dipping sauce featuring dried chilli, garlic oil, salt and sugar, often cooked briefly to blend all the flavours and darken the chilli

น้ำพริกตาแดง
náam phrík taa daeng 'red eye chilli dip'; very dry and hot

น้ำพริกน้ำปู
náam phrík náam puu Northern Thai chilli paste made with **náam puu**, shallots, garlic and dried chillies

น้ำพริกเผา
náam phrík phǎo a thick paste made with dried chillies roasted together with kà-pì and then mortar-blended with fish sauce and a little sugar or honey; often eaten with **kài yâang**

น้ำพริกศรีราชา
náam phrík sǐi raachaa a thick, orange, salty-sweet-sour-spicy bottled chilli sauce from Si Racha (south-east of Bangkok on the Gulf of Thailand)

น้ำพริกหนุ่ม
náam phrík nùm Northern Thai 'young chilli paste' dip made of fresh green chillies and roasted eggplant

น้ำพริกอ่อง
náam phrík àwng Northern Thai chilli paste made by pounding dried red chillies, ground pork, tomatoes, lemongrass and various herbs, then cooking them till the pork is done

น้ำมะขาม
náam mákhǎam tamarind juice

น้ำมะตูม
náam má-tuum an amber drink from the bale fruit, which boasts a long list of health-enhancing properties. Can be rendered as a tea (**chaa**).

น้ำมะพร้าวอ่อน
náam má-phráo àwn juice of a young, green coconut

น้ำมะละกอปั่น
náam málákaw pàn papaya smoothie

น้ำเมี่ยง
náam mîang a ginger, shallot, shrimp paste, fish sauce and honey dip eaten with mîang kham

น้ำยา
náam yaa standard curry topping for khanŏm jiin, which roughly translates as 'herbal sauce'. Ingredients include Chinese key and ground or pounded fish.

น้ำเย็น
náam yen cold water

น้ำร้อน
náam ráwn hot water

น้ำสับปะรดคั้น
náam sàppàrót khán fresh-squeezed pineapple juice

น้ำส้ม
náam sôm orange juice

น้ำส้มพริก
náam sôm phrík sliced green chillies in vinegar

น้ำส้มสายชู
náam sôm sãai chuu vinegar

น้ำอ้อย
náam âwy raw, lumpy cane sugar/sugar cane juice

นึ่ง
nêung steamed

นึ่งข้าว
nêung khâo the task of cooking khâo nĭaw or sticky rice. The uncooked rice must be soaked in cold water overnight or for at least three hours. The rice is then drained and rinsed thoroughly, and placed in a hùat. The narrow end of the hùat is then fitted into the neck of a rounded mâw khàek filled with boiling water and the rice is left to steam for around 30 minutes.

นึ่งปลา
nêung plaa freshwater fish steamed with Thai lemon basil, lemongrass and any other vegetables. The fish is served with some of the water it is steamed in. An Isaan speciality.

เนื้อ
néua beef

เนื้อตุ๋น
néua tŭn steamed beef soup generally featuring a broth darkened by soy sauce and spices such as cinnamon, star anise or Chinese five-spice mixtures. Cabbage or beansprouts give the soup some crunch, while Chinese celery provides fragrance.

เนื้อน้ำตก
néua náam tòk 'waterfall beef'; sliced barbecued beef in a savoury dressing of lime juice, ground chilli and other seasonings popular in the North-East

เนื้อผัดน้ำมันหอย
néua phàt náam-man hãwy beef stir-fried in oyster sauce, a Chinese dish popular in Central Thailand

## บ

บรรพชา
banpaja Buddhist monastic ordination ceremony; also ngaan bùat

บรรยากาศ
banyaakàat ambience

บวบ
bùap gourd

บวบเหลี่ยม
bùap liam sponge gourd

บวบงู
bùap nguu snake gourd

บะหมี่
bà-mìi a yellowish noodle about
1.5mm in diameter made from wheat
flour and sometimes egg

บะหมี่เกี๊ยวปู
bà-mìi kíaw puu a soup containing
**bà-mìi**, won-ton and crab meat

บะหมี่น้ำ
bà-mìi náam bà-mìi with broth,
meat, seafood or vegetables

บะหมี่แห้ง
bà-mìi hâeng bà-mìi served in a bowl
with a little garlic oil, meat, seafood
or vegetables and no liquid

บังตอ
bang taw cleaver

บัวลอย
bua láwy 'floating lotus'; boiled
sticky rice dumplings in a white
syrup of sweetened and slightly salted
coconut milk

บิณฑบาตร
bintàbàat the Theravada Buddhist
'alms round' in which monks receive
food from devotees

บุญ
bun religious merit

เบียร์
bia beer

เบียร์สด
bia sòt 'fresh beer'; draught beer

แบน
baen 375ml bottle (for whisky)

ใบกะเพรา
bai kà-phrao holy basil, called such
due to its sacred status in India. Has
darker leaves and a sharper flavour
than **bai hōhráphaa**

ใบชะพลู
bai chá-phluu wild tea leaf

ใบตอง
bai tawng banana leaves

ใบเตย
bai toey pandan leaves, used primarily to add a vanilla-like flavour to Thai
sweets

ใบมะกรูด
bai ma-krùt kaffir lime leaves

ใบแมงลัก
bai maeng-lák also called Thai basil,
lemon basil or mint basil. Has smaller,
smoother leaves and more delicate
stems than those of sweet basil.
Popular in soups and as a condiment
to **khanōm jiin náam yaa** (rice noodles) and **lâap** (spicy meat salad).

ใบสะระแหน่
bai sá-rá-nàe native spearmint leaves
used in yam and **lâap** and eaten raw
in North-Eastern Thailand

ใบโหระพา
bai hōhráphaa 'sweet basil'; a hardy,
large-leafed plant similar to the basil
found in Italian cuisine. Used in
certain **kaeng** (curries), seafood
dishes and especially **phàt phèt** (hot
stirfries).

# ป

ปอเปี๊ยะ
paw pía egg rolls

| ก | ข | ค | ง | จ | ฉ | ช | ซ | ฌ | ญ | ฎ | ฏ | ฐ | ฑ | ฒ | ณ | ด | ต | ถ | ท |
|---|---|---|---|---|---|---|---|---|---|---|---|---|---|---|---|---|---|---|---|
| k | k/h | kh | ng | j | ch | ch | s | ch | y | d | t | th | th | th | n | d | t | th | th |

ปอเปี๊ยะทอด
paw pía thâwt fried spring rolls

ปอเปี๊ยะสด
paw pía sòt fresh spring rolls

ปลา
plaa fish

ปลากระบอก
plaa krà-bàwk mullet

ปลากะตัก
plaa kà-tàk a type of anchovy used in náam plaa(fish sauce)

ปลากะพง
plaa kà-phong seabass or ocean perch

ปลาเก๋า
plaa kǎo grouper or reef cod

ปลาคลุกขมิ้น
plaa khlúk kha-mîn fresh fish rubbed with a paste of turmeric, garlic and salt before grilling or frying, popular in Southern Thailand

ปลาเค็ม
plaa khem preserved salted fish

ปลาจะละเม็ด
plaa jà-lá-mét pomfret

ปลาช่อน
plaa châwn serpent-headed fish, a freshwater variety

ปลาซาร์ดีน
plaa saa-diin sardine

ปลาดุก
plaa dùk catfish

ปลาแดก
plaa dàek see plaa ráa

ปลาแดดเดียว
plaa tàet diaw half-day dried fish, fried and served with a spicy mango salad

ปลาทอด
plaa thâwt fried fish

ปลาท่องโก๋
paa-thâwng kǒh fried wheat pastry, similar to an unsweetened doughnut and very similar to the Mandarin *youtiao*; often dipped in warm soy milk

ปลาทู
plaa thuu mackerel

ปลานิล
plaa nin tilapia (fish)

ปลาบึก
plaa bèuk giant Mekong catfish

ปลาเผา
plaa phǎo fish wrapped in banana leaves or foil and roasted over (or covered in) hot coals

ปลาร้า
plaa ráa (literally 'rotten fish') an unpasteurised version of náam plaa sold in earthenware jars in North-Eastern Thailand; also known as **pàa dàek**

ปลาสำลี
plaa sǎmlii cottonfish

ปลาสำลีเผา
plaa sǎmlii phǎo fire-roasted cotton-fish

ปลาสำลีแดดเดียว
plaa sǎmlii tàet dìaw 'half-day-dried cottonfish'; a Hua Hin and Prachuap Khiri Khan speciality; whole cotton-fish sliced lengthways and left to dry in the sun for half a day, then fried quickly in a wok. The sun-drying evaporates excess water and oil, and firms up the flesh to produce a

THAI CULINARY DICTIONARY

| ธ | น | บ | ป | ผ | ฝ | พ | ฟ | ภ | ม | ย | ร | ล | ว | ศ | ษ | ส | ห | ฬ | อ | ฮ |
|---|---|---|---|---|---|---|---|---|---|---|---|---|---|---|---|---|---|---|---|---|
| th | n | b | p | ph | f | ph | f | ph | m | y | r | l | w | s | s | s | h | l | aw | h |

toothsome texture. It's always served with spicy mango salad

ปลาหลด
**plaa lòt** saltwater eel

ปลาหมึก
**plaa mèuk** squid; cuttlefish (generic)

ปลาหมึกกระดอง
**plaa mèuk kradawng** cuttlefish

ปลาหมึกกล้วย
**plaa mèuk klûay** squid

ปลาหมึกปิ้ง
**plaa mèuk pîng** dried, roasted squid flattened into a sheet via a hand-cranked press then toasted over hot coals, a favourite night time street vendor snack

ปลาหมึกผัดผงกะหรี่
**plaa mèuk phàt phŏng kà-rìi** squid stirfried in curry powder

ปลาไหล
**plaa lăi** freshwater eel

ปลูกข้าว
**plùuk khâo** to plant rice

ปักษ์ใต้
**Pak Tai** the general term for Southern Thailand

ปิ้งไก่
**pîng kai** Isaan-style grilled chicken; (*see* **kài yâang**)

ปิด
**pìt** to close, closed (adj)

ปู
**puu** crab

ปูทะเล
**puu thaleh** sea crab

ปูนา
**puu naa** field crabs

ปูผัดผงกะหรี่
**puu phàt phŏng kà-rìi** cracked crab in the shell stirfried in curry powder and eggs

ปูอบวุ้นเส้น
**puu òp wún sên** bean thread noodles baked in a lidded, clay pot with crab and seasonings

เป็ด
**pèt** duck

เป็ดตุ๋น
**pèt tŭn** steamed duck soup generally featuring a broth darkened by soy sauce and spices such as cinnamon, star anise or Chinese five-spice mixtures. Cabbage or beansprouts give the soup some crunch, while Chinese celery provides fragrance.

เป็ดย่าง
**pèt yâang** roast duck

เปิด
**pòet** to open, open (adj)

โปงลาง
**ponglang** xylophone-like instrument made of short wooden logs, native to Isaan

โป๊ะแตก
**pó tàek** 'broken fishtrap' soup, **tôm yam** with the addition of either sweet or holy basil and a melange of seafood, usually including squid, crab, fish, mussels and shrimp

# ผ

ผงกะหรี่
**phŏng kàrìi** international 'curry powder'

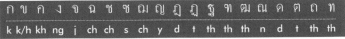

| ก | ข | ค | ง | จ | ฉ | ช | ซ | ฌ | ญ | ฎ | ฏ | ฐ | ฑ | ฒ | ณ | ด | ต | ถ | ท |
|---|---|---|---|---|---|---|---|---|---|---|---|---|---|---|---|---|---|---|---|
| k | k/h | kh | ng | j | ch | ch | s | ch | y | d | t | th | th | th | n | d | t | th | th |

ผงชูรส
**phŏng chuu rót** MSG (monosodium glutamate)

ผลไม้
**phŏn-lá-mái** lit, 'fruit of the tree'; fruit

ผลไม้แช่อิ่ม
**phŏn-lá-mái cháe im** preserved fruit made by drying, salting, pickling or candying the fruit. Also known as '**cháe im**'.

ผัก
**phàk** vegetables

ผักกาดขาวปลี
**phàk kàat khăo plii** long white cabbage

ผักกาดเขียว
**phàk kàat khĭaw** mustard cabbage

ผักกาดน้ำ
**phàk kàat náam** watercress

ผักกาดหอม
**phàk kàat hāwm** lettuce

ผักคะน้า
**phàk kha-náa** Chinese kale

ผักชี
**phàk chii** coriander leaf

ผักชีฝรั่ง
**phàk chii faràng** a strong parsley-like leaf known in English as 'sawtooth coriander'

ผักดอง
**phàk dawng** slightly sour pickled vegetables made by filling a bucket with the leftover starch-filled water used to rinse white rice and soaking cabbage leaves for a few days. An interaction between the rice starch and the fresh vegetables invokes a yeasting process. Used to perk up noodle soups of all kinds.

ผักน้ำ
**phàk náam** a green vegetable grown in creeks, and very high in vitamins and minerals

ผักบุ้ง
**phàk bûng** vine-like plant known as water spinach, water morning glory, water hyacinth, water convolvulus and swamp cabbage

ผักบุ้งไฟแดง
**phàk bûng fai daeng** literally 'red fire water spinach'; water spinach, sliced chillies, black-bean sauce and mashed garlic cloves, and stirfried in a wok of vegetable oil or bacon fat

ผักบุ้งลอยฟ้า
**phàk bûng láwy fáa** 'sky-floating water spinach' or 'flying vegetable'; popular in night markets. A cook fires up a batch of **phàk bûng fai daeng** in the wok and then, by swinging the wok by one handle, flings the **phàk bûng** across the market area to a waiting server who catches it on a plate.

ผักไผ่
**phàk phai** polygonum, or Vietnamese mint

ผัด
**phàt** stirfry

ผัดกระเทียม
**phàt krà-tiam** garlic-fried, a Central Thai cooking style

ผัดกระเทียมพริกไทย
**phàt krà-thiam phrík thai** a stirfry of chicken, pork, beef or shrimp with black pepper and garlic

ผ

ผัดฉ่า
  phàt chàa 'sizzling fried'; a seafood
  stirfry with chillies and ginger

ผัดไทย
  phàt thai stirfried noodles Thai style;
  see kǔaytǐaw phàt thai

ผัดใบกะเพรา
  phàt bai kà-phrao a stirfry of chicken
  or pork with holy basil, garlic and
  fresh sliced chillies, seasoned with soy
  sauce and fish sauce

ผัดผักคะน้า
  phàt phàk kha-ná Chinese kale
  stirfried with black-bean sauce

ผัดผักรวม
  phàt phàk ruam stirfried mixed
  vegetables

ผัดเผ็ด
  phàt phèt 'hot stirfry'; made without
  coconut milk, main ingredients are
  quickly stirfried with red curry paste
  and tossed with sweet basil leaves
  before serving; most often applied to
  seafood or freshwater fish, a Central
  Thai cooking style

ผัดพริกไทยกระเทียม
  phàt phrík thai krà-thiam stirfried
  chicken, pork, beef or shrimp with
  black pepper and garlic

ผัดวุ้นเส้น
  phàt wún sên Northern Thai dish
  featuring mung bean noodles stirfried
  with nǎem (fermented sausage) and
  eggs

ผัดสะตอ
  phàt sà-tàw stirfired sà-tàw (beans)
  with chillies and shrimp paste

ผ้าขาวม้า
  phâakhāmāa a short cotton sarong
  with chequered patterns, worn by
  men

ผ้าซิ่น
  phâa sîn a long cotton sarong with
  small printed patterns, worn by rural
  Thai women

ผี
  phǐi spirits

เผ็ด
  phèt spicy

เผา
  phǎo grilled (chillies, vegetables, fish
  & shrimp only)

เผือกทอด
  phêuak thâwt batter-fried taro

ฝ

ฝรั่ง
  faràng westerner of European
  descent/guava

ฝอยทอง
  fǎwy thawng 'golden threads'; a small
  bundle of sweetened egg-yolk threads
  in Thai desserts

เฝอ
  fǒe Isaan dialect for kǔaytǐaw (rice
  noodles)

พ

พรรษา
  phansǎa the annual three-month
  rains retreat, roughly from late July to
  late October, when many Thai
  Buddhists give up drinking alcohol as
  a show of faith

| ก | ข | ค | ง | จ | ฉ | ช | ซ | ฌ | ญ | ฎ | ฏ | ฐ | ฑ | ฒ | ณ | ด | ต | ถ | ท |
|---|---|---|---|---|---|---|---|---|---|---|---|---|---|---|---|---|---|---|---|
| k | k/h | kh | ng | j | ch | ch | s | ch | y | d | t | th | th | th | n | d | t | th | th |

พระภูมิ
**phrá phum** earth spirits

พริก
**phrík** chilli

พริกขี้หนู
**phrík khîi nūu** 'mouse-dropping' chilli also known as bird's eye chilli, the hottest chilli in Thailand

พริกขี้หนูสวน
**phrík khîi nūu sūan** 'farm' **phrík khîi nūu**

พริกชี้ฟ้า
**phrík chíi fáa** literally 'sky pointing chilli'; also known as spur chilli, Thai chilli and Japanese chilli

พริกไทย
**phrík thai** black pepper; also known as Thai pepper

พริกน้ำปลา
**phrík náam plaa** a standard condiment of sliced fresh red and green **phrík khîi nūu** (chilli) floating in náam plaa or fish sauce; found on nearly every Thai table

พริกน้ำส้ม
**phrík náam sôm** young **phrík yùak** pickled in vinegar, a condiment popular with noodle dishes and Chinese food

พริกปน
**phrík pon** dried red chilli (usually **phrík chíi fáa**), flaked or ground to a near powder

พริกหยวก
**phrík yùak** banana-stalk chilli, a large-size chilli usually cooked or pickled

พริกหวาน
**phrík wāan** 'sweet'; green bell pepper, not spicy

พริกแห้ง
**phrík hâeng** dried chilli

พริกใหญ่
**phrík yài** a large chilli native to Nan Province

พ่อครู
**phâw khruu** male guru or teacher; a term with shamanic undertones

พาย
**phai** 'oar'; a spatula with a curved edge

พิณ
**phin**, a type of small three-stringed lute played with a large plectrum, native to Isaan

พิธีมงคล
**phí-thii mongkhon** blessing ceremony

พิเศษ
**phí-sèht** special

เพลงเพื่อชีวิต
**phleng phêua chiiwít** 'songs for life'; modern Thai folk music with socially conscious lyrics and traditional Thai musical motifs

แพอาหาร
**phae aahāan** 'food raft'; a floating restaurant moored to the bank

## ฟ

ฟัก
**fák** gourd or squash

ฟักเขียว
**fák khīaw** wax gourd

| ธ น | บ | ป | ผ | ฝ | พ | ฟ | ภ | ม | ย | ร | ล | ว | ศ | ษ | ส | ห | ฬ | อ | ฮ |
|---|---|---|---|---|---|---|---|---|---|---|---|---|---|---|---|---|---|---|---|
| th n | b | p | ph | f | ph | f | ph | m | y | r | l | w | s | s | s | h | l | aw | h |

ฟักงู
fák nguu snake or winter melon

ฟักทอง
fák thawng golden squash or Thai pumpkin, similar to the bright orange pumpkin popular in the UK and US except it's smaller and has a mottled, slightly striped shell

# ภ

ภาคกลาง
phâak klaang literally 'central region'; Central Thailand

โภชนา
phochánaa a Thai-Sanskrit term meaning 'meals'; but used in Thai to mean 'restaurant'

# ม

มณฑล
monthon semi-autonomous satellite state in Siam, from the Pali-Sanskrit 'mandala'

มะกอก
ma-kàwk 'ambarella', 'Thai olive' or 'Otaheite apple'; a South-East Asian native, resembles a small mango but has a very clean and astringent flavour that goes well in certain yam salads

มะกรูด
ma-krùt kaffir lime, a small citrus fruit with a bumpy and wrinkled skin

มะขาม
má-khāam tamarind

มะขามเปียก
má-khāam pìak the flesh and seeds of the husked tamarind fruit pressed into red-brown clumps

มะเขือ
mákhēua eggplant/aubergine

มะเขือเทศ
mákhēua-thêht tomatoes

มะเขือเปราะ
má-khēua phráw 'Thai eggplant' about the size of a pingpong ball; a popular curry ingredient

มะเขือพวง
má-khēua phuang 'pea eggplant'; a popular curry ingredient, especially for kaeng khĭaw-wāan

มะเขือยาว
má-khēua yao literally 'long eggplant'; also called Japanese eggplant or Oriental eggplant

มะนาว
má-nao lime

มะตะปะ
mátàbà roti stuffed with chopped chicken or beef with onions and spices

มะพร้าว
má-phráo coconut

มะพร้าวอ่อน
má-phráo àwn young green coconut

มะไฟ
má-fai rambeh fruit

มะม่วง
má-mûang mango

มะละกอ
málákaw papaya

มังคุด
mang-khút mangosteen

| ก | ข | ค | ง | จ | ฉ | ช | ซ | ฌ | ญ | ฏ | ฏ | ฐ | ฑ | ฒ | ณ | ด | ต | ถ | ท |
|---|---|---|---|---|---|---|---|---|---|---|---|---|---|---|---|---|---|---|---|
| k | k/h | kh | ng | j | ch | ch | s | ch | y | d | t | th | th | th | n | d | t | th | th |

มัดหมี่
mát-mìi Thai silk weaving method that involves yarn-dyeing (ikat)

มัน
man fat; oil

มันแกว
man kâew yam root or jicama

มันฝรั่ง
man faràng potatoes

มันฝรั่งทอด
man faràng thâwt fried potatoes

มีด
mîit knife

มีดหมู
mîit mûu 'pig knife'; Chinese-style cleaver

มื้อ
méu meal

เม็ดผักชี
mét phàk chii coriander seed

เม็ดมะม่วงหิมพานต์ทอด
mét má-mûang hìmáphaan thâwt fried cashew nuts

เมา
mao drunk (inebriated)

เมี่ยงคำ
mîang kham do-it-yourself appetiser in which chunks of ginger, shallot, peanuts, coconut flakes, lime and dried shrimp are wrapped in wild tea leaves or lettuce

เมือง
meuang city; also refers to loosely affiliated settlements or principalities in pre-Sukhothai eras

แม่โขง
mâe khŏng Mekong brand rice whisky

แม่โขง
Mekong Mekong brand rice whisky; also the name of South-East Asia's longest river

แม่ครัว
mâe khrua female cook

แม่ครู
mâe khruu female guru or teacher; a term with shamanic undertones

แมงดา
maeng daa water beetle

แมงดานา
maeng daa naa a water beetle found in rice fields and used in certain kinds of náam phrík (chilli & shrimp paste)

แมวขูดมะพร้าว
maew khùut má-phráo literally 'coconut-digging cat'; tool for grating coconut meat

# ย

ย่าง
yâang grilled

ยำ
yam a hot & tangy salad containing a blast of lime, chilli, fresh herbs and a choice of seafood, roast vegetables, noodles or meats

ยำไก่
yam kài hot & tangy salad with chicken and mint

ยำไข่ดาว
yam khài dao hot & tangy salad with fried eggs

ยำถั่วพู
yam thùa phuu hot & tangy salad with angle beans

| ธ | น | บ | ป | ผ | ฝ | พ | ฟ | ภ | ม | ย | ร | ล | ว | ศ | ษ | ส | ห | อ | ฮ |
|---|---|---|---|---|---|---|---|---|---|---|---|---|---|---|---|---|---|---|---|
| th | n | b | p | ph | f | ph | f | ph | m | y | r | l | w | s | s | s | h | aw | h |

ยำเนื้อ
yam néua hot & tangy salad with grilled beef

ยำปลาดุกฟู
yam plaa dùk fuu hot & tangy salad with fried, shredded catfish, chillies, peanuts and a mango dressing

ยำปลาหมึก
yam plaa mèuk hot & tangy salad with squid

ยำสามกรอบ
yam sǎam kràwp fried squid, fish bladder and cashew nuts mixed with **náam plaa** (fish sauce), sugar, lime juice and chilli; a popular **kàp klâem** or drinking food

ยำพริกชี้ฟ้า
yam phrík chíi fáa hot & tangy salad featuring phrík chíi fáa; very spicy

ยำมะเขือยาว
yam má-khěua yao hot & tangy salad created by tossing a fresh-roasted or grilled long eggplant with shrimp, lime juice, ground pork, coriander leaf, chillies, garlic and fish sauce

ยำมะม่วง
yam má-mûang hot & tangy salad with mango

ยำเม็ดมะม่วงหิมพานต์
yam mét má-mûang hìmáphaan spicy cashew nut salad

ยำวุ้นเส้น
yam wún sên a spicy salad made with warm mung bean noodles tossed with lime juice, fresh sliced phrík khîi nǔu, mushrooms, dried or fresh shrimp, ground pork, coriander leaf, lime juice and fresh sliced chillies.

ยำส้มโอ
yam sôm oh hot & tangy salad made with pomelo, a speciality of Chiang Mai

ยำเห็ดหอม
yam hèt hǎwm hot & tangy salad made with fresh shiitake mushrooms

ยี่หร่า
yîiràa cumin

ยุ้งข้าว
yawng khâo round bins for rice storage made of woven bamboo plastered with mud or buffalo dung to keep rice grains from leaking through the bamboo weave

# ร

รถเข็น
rót khěn vendor cart

รวงข้าว
ruang khâo ears of rice

รสจัด
rót jàt rich strong flavours

รสชาดเผ็ดร้อน
Rót châat phèt ráwn 'tastes original spicy hot' often shortened to **rót châat** (from the Pali-Sanskrit *rasa jati*, 'birth flavour'), a highly complimentary term generally applied only to Thai cooking

รังผึ้ง
rang phêung 'honeycomb'; a clay grate used to hold the fuel inside a cooking pot, also known as a **tà-kràp**

รากผักชี
râak phàk chii roots of the coriander/cilantro plant

| ก | ข | ค | ง | จ | ฉ | ช | ซ | ฌ | ญ | ฎ | ฏ | ฐ | ฑ | ฒ | ณ | ด | ต | ถ | ท |
|---|---|---|---|---|---|---|---|---|---|---|---|---|---|---|---|---|---|---|---|
| k | k/h | kh | ng | j | ch | ch | s | ch | y | d | t | th | th | th | n | d | t | th | th |

ราดข้าว
râat khâo 'over rice'

ราดพริก
râat phrík smothered in garlic, chillies and onions; usually for freshwater fish

ราดหน้า
râat nâa the shortened name for any kǔaytǐaw râat nâa dish, frequently used when ordering (pronounced 'lâat nâa' in Bangkok and Central Thailand)

---

## L & R

l and r are often interchanged in speech. For example **raat** might be rendered as laat.

---

ร้านก๋วยเตี๋ยว
ráan kǔaytǐaw noodle shop

ร้านของชำ
ráan khǎwng cham sundries shop

ร้านข้าวแกง
ráan khâo kaeng rice & curry shop

ร้านข้าวต้ม
ráan khâo tôm khâo tôm shop

ร้านอาหาร
ráan aahǎan food shop

ร้านอาหารตามสั่ง
ráan aahǎan taam sàng food-to-order shop

ร้านอาหารมังสวิรัติ
ráan aahǎan mangsàwírát vegetarian restaurant

รายการอาหาร
raai kaan aahǎan menu

รำข้าว
ram khâo rice chaff

เรือของชำ
reua khǎwng cham sundries shop on water

เรืออาหาร
reua aahǎan riverside restaurants which operate dinner boat cruises

โรงสี
rohng sǐi rice mills

โรตี
roti fried round, flat wheat bread descended from the Indian *paratha*; popular in the South

โรตีกล้วย
roti klûay roti stuffed with fresh banana chunks or banana paste and sprinkled with sugar and condensed milk

โรตีแกง
roti kaeng roti dipped in the sauce from a chicken, beef or crab curry

โรตีไข่
roti khài roti cooked with egg

# ล

ลวก
lûak parboil

ละมุด
lámút sapodilla fruit

ลังถึง
lang thěung round flat steamer of steel or bamboo

ลางสาด
langsat an oval-shaped fruit with

| ธ | น | บ | ป | ผ | ฝ | พ | ฟ | ภ | ม | ย | ร | ล | ว | ศ | ษ | ส | ห | ฬ | อ | ฮ |
|---|---|---|---|---|---|---|---|---|---|---|---|---|---|---|---|---|---|---|---|---|
| th | n | b | p | ph | f | ph | f | ph | m | y | r | l | w | s | s | s | h | l | aw | h |

white fragrant flesh, grown in Utaradit Province

ลาบ
lâap North-Eastern spicy minced meat salad made by tossing minced meat, poultry or freshwater fish with lime juice, fish sauce, chillies, fresh mint leaves, chopped spring onion and **khâo khûa pòn** (pulverised rice)

ลาบเป็ด
lâap pèt duck **lâap**, an Ubon Ratchathani speciality

ลาบเป็ดขาว
lâap pèt khâo white duck **lâap**

ลาบเป็ดแดง
lâap pèt daeng red duck **lâap**, which uses duck blood as part of the sauce

ลาบสุก
lâap sùk cooked **lâap**

ลำแต้
lam tâe 'very tasty' in Northern Thai dialect

ลำใย
lam yài longan fruit, also known as 'dragon's eyes'

ลูก
lûuk unit of measure for an individual fruit or vegetable

ลูกกระวาน
lûuk krà-waan cardamom

ลูกชิ้นปลา
lûuk chín plaa fish balls

ลูกชุบ
lûuk chúp 'dipped fruit'; sweets made of soybean paste, sugar and coconut milk that are boiled, coloured and fashioned to look exactly like miniature fruits and vegetables

ลูกทุ่ง
lûuk thûng literally 'children of the fields'; a contemporary syncopated Isaan song form

## ว

วัฒนธรรม
wátánátham culture, with an emphasis on fine arts and religious ceremonies

วัด
wát monastery

วุ้นเส้น
wún sên noodles made from mung bean and water to produce an almost clear noodle; sometimes called 'cellophane noodles'; 'glass noodles' or 'bean thread noodles' in English

ไวน์ขาว
wain khâo white wine

ไวน์แดง
wain daeng red wine

## ศ

ศิลปอาหาร
sìlàpaahǎan food arts

## ส

สงกรานต์
Songkran water festival

สด
sòt fresh (not stale)

สนุก
sanùk fun

ส้มเขียวหวาน
sôm khǐaw-wǎan mandarin orange

| ก | ข | ค | ง | จ | ฉ | ช | ซ | ฌ | ญ | ฎ | ฏ | ฐ | ฑ | ฒ | ณ | ด | ต | ถ | ท |
|---|---|---|---|---|---|---|---|---|---|---|---|---|---|---|---|---|---|---|---|
| k | k/h | kh | ng | j | ch | ch | s | ch | y | d | t | th | th | th | n | d | t | th | th |

ส้มตำ
**sômtam** a tart and spicy salad usually made with green papaya; also known as **tamsôm** or **tam màak hûng**

ส้มโอ
**sôm oh** pomelo, popular in Northern Thailand

สมุนไพร
**samūn phrai** indigenous culinary or medicinal herbs

สวน
**sūan** garden

ส้อม
**sâwm** fork

สะตอ
**sà-tàw** a large, flat, Southern Thai bean with a bitter taste

สะเต๊ะ
**sà-té** satay, short skewers of barbecued beef, pork or chicken that are served with a spicy peanut sauce

สะเต๊ะหมู
**sà-té kài** chicken sà-té

สะเต๊ะเนื้อ
**sà-té néua** beef sà-té

สะเต๊ะหมู
**sà-té mūu** pork sà-té

สะระแหน่
**sàránàe** mint

สั่ง
**sàng** to order

สังขยา
**sāngkhayāa** custard

สังขยาฟักทอง
**sāngkhayāa fák thawng** custard-filled pumpkin

สังฆ
**Sangha** Buddhist community

สับปะรด
**sàppàrót** pineapple

สาก
**sàak** pestle

สากไม้
**sàak mái** large wooden pestle dedicated to the making of **sômtam** (spicy papaya salad)

สุกี้ยากี้/สุกี้
**sukiyaki/sùkîi** 'hot pot'; a peculiar Thai-Japanese hybrid popular in Central Thailand involving a large stationary pot sitting on a gas burner to which diners add raw ingredients such as mung bean noodles, egg, water spinach and cabbage. Thin-sliced beef and shrimp are cooked on a metal dome in the centre of the pot, well above the surface of the broth. As the ingredients cook, they are removed from the pot with chopsticks and eaten with very Chinese- or Japanese-style sauces on the table, while further raw ingredients are put into the pot.

สูตร
**sutta** discourses of the Buddha

เส้นเล็ก
**sên lék** 'small line' rice noodles about 5mm wide

เส้นหมี่
**sên mìi** 'noodle line' rice noodles only 1 or 2mm wide

เส้นใหญ่
**sên yài** flat 'wide line' rice noodles 2 to 3cm wide

| ธ | น | บ | ป | ผ | ฝ | พ | ฟ | ภ | ม | ย | ร | ล | ว | ศ | ษ | ส | ห | ฬ | อ | ฮ |
|---|---|---|---|---|---|---|---|---|---|---|---|---|---|---|---|---|---|---|---|---|
| th | n | b | p | ph | f | ph | f | ph | m | y | r | l | w | s | s | s | h | l | aw | h |

เสื่อ
**sèua** rice mat

เสื้อหม้อฮ่อม
**sèua mâw hâwm** rice farmer's collarless blue cotton tunic, hand-sewn in Northern Thailand's Phrae Province

แสงทิพย์
**sǎeng thíp** Sang Thip brand rice whisky

ใส่ไข่
**sài khài**, 'add egg'

ใส่ถุง
**sài thǔng** 'put in a bag'; for takeaway orders

ใส้อั่ว
**sâi ùa** Northern Thai sausage made from a curry paste of dried chillies, garlic, shallots, lemongrass and kaffir lime peel, blended with ground pork, stuffed into pork intestines and then fried to produce a spicy red sausage

# ห

หน่อไม้
**nàw mái** bamboo shoots

หน่อไม้เปรี้ยว
**nàw mái prîaw** pickled bamboo shoots

หนังใหญ่
**nǎng yài** life-size shadow puppets carved from buffalo hide, found in the Southern towns of Nakhon Si Thammarat and Phattalung

หมวดทอด
**mùat thâwt** deep-fried dishes

หมวดผัด
**mùat phàt** stirfried dishes

หม้อ
**mâw** cooking pot traditionally made of fired clay or other earthenware, but nowadays from aluminium or porcelain-laminated steel

หม้อดิน
**mâw din** claypot used to bake certain rice and mung bean noodle dishes

---

## Tone

Tone, the pitch at which a syllable is pronounced, often determines its meaning. For example, depending on the tone, the syllable mai can mean 'new', 'burn', 'wood', 'not?' or 'not', from which we can make the sentence **mái, mài mâi mâi mǎi**, 'new wood doesn't burn, does it?'

---

หม้อแขก
**mâw khàek** rounded, narrow-necked 'Indian pot' for preparing sticky rice

หมอนทอง
**mǎwn thawng** 'golden pillow' durian

หมี่พัน
**mìi pan** a spicy mix of thin rice noodles, bean sprouts and coriander leaf wrapped into a rice paper roll, a speciality of Laplae district in Utaradit Province

หมู
**mǔu** pork

หมูแดง
**mǔu daeng** strips of bright red barbecued pork

| ก | ข | ค | ง | จ | ฉ | ช | ซ | ฌ | ญ | ฎ | ฏ | ฐ | ฑ | ฒ | ณ | ด | ต | ถ | ท |
|---|---|---|---|---|---|---|---|---|---|---|---|---|---|---|---|---|---|---|---|
| k | k/h | kh | ng | j | ch | ch | s | ch | y | d | t | th | th | th | n | d | t | th | th |

หมูปิ้ง
**mǔu pîng** toasted pork

หมูยอ
**mǔu yǎw** Northern Thai sausage resembling a large German frankfurter

หมูย่าง
**mǔu yâang** a **kàp klâem** (drinking food) dish, grilled strips of pork eaten with spicy dipping sauces

หมูสับ
**mǔu sàp** ground pork

หมูสามชั้น
**mǔu sǎam chán** 'three level pork'; meaning cuts that include meat, fat and skin

หร่อยจังฮู้
**ràwy jang hûu** 'very tasty' in Southern dialect

หลักเมือง
**làk meuang** city pillar associated with the founding of the city and where the city's guardian spirit is thought to reside

หวด
**hùat** crescent-shaped bamboo steamer

หวาน
**wǎan** sweet

ห้องครัว
**khrua** kitchen

ห้องแถว
**hâwng thǎew** literally, row house; a two storey affair in which the ground floor is reserved for stocking and selling, while the upper floor serves as a residence for the merchant's family

หอมแดง
**hǎwm daeng** shallots

หอย
**hǎwy** clams & oysters (generic)

หอยแครง
**hǎwy khraeng** cockle

หอยทอด
**hǎwy thâwt** fresh oysters quickly fried with beaten eggs, mung bean sprouts and sliced spring onions. A Central Thai dish.

หอยนางรม
**hǎwy naang rom** oyster

หอยพัด
**hǎwy phát** scallop

หอยแมลงภู่
**hǎwy malaeng phùu** green mussel

ห่อหมก
**hàw mòk** souffle-like dish made by steaming a mixture of red curry paste, beaten eggs, coconut milk and fish in a banana-leaf cup. A Central Thai dish.

ห่อหมกทะเล
**hàw mòk thaleh hàw mòk** made by steaming a mixture of red curry paste, beaten eggs, coconut milk and mixed seafood in a banana-leaf cup

ห่อหมกหอยแมลงภู่
**hàw mòk hǎwy malaeng phuu hàw mòk** cooked inside green mussel shells

หัว
**hǔa** head

หัวกะทิ
**hǔa kà-thí** 'coconut head'; coconut cream

หัวไชเท้า
**hǔa chai tháo** Chinese radish

| ธ | น | บ | ป | ผ | ฝ | พ | ฟ | ภ | ม | ย | ร | ล | ว | ศ | ษ | ส | ห | อ | ฮ |
|---|---|---|---|---|---|---|---|---|---|---|---|---|---|---|---|---|---|---|---|
| th | n | b | p | ph | f | ph | f | ph | m | y | r | l | w | s | s | s | h | aw | h |

หัวปลี
hŭa plii banana flower, a purplish, oval-shaped bud that has a tart and astringent mouth feel when eaten raw as an accompaniment to lâap in the North-East. Blanching the bud removes most of the bud's astringency and makes it very suitable for use in yam.

หัวผักกาด
hŭa phàk kàat giant white radish

หางกะทิ
hăang kà-thí 'coconut tail'; coconut milk

หุงข้าว
hŭng khâo the task of preparing white rice by boiling it in water in a lidded pot

หู
hŭu ear; pot handle

เห็ดฟาง
hèt faang straw mushrooms

เห็ดหอม
hèt hăwm shiitake mushrooms

เหล้า
lâo distilled spirits

เหล้าขาว
lâo khăo 'white liquor' spirits distilled from sticky rice or, in the case of lâo thèuan, other agricultural products

เหล้าเถื่อน
lâo thèuan 'wild liquor'; illegal lâo khăo made from products such as sugar palm sap, coconut milk, coconut sap, sugar cane, taro and sticky rice

เหล้ายาดอง
lâo yaa dawng 'pickled herb liquor'; herbal liquors made by adding herbs, roots, seeds, fruit or bark to lâo khăo and allowing it to steep for a number of days

แห้ง
hâeng dried, dry

แหนมหม้อ
nãem mâw Nothern Thai 'pot sausage' requires no cooking, instead ground pork, pork rind and cooked sticky rice are mixed with salt, garlic and chilli, then pressed into a clay pot and left to stand exactly three days. After three days it is wrapped in banana leaves and served or sold. The fermenting effects of the garlic and chilli 'cook' the mixture into a sour-tasting sausage, which must be eaten on the third day or disposed of before it spoils.

# อ

อบ
òp baked

อบเชย
òp choei a variety of cinnamomum, correctly called cassia but often called cinnamon

อบหม้อดิน
òp mâw din baked in a clay pot, a Central Thai cooking style

อยากได้
yàak dâi to want (something)

อร่อยมาก
àràwy mâak 'very tasty' in Central Thai

| ก | ข | ค | ง | จ | ฉ | ช | ซ | ฌ | ญ | ฏ | ฎ | ฐ | ฑ | ฒ | ณ | ด | ต | ถ | ท |
|---|---|---|---|---|---|---|---|---|---|---|---|---|---|---|---|---|---|---|---|
| k | k/h | kh | ng | j | ch | ch | s | ch | y | d | t | th | th | th | n | d | t | th | th |

อาหาร
aahǎan food

อาหารกลางวัน
aahǎan klaang wan lunch

อาหารเช้า
aahǎan cháo breakfast

อาหารทะเล
aahǎan tháleh seafood

อาหารไทย
aahǎan thai Thai food

อาหารเหนือ
aahǎan něua Northern Thai food

อาหารปักษ์ใต้
aahǎan pàk tâi Southern Thai food

อาหารป่า
aahǎan pàa 'forest food'; ie wildlife
that is bought and sold for food

อาหารภาคกลาง
aahǎan phâak klaang Central Thai
food

อาหารมังสวิรัติ
aahǎan mangsàwírát vegetarian food

อาหารเย็น
aahǎan yen dinner

อาหารว่าง
aahǎan wâang 'empty food'; snacks

อาหารหลัก
aahǎan làk staple

อาหารอีสาน
aahǎan isǎan North-Eastern Thai food

อำเภอเมือง
amphoe meuang provincial capitals

อิ่ม
ìm to feel full

อิ่มใจ
ìm jai 'full heart'; an expression that
fuses culinary satisfaction with general
contentment

อีโต้
ii-tôh hatchet-like utility knife with a
wide, curved-top blade used for
splitting coconut shells or chopping
kindling for the firepot

อีสาน
isǎan the general term for North-
Eastern Thailand, from the Sanskrit
name for the medieval kingdom
Isana, which encompassed parts of
Cambodia and North-Eastern
Thailand

โอเลี้ยง
oh-líang iced coffee with sugar, no
milk

# ฮ

ฮ้านน้ำ
háan náam a small roofed platform
holding clay water jars from which
visitors or passers-by are welcome to
quench their thirst; traditionally
found in front of houses throughout
Northern Thailand

THAI CULINARY DICTIONARY

| ธ | น | บ | ป | ผ | ฝ | พ | ฟ | ภ | ม | ย | ร | ล | ว | ศ | ษ | ส | ห | ฬ | อ | ฮ |
|---|---|---|---|---|---|---|---|---|---|---|---|---|---|---|---|---|---|---|---|---|
| th | n | b | p | ph | f | ph | f | ph | m | y | r | l | w | s | s | s | h | l | aw | h |

**Jerry Alexander** Front & back cover, p1, p5, p8, p9, p14, p17, p18, p19, p23, p26, p27, p33, p34, p36, p40, p43, p44, p48, p50, p51, p53, p54, p56, p57, p58, p62, p66, p67, p68, p69, p70, p71, p73, p78, p83, p88, p89 right, p91, p98, p103, p104, p107 left, bottom, p110, p111, p112, p116, p117 left, p120, p123, p127, p131, p132, p135, p137 top right, bottom, p142, p144, p146, p152, p154, p156, p159, p161, p163, p164, p168, p171, p175, p178, p180, p182, p189, p191, p194, p199, p204, p207, p211, p213, p215, p222.

**John Hay** p12, p89 left, p137 top left, p186, p216.

**Richard I'Anson** p122, p173, p183.

**S. J. Cleland** p117 right, p118.

**Mick Elmore** p176, p197.

**Chris Mellor** p20, p86.

**Richard Nebesky** p107 top right.

**John Borthwick** p24.

**Nicholas Reuss** p29.

**Juliet Coombe** p64.

**Patrick Horton** p181.

### Boxed Text

---

## Maps

---

## Recipes

# More World Food Titles

Brimming with cultural insight, the World Food series takes the guesswork out of new cuisines and provide the ideal guides to your own culinary adventures. The books cover everything to do with food and drink in each country – the history and evolution of the cuisine, its staples & specialities, and the kitchen philosophy of the people. You'll find definitive two-way dictionaries, menu readers and useful phrases for shopping, drunken apologies and much more.

The essential guides for travelling and non-travelling food lovers around the world, look out for the full range of World Food titles including:

**Deep South (USA),**
**Italy,**
**Mexico,**
**Morocco,**
**Spain,**
**Turkey,**
**Vietnam,**
**France,**
**Ireland &**
**Hong Kong.**

# Out to Eat Series

Lonely Planet's Out to Eat series takes its food seriously but offers a fresh approach with independent, unstuffy opinion on hundreds of hand-picked restaurants, bars and cafes in each city. Along with reviews, Out to Eat identifies the best culinary cul-de-sacs, describes cultural contexts of ethnic cuisines, and explains menu terms and ingredients.

Updated annually, new Out to Eat titles include:
**Melbourne, Paris, Sydney, London and San Francisco.**

# Planet Talk

Our FREE quarterly printed newsletter is full of tips from travellers and anecdotes from Lonely Planet guidebook authors. Every issue is packed with up-to-date travel news and advice, and includes:

- a postcard from Lonely Planet co-founder Tony Wheeler
- a swag of mail from travellers
- a look at life on the road through the eyes of a Lonely Planet author
- topical health advice
- prizes for the best travel yarn
- news about forthcoming Lonely Planet events
- a complete list of Lonely Planet books and other titles

To join our mailing list, residents of the UK, Europe and Africa can email us at go@lonelyplanet.co.uk; residents of North and South America can do so at info@lonelyplanet.com; the rest of the world can email talk2us@lonelyplanet.com.au, or contact any Lonely Planet office.

## The Lonely Planet Story

Lonely Planet published its first book in 1973 in response to the numerous 'How did you do it?' questions Maureen and Tony Wheeler were asked after driving, bussing, hitching, sailing and railing their way from England to Australia. Written at a kitchen table and hand collated, trimmed and stapled, *Across Asia on the Cheap* became an instant local bestseller.

Eighteen months in South-East Asia resulted in their second guide, *South-East Asia on a Shoestring*, which they put together in a backstreet Chinese hotel in Singapore in 1975. The 'yellow bible', as it quickly became known to backpackers around the world, soon became the guide to the region. It has sold well over ¾ million copies and is now in its 10th edition, still retaining its familiar yellow cover.

Today there are over 400 titles, including travel guides, walking guides, language kits & phrasebooks, travel atlases & maps, diving guides, restaurant guides, first time travel guides, condensed guides, illustrated pictorials and travel literature. The company is the largest independent travel publisher in the world.

The emphasis continues to be on travel for independent travellers. Tony and Maureen still travel for several months of each year and play an active part in the writing, updating and quality control of Lonely Planet's guides.

They have been joined by over 120 authors and over 400 staff at our offices in Melbourne (Australia), Oakland (USA), London (UK) and Paris (France). Travellers themselves also make a valuable contribution to the guides through the feedback we receive in thousands of letters each year and on our web site.

The people at Lonely Planet strongly believe that travellers can make a positive contribution to the countries they visit, both through their appreciation of the countries' culture, wildlife and natural features, and through the money they spend. In addition, the company makes a direct contribution to the countries and regions it covers. Since 1986 a percentage of the income from each book has been donated to ventures such as famine relief in Africa; aid projects in India; agricultural projects in Central America; Greenpeace's efforts to halt French nuclear testing in the Pacific.

## Lonely Planet Offices

**Australia**
PO Box 617, Hawthorn, Victoria 3122
☎ 03-9819 1877
fax 03-9819 6459
email:talk2us@lonelyplanet.com.au

**USA**
150 Linden St, Oakland, CA 94607
☎ 510-893 8555  TOLL FREE: 800 275 8555
fax 510-893 8572
email: info@lonelyplanet.com

**UK**
10a Spring Place, London NW5 3BH
☎ 020-7428 4800
fax 020-7428 4828
email: go@lonelyplanet.co.uk

**France**
1 rue du Dahomey, 75011 Paris
☎ 01 55 25 33 00
fax 01 55 25 33 01
email: bip@lonelyplanet.fr